Adopting
AFTER
Infertility

by the same editors

Sexuality and Fertility Issues in Ill Health and Disability
From Early Adolescence to Adulthood
Edited by Rachel Balen and Marilyn Crawshaw
ISBN 978 1 84310 339 4

of related interest

Making Babies the Hard Way
Living with Infertility and Treatment
Caroline Gallup
ISBN 978 1 84310 463 6

Faith and Fertility
Attitudes Towards Reproductive Practices in Different
Religions from Ancient to Modern Times
Edited by Eric Blyth and Ruth Landau
Foreword by Richard Harries
ISBN 978 1 84310 535 0

Big Steps for Little People
Parenting Your Adopted Child
Celia Foster
Forewords by David Howe and Daniel A. Hughes
ISBN 978 1 84310 620 3

Life Story Books for Adopted Children
A Family Friendly Approach
Joy Rees
Illustrated by Jamie Goldberg
Foreword by Alan Burnell
ISBN 978 1 84310 953 2

Nurturing Attachments
Supporting Children who are Fostered or Adopted
Kim S. Golding
ISBN 978 1 84310 614 2

New Families, Old Scripts
A Guide to the Language of Trauma and Attachment in Adoptive Families
Caroline Archer and Christine Gordon
ISBN 978 1 84310 258 8

Understanding Looked After Children
An Introduction to Psychology for Foster Care
Jeune Guishard-Pine, Suzanne McCall and Lloyd Hamilton
Foreword by Andrew Wiener
ISBN 978 1 84310 370 7

EDITED BY MARILYN CRAWSHAW AND RACHEL BALEN

Adopting
AFTER
Infertility

MESSAGES FROM PRACTICE, RESEARCH
AND PERSONAL EXPERIENCE

Jessica Kingsley Publishers
London and Philadelphia

First published in 2010
by Jessica Kingsley Publishers
116 Pentonville Road
London N1 9JB, UK
and
400 Market Street, Suite 400
Philadelphia, PA 19106, USA

www.jkp.com

Copyright © Jessica Kingsley Publishers 2010

Library of Congress Cataloging in Publication Data
Adopting after infertility : messages from practice, research, and personal experience / edited by Marilyn Crawshaw and Rachel Balen.
p. cm.
Includes bibliographical references and index.
ISBN 978-1-84905-028-9 (alk. paper)
1. Adoption. 2. Infertility--Psychology. 3. Counseling. I. Crawshaw, Marilyn, 1949- II. Balen, Rachel, 1954-
HV875.A326 2010
362.734--dc22

2010001264

British Library Cataloguing in Publication Data
A CIP catalogue record for this book is available from the British Library

ISBN 978 1 84905 028 9

Printed and bound in Great Britain by
MPG Books Group

Acknowledgement

We would like to thank Sue Hanson of the Centre for Applied Childhood Studies, University of Huddersfield, for her assistance in the preparation of this book.

Contents

Introduction

The majority of adoptive parents around the world turn to adoptive family life as a result of finding out that they cannot have their own biological children. So does second choice always mean second best? Do infertile people feel haunted by thoughts of 'what might have been'? Do adopted children feel that they can never quite satisfy their (infertile) parents' needs? Is it good professional practice to ignore fertility issues once adopters are approved or to continue proactively to explore such issues? These are just some of the questions about which we hope this edited collection will provide information, stimulate thinking and prompt debate.

When one searches the adoption literature, as we have done, the absence of theoretical or research attention to the influence of fertility experiences on adoptive family life is resounding. By contrast, the literature on the experience of coping with fertility difficulties at diagnosis or during fertility treatments is burgeoning – but, interestingly, stops short of considering what happens to those who move on to adoption. So what is happening? Why do we not seem to want to hear about and study this potential key influence on the ability to form and maintain emotionally and socially healthy adoptive family relationships? Even though pronatalist messages have become less overt in Western societies, the 'right' to exercise reproductive choice remains a closely guarded one. Adults who choose to remain child-free may be less frowned on than in the past and the plight of those whose choice has been removed is covered more sympathetically than ever. However, to be 'infertile' invokes not only sympathy but pity. Perhaps what we are looking at here are deep-seated psychological reactions to the inability to procreate, among those directly affected and those 'looking on', and deep-seated sociological influences that put infertile people into a socially undesirable 'other' category akin to that of Goffman's (1963) classic 'spoiled identity'.

When such forces combine with feelings towards children who are also seen as society's casualties – those in the state care system who have been abandoned, neglected or abused – then the desire to look away from all but altruistic 'rescuer' adopter motivations may be heightened. Recent adoption literature has instead focused heavily on the influences that the adopted child alone brings to their new family. Growing awareness of attachment disorders in particular has fuelled this tendency.

Understandably, difficulties in forming attachments are thought of first and foremost as located in the child, with any negative influence that adoptive parents may have being seen, if at all, as stemming from them having too high expectations of this child who is not of their genes.

Debates about the relative influences of nature and nurture are, however, now starting to come more to the fore. The prominence of social workers among those professional groups trained to see the importance of environmental influences on human development may explain their tendency hitherto to downplay the possible transmission of genetic traits. The essentialist language of early writings in the field of genetics with its implication that humans are at the mercy of their genetic make-up has no doubt also contributed. That said, the complexity of the interplay is now starting to be engaged with more fully and the next few years are likely to bring more sophisticated levels of understanding and debate among professionals and members of the public alike.

In this collection we have put together an international, interdisciplinary set of chapters that take the reader through the life of an adoptive family. Through the particular lens of (in)fertility, we consider the range of influences that the family might encounter. In doing so, our compilation runs the danger of privileging fertility but we hope that this is tempered by the fact that the chapters themselves weave in and out of the fertility focus, thus illustrating its often enmeshed nature.

We also need to acknowledge the limitations of language. We have struggled to decide whether to use 'infertility', 'fertility difficulties', 'subfertility' or 'fertility impairment'. None quite hit the mark. The reality for many of those directly affected is that they too do not know how to describe themselves – a small number of individuals will know that they will never be able to have biological children; the majority will not. Many, but not all, will be part of a couple: some will have been told that only one has fertility difficulties (meaning that the other could have children with a different partner) while others may have been advised that it is them as a couple that has the problem (and hence that both could have children with someone else). Some will have been told that their situation is not yet understood by medical science and that their inability to conceive is 'unexplained'. We decided on the term 'infertility' for its simplicity rather than its accuracy.

The collection starts with an academic psychologist's review of research into the impact of fertility investigations and treatments. Lone Schmidt offers a concise outline of available medical tests and fertility treatments before moving on to consider the research into some of the psychosocial implications, stressors and coping mechanisms that may be relevant to those affected. Sociology too has much to offer in aiding understanding of the social forces that influence personal experience. Gayle Letherby, in Chapter 2, draws from her own qualitative research to explore such concepts and experiences as they relate to choosing whether or not to have children, pursuing and ending fertility treatment and deciding what to do next.

Turning from the world of academia, Petra Thorn, in Chapter 3, takes the reader through accounts of her practice experiences as an infertility counsellor with couples struggling to decide whether to leave behind the world of medical treatment and commit to adoption. Her discussion thoughtfully explores the meanings of (in)fertility for the individuals and couples with whom she works and includes examples of issues raised and related activities used in her practice.

Next, we ourselves have drawn on our backgrounds straddling academia and practice to consider, in Chapter 4, the unique aspects facing those whose infertility arises because of a health condition or physical impairment that is either congenital or acquired later in childhood or adulthood. Growing numbers are now surviving to the point where they wish to be considered as adopters. Our chapter includes consideration of such issues as the impact on personal relationships, disclosing infertility, views about alternative routes to parenthood and the attitudes of those affected and of professionals towards those who (wish to) parent.

Assessment and preparation are stages in the adoption journey when professionals are required to satisfy themselves and others that applicants have resolved their feelings about their infertility sufficiently to move unfettered into adoptive parenthood. In Chapter 5, one of us (Marilyn) looks further into some of the theoretical frameworks that may help the assessing social worker and introduces tools to augment 'talking' sessions. This links closely to Chapter 6 where Jenny Gwilt approaches the question of suitability from the point of view of the adoption panel. Not all jurisdictions have such panels but most have a comparable scrutiny process. The need to pay comprehensive attention to infertility, both when deciding whether to recommend approval of adopters or approval of a proposed match with a child, is a sensitive and challenging task.

Next, the collection has two chapters that explore the particular context for those coming to adoptive parenthood from minority ethnic communities that maintain a strongly pronatalist culture in which genetic relatedness is highly valued. In Chapter 7, Lorraine Culley and Nicky Hudson bring sociological understanding to their account of research into beliefs about adoption and infertility within South Asian communities and Sally Baffour, in Chapter 8, offers a more personal account in which she relates her own experience as an infertile Black African woman of adopting twins, interwoven with understandings drawn from her extensive experience of supporting other adopters from the Black community over many years. The question of the interplay of ethnicity, culture and infertility is dealt with from a different but equally fascinating angle in Chapter 9. Gill Haworth, Peter Selman and Jan Way bring their practitioner and academic insights together in looking at the controversial area of inter-country adoption. In a fascinating account that starts with charting its changing profile across Europe from the 1960s to the present day, the complexities of going overseas as an infertile couple and meeting the unique challenges and rewards of adopting through this route are explored.

The life of the adoptive family starts with placement(s) but many of the chapters so far make clear that the journey is then only just beginning. In their highly sensitive account, in Chapter 10, of practice experiences in child and adolescent mental health services when working with adoptive families at different stages of their life together, Anthea Hendry and Penny Netherwood consider the need to be attentive to residual and newly awakened feelings arising from infertility that can affect personal and family dynamics.

We alluded earlier to fast-changing debates about the relative influences of nature and nurture. In Chapter 11, Olga van den Akker helps to make sense of these by drawing on findings from research with families without full genetic links, not only as a result of adoption but also through donor-assisted conception and surrogacy. In the final chapter in the collection, Chapter 12, Julia Feast looks at the experiences of adopters whose children have reached adulthood. She outlines findings from her own research and practice into the impact on infertile adoptive parents when their adult children search for birth relatives and when they themselves become grandparents.

Many of the chapters bring alive the experiences of those negotiating the worlds of infertility and adoption and three sets of adopters have contributed specifically to this book – Joanne and John who adopted their sons three years ago at the ages of two and one; Louise and Oliver who, at the time of contributing to this book, had recently had an eleven-month-old girl and her eight-week-old brother placed with them for adoption; and Mary who adopted her son, now aged 12, as a single parent 11 years ago.

We hope that readers – practitioners, academics and those directly affected – will enjoy this collection as much as we have enjoyed putting it together. We hope too that it will redress in some way the gap in the literature that has been there for too long.

We end with the words of Joanne and John, Mary, and Louise and Oliver:

Joanne and John said:

> We'll always be sad that we never went through a pregnancy and gave birth and all that, that will always be there. It's there but we've learnt to deal with it; it's not as important as it used to be. We've realised that being a parent is more than nine months pregnancy.
>
> We just know these two are our little boys. We don't have anything to compare it to but we just know that we are a family. We'll always have the adoption issues in the background but we'll deal with them as and when. I suppose we sometimes think it would have been easier if we'd had biological children in the same way that people with two biological children sometimes think it would be easier with one. But these kids were made for us; they're just our children.

Mary said:

> When I held my child for the first time I wept again at the fact that my joy was only possible because of the unimaginable pain of another woman. My child's beautiful smile, his eyes, his smell came from her, his skin, his life…came from her (and a man I had little knowledge of). How could part of me not love her too?
>
> I was determined that not just me, but other people in my child's life would cherish and respect her – and that we would let my child know that she was cherished by us.

And Louise (and Oliver) said:

> I now sit here watching my beautiful daughter playing with the dogs and talking to them in a language I don't understand. Every so often she stops and looks up at me with a cheeky look on her face. She grips my heart and brings tears to my eyes. My black thunder cloud is always with me, more often than not it's on the horizon, still watching, staring at me. I'm always aware of it, even now; it comes closer from time to

time to empty its anger over me and then retreat back to the horizon, giving me peace again. In many ways I wish we'd pursued adoption earlier but if we had we wouldn't have had the wonderful daughter we have now. I'm a strong believer in fate – whatever will be will be and we both know she was meant to be and definitely worth waiting for.

We trust that this collection will contribute to enabling all involved in the adoption process neither to be afraid of the 'black thunder clouds' nor to forget that they can sometimes be there.

Marilyn Crawshaw
Rachel Balen

Reference

Goffman, E. (1963) *Stigma: Notes on the Management of Spoiled Identity.* Englewood Cliffs, NJ: Prentice-Hall.

CHAPTER 1

The Impact of Infertility and Treatment on Individuals and Couples

Lone Schmidt

Infertility

Studies among childless women and men aged between 23 and 25 years show that around 95 per cent expect to become parents in the future (Statistics Sweden 2001). However, for many different reasons, including biologically reduced fecundity, not all people will achieve parenthood. Further, not all people will be able to achieve their desired number of children. Infertility is defined as a 'lack of conception after at least 12 months of unprotected intercourse' (Rowe *et al.* 1993, p.7). Population-based studies show that among those couples who have tried to achieve childbirth, around 17–28 per cent will experience infertility during one or more periods (Jacob, McQuillan and Greil 2007; Schmidt 2006). According to a review of population-based studies (Schmidt 2006), around 3–6 per cent of women will, for biological causes, never involuntarily deliver a first child. A further 4–6 per cent will, due to infertility, not be able to deliver a subsequent desired child.

Infertility risk factors are on the increase. In many European countries there is a continuous increase in the proportion of people who postpone childbearing. In 2005 in Western European countries, the mean age of women at first birth varied between 28 and 30 years (Commission of the European Communities 2008). This indicates that an increasing proportion of women will, because of advanced age, have a lower fecundity due to both the physiological decline in fertility with age and an increased risk, during the years, of getting other diseases that may impact on fertility. As a consequence, the risk of infertility will increase. Further, many populations are reporting an increase in numbers who are overweight or obese, factors that are known among both women and men to delay conception or lead to infertility (Ramlau-Hansen *et al.* 2007). Another infertility risk factor – smoking (especially among females) – remains highly prevalent among people in the fertile age groups (The Practice Committee of the American Society for Reproductive Medicine 2004). Further, pregnant women who smoke increase the risk of their male foetus having reduced semen quality as an adult (Jensen et al. 2005). Finally, a rise in chlamydia infections may occur, partly due to a perception that HIV is not as deadly as before, and hence there is a lack of adequate protection from sexually transmitted diseases.

Despite the relevance of studying infertility in populations over time, only a few studies have repeatedly investigated the infertility prevalence in the same geographical region. Rostad, Schei and Sundby (2006) reported, based on data from Norway, an increase in the prevalence of infertility among the younger cohorts when population-based data were sampled 20 years apart.

Fertility treatment

On average 56 per cent of infertile people in the developed countries seek medical advice in the health care system (Boivin et al. 2007). Fertility treatment covers assisted reproductive technologies (ARTs) with a range of in vitro techniques where fertilisation takes place in the laboratory outside the female body: in vitro fertilisation (IVF), intracytoplasmic sperm injection (ICSI), egg donation (ED), and frozen embryo replacement (FER). Additionally, there are in vivo treatments with intrauterine insemination with the partner's semen (IUI-H) or donor semen (IUI-D). Depending on the kind of treatment, the delivery rates after each treatment attempt vary between 10 and 25 per cent (see Table 1.1). Fertility treatment is on the increase across Europe. Based on the most recent published data from 2005, in certain European countries up to 4 per cent of all children are now conceived after ARTs. In the UK it was 1.6 per cent (Nyboe Andersen et al. 2009). Additionally, in vivo treatments like intrauterine inseminations may, in certain countries like Denmark, add another 2–3 per cent to the annual birth rates. The latest data from Denmark showed that ART and non-ART treatments accounted for 7–8 per cent of all children born in 2008 (The Danish Fertility Society 2008).

Access to treatment is organised differently in different countries and its availability also differs. In some countries, for example Belgium, the Netherlands, Spain, France, Germany and the Nordic countries, fertility treatments are offered within the National Health Programme. In other countries only self-financed treatment is available. One study (Pinborg et al. 2009) investigated the delivery and adoption rates in a large cohort of

Table 1.1: Assisted reproductive technologies (ARTs)

(i) 'In vitro' techniques

In vitro fertilisation (IVF)
Hormone stimulation of the woman in order to increase the number of eggs
Eggs retrieved
Eggs and semen (partner or donor) are placed together in Petri dish
Fertilisation
One or two embryos transferred to the uterus
Delivery rate per treatment cycle: 20–25 per cent

Intracytoplasmic sperm injection (ICSI)
As IVF except that one single spermatozoa is induced in each egg
Delivery rate per treatment cycle: 20–25 per cent

Frozen embryo replacement (FER)
Initiated by an IVF or ICSI treatment
One or two frozen, thawed embryos transferred to the uterus
Delivery rate per transfer: 15–18 per cent

(ii) 'In vivo' techniques

Intrauterine insemination with partner's semen (IUI-H)
+/- hormonal stimulation of the woman
Partner's semen inseminated in the uterus
Pregnancy rate per treatment cycle: 10–15 per cent

Intrauterine insemination with donor semen (IUI-D)
+/- hormonal stimulation of the woman
Donor semen inseminated in the uterus
Pregnancy rate per treatment cycle: around 20 per cent

Sources: The Danish Fertility Society (2008); Nyboe Anderson *et al.* (2009), among others.

people who had initiated fertility treatment five years earlier in a country with access to three fully reimbursed IVF/ICSI cycles and an unlimited number of insemination and frozen embryo cycles. At the time of entering the study, participants had been infertile for an average of four years and only around 4 per cent had a child together. In total, 69.4 per cent of the complete cohort of women invited to participate in the study had achieved at least one live born child. For women younger than 35 years, three-quarters (74.9%) had delivered compared with just over half (52.2%) of those aged 35 years or older. In total, 18.2 per cent of the women had a non-treatment dependent delivery, i.e. a spontaneous conception. Overall, only 3.1 per cent delivered after a spontaneous conception without any fertility treatment prior to this conception. During the five-year study period 5.8 per cent of the participants had adopted at least one child.

Seeking treatment

Only a few studies have investigated why infertile people seek medical advice and what treatment they expect from the fertility clinics before they have initiated examinations and treatment. Glover *et al.* (1999) asked 29 men attending a specialist male subfertility clinic and the most important reason was to increase their partner's chance of conceiving. Additionally, 75–88 per cent of the men expected general information, information about their specific problem, discussion of possible alternatives, having their questions answered and help with decision-making. Finally, 52 per cent found it important to be able to discuss their feelings about infertility and the way it was treated. Schmidt *et al.* (2003) included 2250 men and women immediately before they initiated fertility treatment at a specialised fertility clinic. Almost all stated that achieving a pregnancy was important and around 77 per cent stated that having a child was important. Women reported undertaking treatment for both themselves (73%) and their partners (70%) while men were having treatment mainly for their partner (79%) and to a lesser extent for themselves (56%). Almost all participants found it important for information about test results and treatment options to be explained by medical staff. Fewer were interested in receiving medical take-home treatment information (women 82%, men 76%).

Significantly more women than men found patient-centred care important. This included fertility clinic staff showing concern and understanding, and receiving written information about the psychosocial consequences of infertility and contact information for infertility associations. However, women and men had similar importance ratings across the different aspects of care. The participants considered staff concern about emotional welfare to be more important than receiving written psychosocial information.

Psychosocial consequences

Only a few studies on the psychosocial consequences of infertility are based on samples from the general population. King (2003) found that subfecundity was positively associated with increased odds of fulfilling the diagnostic criteria for generalised anxiety disorder; having had fertility treatment did not change this relationship. Jacob *et al.* (2007) reported that more women with fertility barriers (infertility and other fertility problems) had elevated general distress compared to women without fertility barriers. The remaining text in this chapter is based on studies among clinical samples.

Loss of life expectations

Qualitative interview studies among fertility patients show that the core of the infertility experience is a loss of expectations and life possibilities (Schmidt 1996; Wirtberg 1992). Infertile people lose the sense that they have a healthy body capable of reproducing the dream of becoming parents together with their partner and planning for how to raise a family, and the feeling that they have control over how their life will continue. Their infertility reduces the possibility of moving into the 'next' generation by becoming parents themselves and hence turning their own parents into grandparents. Many infertile people find that infertility challenges the existential meaning of life and they experience repeated periods of existential crisis. What is life all about if parenthood is not possible? Infertility is for many a deep grief and a substantial loss of existential life expectations.

A stressor

Infertility is a chronic stressor, that is, a stressor that develops slowly as a continuous and problematic state in our social conditions or social roles (Wheaton 1999). Further, infertility is a low-control stressor, that is, a stressful situation where the infertile couple can do little or nothing to influence the outcome of their situation (Terry and Hynes 1998). However, not all studies comparing the level of distress and self-esteem between infertile people and the background population find differences. In Greil's critical review of this literature he concluded that 'it may be safe to assert that the infertile seem to be distressed compared to other individuals but not in a clinically significant way' (Greil 1997, p.1683).

Depression and anxiety

Fertility treatment is in itself a further multidimensional stressor. According to Verhaak et al. (2007a) the treatment constitutes a primary stressor that is most likely to evoke anxiety, whereas the unpredictable outcome of treatment is more likely to evoke feelings of depression. A systematic review of women's emotional adjustment to IVF (Verhaak et al. 2007a) showed that, in general, women did not differ from norm groups with respect to depression levels before the start of fertility treatment. Longitudinal studies measuring pre- and post-treatment emotional adjustment reported an increase in depression levels after one or more unsuccessful cycles. The results regarding anxiety were less consistent, with some studies reporting an increase in anxiety levels. When making gender comparisons of the prevalence of depressive symptoms in people initiating fertility treatment, studies usually identify women as being two to three times more likely than men to report having severe depressive symptoms (Volgsten *et al.* 2008). A one-year follow-up study among fertility patients having unsuccessful treatment showed that, when participants with severe depressive symptoms at baseline were excluded, 14.8 per cent of the women and 5.7 per cent of the men reported having developed severe depressive symptoms (Lund *et al.* 2009).

Only one study (Verhaak *et al.* 2005) evaluated anxiety and depression levels six months after the final treatment cycle. They found that, among women, there was no recovery from enhanced anxiety and depression levels after unsuccessful treatment but a decrease after successful treatment. In the same study, men showed no change in anxiety and depression either after successful or unsuccessful treatment. From their last follow-up study three to five years after having initiated IVF/ICSI treatment, Verhaak *et al.* (2007b) found that the depression level among those women who failed to give birth did not differ significantly between pre-treatment and last follow-up. However, significantly higher depression levels were found among those women still pursuing a desire for pregnancy compared to the women who had abandoned their active pursuit of pregnancy.

Depressive symptoms are also suggested to be associated with the hormones used in fertility treatment. De Klerk *et al.* (2007) found that when IVF treatment using mild ovarian hormone stimulation and single embryo transfer was compared with standard treatment (long-protocol ovarian stimulation and double embryo transfer) among women in unsuccessful treatment cycles, the levels of depressive symptoms were lower among the women having had the mild ovarian hormone stimulation IVF treatment. It is still not clear whether depressive symptoms among women in treatment are a predictor of a lower chance of achieving a pregnancy. According to a recent published review (Williams, Marsh and Rasgon 2007) many studies, but not all, have found that depressive symptoms may decrease success rates of fertility treatment.

Infertile couples
Strains and benefits
Infertile couples often experience a serious strain on their interpersonal relationship (Greil 1997), and some couples see infertility as a fundamental threat for continuing their relationship (Schmidt 1996). As infertility

is a shared couple problem, being able to discuss the impact of infertility and the possible different solutions with the partner seems important (Newton, Sherrard and Glavac 1999; Pasch, Dunkel-Schetter and Christensen 2002). The latter study reported that the more that husbands saw having children as important, were involved in trying to have a baby or wanted to talk with their wives about trying to have a baby, the greater the positive impact on the quality of marital communication and hence the more their wives perceived a more positive effect of infertility on their marriage (Pasch *et al.* 2002).

Most people report that they are able to talk to their partner about infertility and its treatment. However, in a large cohort study among fertility patients 27 per cent of the women and 22 per cent of the men reported, prior to their first treatment attempt at a specialised fertility clinic, that they were having difficulties in their partner communication (Schmidt 2006). The longitudinal one-year follow-up analyses among couples in unsuccessful treatment showed that difficulties in partner communication when initiating treatment were a significant risk factor for a high level of fertility-problem stress one year later (Schmidt *et al.* 2005a). Lund *et al.* (2009) reported, in the same study population, predictors of developing severe depressive symptoms after unsuccessful treatment. Among men, not being able always to talk to their partner when emotional support was needed was a significant risk factor for developing severe depressive symptoms. Also, not feeling appreciated by and/or sometimes experiencing excessive demands from their partner were identified as risk factors. None of these factors were identified as risk factors among women. Newton *et al.* (1999) measured relationship concern, which included items about marital communication, and found a positive relationship between relationship concern and higher ratings of depression. In line with this, Abbey, Andrews and Halman (1995) showed that increased 'received' emotional support between partners was associated with increased quality of marital life.

It is important to be aware that, for many couples, infertility and its treatment are at the same time both a threat and a situation that can bring the partners closer together and strengthen their relationship (Greil, Leitko and Porter 1988; Schmidt 1996; Tjørnhøj-Thomsen 1999). The infertility experience forces the partners to talk about existential aspects of life, to talk about the emotional aspects of infertility and to learn a new terminology to be able to talk about the different fertility treatment methods. These conversations are reported to have the effect of bringing the partners closer together and strengthening their marriage (Tjørnhøj-Thomsen

1999). This positive effect on the partnership has later been called marital benefit (Schmidt *et al.* 2005b). Around 25 per cent of couples initiating fertility treatment reported having high marital benefit. Among men only, having difficulties in partner communication was associated significantly with low marital benefit (Schmidt *et al.* 2005b).

Sexual life

Many infertile couples experience infertility as putting a serious strain on their sexual life. Pleasure and joy can, during the long time spent trying to achieve a pregnancy, change to become more 'organised' intercourse focused on ovulation, timing and reproduction. Some couples find it a relief on initiating fertility treatment where the clinical staff take over responsibility for producing a conception, whereas others experience treatment as a further threat to the spontaneity and pleasure of their sexual life (Tjørnhøj-Thomsen 1999). Long-term follow-up studies among women who have been through fertility treatment show that infertility can have severe long-lasting negative effects on the couples' sexual life (Sundby *et al.* 2007; Wirtberg *et al.* 2007).

Social interactions with other people
Supportive and unsupportive interactions

Besides being a medical condition infertility is a social situation and it is important to study the infertility experience as a socially constructed life crisis, that is, to study how infertility is experienced in everyday life (Greil 1997). One of the challenges infertile people face is to learn how to manage infertility in their social interactions with other people (Schmidt 1996). Across all studies investigating infertility and social interactions, infertile people report both supportive and unsupportive interactions (Akizuki and Kai 2008; Mindes *et al.* 2003; Sandelowski and Jones 1986; Schmidt 1996). Slade *et al.* (2007) found that among female and male new attendees at an infertility clinic, greater perceived social support was associated with a lower level of anxiety, depression and overall infertility distress. This is in accordance with a longitudinal study among infertile women, which found that unsupportive social interactions at baseline were positively related to depressive symptoms and overall psychological distress at follow-up among those women who did not achieve a pregnancy (Mindes *et al.* 2003). Others have studied the effects of perceived relational strains, that is, having conflicts with other people and/or experiencing excessive demands from others (Lund *et al.* 2009). Among both men and women, having conflicts with family, friends and/or neighbours was a significant risk factor for developing severe depressive symptoms; the closer the relationship (family vs. friends vs. neighbours), the higher the risk of developing severe depressive symptoms. Furthermore, the experience of conflict with other people was significantly associated with severe depressive symptoms during unsuccessful treatment. Lechner, Bolman and van Dalen (2007) conducted a cross-sectional study and found that, among involuntarily childless people, dissatisfaction with social support was positively associated with health complaints, depression, anxiety and 'complicated' grief reactions.

Communication – disclosure and non-disclosure

Most infertile people talk to other people about their infertility (Abbey, Andrews and Halman 1991; van Balen and Trimbos-Kemper 1994; Schmidt 2006). Abbey et al. (1991) reported that more women than men had spoken with their friends and family about the fertility problem. Women described more benefits and costs to these interactions than men did, while men described more reasons to be indifferent to the responses from other people than women did. Van Balen and Trimbos-Kemper (1994) showed that 10 per cent of men kept infertility a secret and reported lower well-being. Slade et al. (2007) tested a model suggesting that high perception of stigma was associated with reduced disclosure to others, leading to lower social support and higher distress. Among new attendees at a fertility clinic application of this model revealed that, for women, greater disclosure was linked to higher generic stress and that stigma and disclosure were unrelated. Among men, higher stigma was associated with lower disclosure.

The studies mentioned above measured whether or not the participants talked to others about their infertility. A qualitative interview study among infertile people showed that it is also important to measure what people talk about and what they do not disclose to others (Schmidt 1996). Three different strategies were identified:

1. an open-minded strategy, including sharing both formal information and emotional reactions related to infertility and its treatment

2. a formal strategy, in which only formal information was shared, for example date of treatment, number of eggs retrieved

3. secrecy, in which infertility and its treatment were kept secret from others.

In a later epidemiological study (Schmidt *et al.* 2005a) the participants' communication with others was separated into these three strategies. Among participants in unsuccessful treatment, the use of the formal communication strategy in comparison with the open-minded strategy was a risk factor for a high level of fertility problem stress at the one-year follow-up. On the other hand, keeping the infertility and its treatment a secret was not associated with fertility problem stress. However, keeping the infertility a secret was, among men, related to low marital benefit at the one-year follow-up (Schmidt *et al.* 2005b).

An intervention study using a communication and stress management programme with fertility patients (Schmidt *et al.* 2005c) showed that it is possible for people to learn to change the frequency and content of their communication about infertility and its treatment, especially with close other people. It was not necessarily better to talk more rather than less often. What was important was that the participants achieved skills to actively moderate their communication pattern according to the demands of different social arenas.

Coping strategies

Review studies have often concluded that coping strategies for managing negative emotions in stressful encounters are maladaptive (Austenfeld and Stanton 2004). However, in response to low-control stressors such as infertility and its treatment, it is likely that problem-focused coping strategies aimed at managing the situation actively may have deleterious effects, while emotion-focused strategies could be more effective (Terry and Hynes 1998). Empirical studies among fertility patients support this hypothesis.

Both women and men in fertility treatment use a variety of different coping strategies at the same time, although women use each coping strategy to a greater extent compared to men (Peterson *et al.* 2006a; Schmidt *et al.* 2005a). Longitudinal studies with pre- and post-treatment measures found that, among women in IVF treatment, problem-appraisal coping strategies (e.g. trying to step back and be more objective, trying to see the positive side of the situation) were predictive of better adjustment (Terry and Hynes 1998) and approach-oriented coping (including problem-focused coping, emotional processing and expression) was related to lower distress (Berghuis and Stanton 2002). Schmidt *et al.* (2005a) found that, among men, active-confronting coping (e.g. letting feelings out, accepting sympathy and understanding, asking others for advice, talking to someone about emotional reactions) was a significant predictor of low fertility problem stress in the marital domain. Further, among women the use of meaning-based coping (e.g. thinking about the infertility problem in a positive light, finding other goals in life) was a determinant for lower fertility problem stress.

Conversely, longitudinal studies have shown that avoidance or escape-coping are predictors of poor adjustment to infertility (Terry and Hynes 1998) and of increased stress after one treatment attempt (Berghuis and Stanton 2002). Further, high use of active-avoidance coping (e.g. avoiding being with pregnant women, leaving when people are talking about pregnancies and deliveries, turning to work or substitute activity to take one's mind off things) among both men and women initiating fertility treatment was a significant predictor of high fertility problem stress in the personal domain and the social domain (Schmidt *et al.* 2005a).

From cross-sectional studies among couples seeking fertility treatment, it is reported that both women and men who engaged in a disproportionate degree of escape/avoidance-coping and who felt responsible for infertility were more vulnerable to symptoms of depression (Peterson *et al.* 2006b). Further, these coping strategies were positively associated with infertility stress (Peterson *et al.* 2006a). In line with this, Lechner *et al.* (2007) found that, among involuntarily childless couples, a passive coping style was positively associated with health complaints, depression and anxiety.

As well as the fact that the use of different coping strategies appears related to the level of fertility problem stress, depression and anxiety, such coping strategies are also related to the level of marital benefit, in that the infertility experience has brought the partners closer together and strengthened their marriage. Among men, a longitudinal study showed that high use of active avoidance-coping is both a risk factor of having low marital benefit and a risk factor of high fertility problem stress. On the other hand, high use of active-confronting coping was a determinant for having both high marital benefit and low fertility problem stress (Schmidt *et al.* 2005a, 2005b).

Conclusion

Infertility is a common health problem and on average 56 per cent of infertile couples seek medical advice. Infertility and its treatment are severe low-control stressors often leading to repeated existential life crises and increased levels of anxiety and depression. Infertility and its treatment have a paradoxical effect on couples. At the same time they are both a strain and offer the possibility of strengthening the relationship. Besides being a medical condition, infertility has implications for the social situation of those affected. Infertile people's social interactions with other people in relation to their infertility have an impact on their mental well-being. Women and men have many similarities in their experience of infertility and in how they manage the situation, although it appears that women report higher levels of stress, anxiety and depressive symptoms and a higher level of use of each of the coping strategies than men do. However, it is not clear whether these gender differences reflect how women and men respond to questionnaire scales and how well the developed scales are able to capture both genders' emotional responses to infertility and its treatment.

References

Abbey, A., Andrews, F.M. and Halman, L.J. (1991) 'The Importance of Social Relationships for Infertile Couples' Well-being.' In A.L. Stanton and C. Dunkel-Schetter (eds) *Infertility: Perspectives from Stress and Coping Research.* New York, NY: Plenum Press.

Abbey, A., Andrews, F.M. and Halman, L.J. (1995) 'Provision and receipt of social support and disregard: What is their impact on the marital life quality of infertile and fertile couples?' *Journal of Personality and Social Psychology 68*, 3, 455–469.

Akizuki, Y. and Kai, I. (2008) 'Infertile Japanese women's perception of positive and negative social interactions within their social network.' *Human Reproduction 23*, 12, 2737–2743.

Austenfeld, J.L. and Stanton, A.L. (2004) 'Coping through emotional approach: A new look at emotion, coping, and health-related outcomes.' *Journal of Personality 72*, 6, 1335–1363.

van Balen, F. and Trimbos-Kemper, T.C.M. (1994) 'Factors influencing the well-being of long-term infertile couples.' *Journal of Psychosomatic Obstetrics and Gynecology 15*, 157–164.

Berghuis, J.P. and Stanton, A.L. (2002) 'Adjustment to a dyadic stressor: A longitudinal study of coping and depressive symptoms in infertile couples over an insemination attempt.' *Journal of Consulting and Clinical Psychology 70*, 2, 433–438.

Boivin, J., Bunting, L., Collins, J.A. and Nygren, K.G. (2007) 'International estimates of infertility prevalence and treatment-seeking: Potential need and demand for infertility medical care.' *Human Reproduction 22*, 6, 1506–1512.

Commission of the European Communities (2008) *Demography Report: Meeting Social Needs in an Ageing Society.* Brussels: Commission of the European Communities.

The Danish Fertility Society (2008) *Annual Report.* Available at www.fetilitetsselskab.dk/index. php?option=com_content&view=article&id=93&Itemid=104, accessed on 26 April 2010.

Glover, L., Gannon, K., Platt, Z. and Abel, P.D. (1999) 'Male subfertility clinic attenders' expectations of medical consultation.' *British Journal of Health Psychology 4*, 53–61.

Greil, A.L. (1997) 'Infertility and psychological distress: A critical review of the literature.' *Social Science and Medicine 45*, 11, 1679–1704.

Greil, A.L., Leitko, T.A. and Porter, K.L. (1988) 'Infertility: His and hers.' *Gender and Society 2*, 172–199.

Jacob, M.C., McQuillan, J. and Greil, A.L. (2007) 'Psychological distress by type of fertility barrier.' *Human Reproduction 22*, 3, 885–894.

Jensen, M.S., Mabeck, L.M., Toft, G., Thulstrup, A.M. and Bonde, J.P. (2005) 'Lower sperm counts following prenatal tobacco exposure.' *Human Reproduction 20*, 9, 2559–2566.

King, R.B. (2003) 'Subfecundity and anxiety in a nationally representative sample.' *Social Science and Medicine 56*, 739–751.

de Klerk, C., Macklon, N.S., Heijnen, E.M.E.W., Eijkemans, M.J.C. *et al.* (2007) 'The psychological impact of IVF failure after two or more cycles of IVF with a mild versus standard treatment strategy.' *Human Reproduction 22*, 9, 2554–2558.

Lechner, L., Bolman, C. and van Dalen, A. (2007) 'Definite involuntary childlessness: Associations between coping, social support and psychological distress.' *Human Reproduction 22*, 1, 288–294.

Lund, R., Sejbaek, C.S., Christensen, U. and Schmidt, L. (2009) 'The impact of social relations on incident severe depressive symptoms among infertile women and men.' *Human Reproduction 24*, 11, 2810–2820.

Mindes, E.J., Ingram, K.M., Kliewer, W. and James, C.A. (2003) 'Longitudinal analyses of the relationship between unsupportive social interactions and psychological adjustment among women with fertility problems.' *Social Science and Medicine 56*, 2165–2180.

Newton, C.R., Sherrard, W. and Glavac, I. (1999) 'The fertility problem inventory: Measuring perceived infertility-related stress.' *Fertility and Sterility 72*, 1, 54–62.

Nyboe Andersen, A., Goosens, V., Bhattacharya, S., Ferraretti, A.P. *et al.* (2009) 'Assisted reproductive technology and intrauterine inseminations in Europe, 2005: Results generated from European registers by ESHRE.' *Human Reproduction 24*, 6, 1267–1287.

Pasch, L.A., Dunkel-Schetter, C. and Christensen, A. (2002) 'Differences between husbands' and wives' approach to infertility affect marital communication and adjustment.' *Fertility and Sterility 77*, 6, 1241–1247.

Peterson, B.D., Newton, C.R., Rosen, K.H. and Skaggs, G.E. (2006a) 'Gender differences in how men and women who are referred for IVF cope with infertility stress.' *Human Reproduction 21*, 9, 2443–2449.

Peterson, B.D., Newton, C.R., Rosen, K.H. and Skaggs, G.E. (2006b) 'The relationship between coping and depression in men and women referred for in vitro fertilization.' *Fertility and Sterility 85*, 3, 802–804.

Pinborg, A., Hougaard, C.O., Nyboe Andersen, A., Molbo, D. and Schmidt, L. (2009) 'Prospective longitudinal cohort study on cumulative 5 year delivery and adoption rates among 1338 couples initiating infertility treatment.' *Human Reproduction 24*, 4, 991–999.

The Practice Committee of the American Society for Reproductive Medicine (2004) 'Smoking and infertility.' *Fertility and Sterility 81*, 4, 1181–1186.

Ramlau-Hansen, C.H., Thulstrup, A.M., Nohr, E.A., Bonde, J.P., Sørensen, T.I.A. and Olsen, J. (2007) 'Subfecundity and overweight in obese couples.' *Human Reproduction 22*, 6, 1634–1637.

Rostad, B., Schei, B. and Sundby, J. (2006) 'Fertility in Norwegian women: Results from a population-based health survey.' *Scandinavian Journal of Public Health 34*, 5–10.

Rowe, P.J., Comhaire, F.H., Hargreave, T.B. and Mellow, H.J. (1993) *WHO Manual for the Standardized Investigation and Diagnosis of the Infertile Couple*. New York, NY: Cambridge University Press.

Sandelowski, M. and Jones, L.C. (1986) 'Social exchanges of infertile women.' *Issues of Mental Health Nurses 40*, 173–189.

Schmidt, L. (1996) *Psykosociale konsekvenser af infertilitet og behandling [Psychosocial Consequences of Infertility and Treatment]*. In Danish. Copenhagen: FADL's Forlag.

Schmidt, L. (2006) *Infertility and Assisted Reproduction in Denmark: Epidemiology and Psychosocial Consequences*. Copenhagen: Lægeforeningen's Forlag.

Schmidt, L., Holstein, B.E., Boivin, J., Sångren, H. *et al.* (2003) 'Patients' attitudes to medical and psychosocial aspects of care in fertility clinics: Findings from the Copenhagen Multi-centre Psychosocial Infertility (COMPI) Research Programme.' *Human Reproduction 18*, 3, 628–637.

Schmidt, L., Holstein, B.E., Christensen, U. and Boivin, J. (2005a) 'Communication and coping as predictors of fertility problem stress: A cohort study of 816 participants who did not achieve a delivery after 12 months of fertility treatment.' *Human Reproduction 20*, 11, 3248–3256.

Schmidt, L., Holstein, B.E., Christensen, U. and Boivin, J. (2005b) 'Does infertility cause marital benefit? An epidemiological study of 2250 women and men in fertility treatment.' *Patient Education and Counseling 59*, 244–251.

Schmidt, L., Tjørnhøj-Thomsen, T., Boivin, J. and Nyboe Andersen, A. (2005c) 'Evaluation of a communication and stress management training programme for infertile couples.' *Patient Education and Counseling 59*, 252–262.

Slade, P., O'Neill, C., Simpson, A.J. and Lashen, H. (2007) 'The relationship between perceived stigma, disclosure patterns, support and distress in new attendees at an infertility clinic.' *Human Reproduction 22*, 8, 2309–2317.

Statistics Sweden (2001) *Why so Few Babies?* [in Swedish]. Demographic Reports 2001:1. Örebro: Statistics Sweden.

Sundby, J., Schmidt, L., Heldaas, K., Bugge, S. and Tanbo, T. (2007) 'Consequences of IVF among women: 10 years post-treatment.' *Journal of Psychosomatic Obstetrics and Gynecology 28*, 2, 115–120.

Terry, D.J. and Hynes, G.J. (1998) 'Adjustment to a low-control situation: Re-examining the role of coping responses.' *Journal of Personality and Social Psychology 74*, 4, 1078–1092.

Tjørnhøj-Thomsen, T. (1999) *Tilblivelseshistorier: Barnløshed, slægtskab og forplantningsteknologi i Danmark [Genesis: Childlessness, Kinship and Reproductive Technology in Denmark].* In Danish. Copenhagen: University of Copenhagen.

Verhaak, C.M., Smeenk, J.M.J., Evers, A.W.M., Kremer, J.A.M., Kraaimaat, F.W. and Braat, D.D. (2007a) 'Women's emotional adjustment to IVF: A systematic review of 25 years of research.' *Human Reproduction Update 13*, 1, 27–36.

Verhaak, C.M., Smeenk, J.M.J., van Minnen, A., Kremer, J.A.M. and Kraaimaat, F.W. (2005) 'A longitudinal, prospective study on emotional adjustment before, during and after consecutive fertility treatment cycles.' *Human Reproduction 20*, 8, 2253–2260.

Verhaak, C.M., Smeenk, J.M.J., Nahuis, M.J., Kremer, J.A.M. and Braat, D.D.M. (2007b) 'Long-term psychological adjustment to IVF/ICSI treatment in women.' *Human Reproduction 22*, 1, 305–308.

Volgsten, H., Skoog Svanberg, A., Ekselius, L., Lundkvist, Ö. and Sundström Poromaa, I. (2008) 'Prevalence of psychiatric disorders in infertile women and men undergoing in vitro fertilization treatment.' *Human Reproduction 23*, 9, 2056–2063.

Wheaton, B. (1999) 'Social Stress.' In C.S. Aneshensel and J.C. Phelan (eds) *Handbook of the Sociology of Mental Health.* New York, NY: Kluwer Academic/Plenum Publishers.

Williams, K.E., Marsh, W.K. and Rasgon, N.L. (2007) 'Mood disorders and fertility in women: A critical review of the literature and implications for future research.' *Human Reproduction Update 13*, 13, 607–616.

Wirtberg, I. (1992) *His and Her Childlessness.* Stockholm: Karolinska Institute, University of Stockholm.

Wirtberg, I., Möller, A., Hogström, L., Tronstad, S-E. and Lalos, A. (2007) 'Life 20 years after unsuccessful infertility treatment.' *Human Reproduction 22*, 2, 598–604.

CHAPTER 2

When Treatment Ends: The Experience of Women and Couples

Gayle Letherby

Introduction

'Infertility' is generally thought of as a medical condition and 'involuntary childlessness' a social experience. It is possible for both to be present at the same time, such as when a woman is unable to conceive after 12 months of unprotected sex and/or is unable to carry a baby to term and is not in a social caring relationship with a child. It is also possible to be medically defined as 'infertile' and yet have a biological child following medical assistance such as in vitro fertilisation or to be caring for a child as a step-, adoptive or foster parent. An individual who defines themselves as 'voluntarily' biologically childless may likewise find themselves in a parenting relationship with children. Furthermore, just as the experiences of motherhood and fatherhood are complex and varied, so is the experience of non-motherhood and non-fatherhood. For this reason I write 'infertility' and 'involuntary childless/ness' in single quotation marks.

In the early 1990s I undertook a UK-based sociological study focusing on issues of definition and identity in relation to 'infertility' and 'involuntary childlessness'. Using qualitative methods – single and dyad interviews and research by correspondence – with 65 women and 8 men, my study group included parents who had achieved parenthood through unaided biological conception, as a result of assisted conception, through adoption and step-parenthood and non-parents. The majority, but not all, had had tests and/or some medical treatment which related to their 'infertility'/'involuntary childlessness'. Twenty of the 65 women were mothers: 12 biologically (5 following medical assistance) and 8 socially; ages ranged from early 20s to early 70s. As well as these differences of experience and age, different economic groupings were also represented. However, there were some differences that were not represented, for example my respondents were predominantly white and heterosexual.

In this chapter I reflect again on my own findings and draw on the research of others to undertake a sociological consideration of the experience of '"choosing" to have children'; 'having treatment and deciding to stop'; and 'following treatment' for individuals and couples experiencing 'infertility' and/or 'involuntary childlessness'.

'Choosing' to have children

In contemporary Western society there are more women (and couples) choosing to remain childless and higher numbers of 'infertility' cases than ever before. Those who do have children have fewer and have them later. Increasing numbers of babies are born following some form of 'assistance': from self-administered donated sperm to medically sophisticated procedures such as egg donation. As Culley, Hudson and van Rooij (2009, p.1) note: 'Differences in definitions, measurement criteria and healthcare systems between countries make global estimates of the prevalence of infertility difficult.' However, a recent and comprehensive review of 25 population surveys of 'infertility' concluded that overall around 9 per cent of women aged between 20 and 44 experience infertility, which equates to 72.4 million worldwide (Boivin *et al.* 2007). Despite this, only around half of those experiencing fertility problems seek any 'infertility' care, and even in more developed societies less than one quarter actually receive any specialist infertility treatment (Boivin *et al.* 2007).

With reference to the desire to parent, Oakley (1981) argued that, for many women, children represent their main possibility of achievement and power. So, children could be viewed as a form of 'property' for women, a group who are otherwise placed by society in a property-less condition. Many writers continue to argue that motherhood is key to women's identity in a way that fatherhood is not to that of men (Gillespie 2000; Letherby and Williams 1999; McAllister and Clarke 1998).

For many people, 'childless' implies a person with something missing from their life:

> mothers are perceived as 'proper' women, while women without children are perceived as 'improper' and treated as 'other'. They are also treated as childlike rather than fully adult... Thus, women who have no children are considered to have no responsibilities and thus to be like children themselves. (Letherby and Williams 1999, pp.722–723).

Further to this, 'choice' in this area for women is something of a misnomer given societal expectations:

> In Western society, all women live their lives against a background of personal and cultural assumptions that all women are or want to be mothers and that for women motherhood is proof of adulthood and a natural consequence of marriage or a permanent relationship with a man. (Letherby 1994, p.525)

While the identity of mother has always been closely identified with caring and nurturing, the identity of father has traditionally been primarily linked to the biological: the father as the provider of seed and significant in terms of genetic ties and family lines. Indeed, in a patriarchal society a child without a father is considered lesser, is illegitimate (e.g. Katz Rothman 1988; Walker 1985). Fatherhood has also been associated with power, authority and status and 'good' fathers are 'good providers'. Thus, the implication is that the biological aspect of fatherhood is important for men and for masculine identity, as is their status as patriarch, but other social and emotional elements of fathering such as caring and nurturing are less important.

The concept of 'capital' can be usefully adapted here. Bourdieu (1986) distinguished between economic capital as command over economic resources (money, assets); social capital as possession of resources based on group membership, relationships, networks of influence and support; and cultural capital represented by the forms of knowledge, skills, education and advantages that a person has which give them a higher status in society. Bourdieu and others have further developed the concept with one of the most recent additions being Urry's (2007) network capital, which is the capacity to sustain networks in situations where people are not always physically proximate. In addition, I would suggest that those who parent children are seen to hold maternal/paternal and parental capital, although the level of status may vary with reference to how parenthood is achieved.

Coppock, Haydon and Richter (1995, p.32) suggest that women's 'rightful' role as mothers has been espoused historically as 'natural' by virtue of their capacity to bear children. Thus motherhood is a 'rite of passage' invariably equated with 'womanhood' and glorified as women's chief vocation. In addition, despite the continued focus on men as providers, both of sperm and money, contemporary fathers are expected to have and also desire more involved fatherhood (Dermott 2003, 2008). All of this is reflected in the stigma and pity that is conferred on women and men who are childless – whether by 'choice' or through 'infertility' (Letherby 1999, 2002a; Throsby 2004) – and in the hostile humour sometimes directed at childless men and their 'manhood' (Exley and Letherby 2001).

Within many non-Western settings and non-white communities in the West, women are arguably even more likely to be 'blamed' for childlessness, and 'infertility' is sometimes thought to be 'good grounds' for divorce for men (Culley and Hudson 2009).

Thus, well-established gendered expectations remain dominant and, while parenthood, especially biological parenthood, is valued for all, there remain differential expectations for women/mothers and men/fathers. Individuals who fail to fulfil these expectations are likely to be viewed as strangers, a concept developed by Simmel (cited by Wolff 1950) which draws on notions of belonging and not belonging, commonality and difference, acceptance and exclusion as a reflection of social ordering. Individuals or couples who are 'involuntarily' or 'voluntarily childless', who parent children to whom they are not biologically related or who parent unconventionally (for example, father as primary carer) may therefore be close to the mainstream group in so far as they have common features in relation, for example, to national, social and occupational identity, but nevertheless feel themselves to be 'strangers', not quite belonging or accepted.

Having treatment and deciding to stop

It is still commonly assumed that reproductive health is 'women's business' and, for some women, this assumption has been instrumental in their control over reproduction. It has also been the cornerstone of many feminist campaigns which have demanded the right for women to 'control their own bodies' (for example, Earle and Letherby 2003; Petchesky 1987). Yet the majority of women do not make reproductive choices in isolation from men (Earle and Letherby 2003) and men, both as medics and as partners, have significant influence on the reproductive choices and experience of women. Furthermore, as evidenced above, the labelling of an illness or a condition as 'women's business' can have serious medical, social and emotional consequences for women. Van Balen and Inhorn's (2002) comment on 'infertility' – a condition that has been seen by some to have its roots in psychological 'disorders' and therefore to be women's rather than men's business – highlights this further:

> women worldwide appear to bear the major burden of infertility, in terms of blame for the reproductive failing; personal anxiety, frustration, grief, and fear; marital duress, dissolution, and abandonment; social stigma and community ostracism; and, in some cases, life-threatening medical interventions. (van Balen and Inhorn 2002, pp.7–8)

Data from research supports this. Throsby (2004), in her study of 15 women and 13 couples who had experienced unsuccessful IVF treatment, notes the following exchange in one interview:

> *Graham:* It's easier being childless for a man. A woman's expected to be a mother figure. You reach a stage, you know married – you're engaged, married, house, kids. You know, nice loving mum and kids. It's just…there is more pressure as well.
>
> *Denise:* Or do you think it's more acceptable that men haven't got children?
>
> *Graham:* Yeah, because there are a lot of men about that are divorced, that are part-time, weekend dads. Men sort of…you know I think it's more of a woman thing. They're supposed to be mothers. (p.68)

Data from my own research suggests that women do not anticipate having difficulties conceiving:

> I don't remember deciding to have children. I had always wanted children of my own and assumed this would happen one day in the same way I assume I will grow old and die one day. It was simply a matter of waiting till I felt secure enough to have children, lived somewhere with sufficient space and had a steady partner. (Steph)
>
> I never thought I'd have any problems – it's the most natural thing in the world. (Sara)
>
> As women grow up we spend half our lives trying to stop ourselves having children and then… [stops talking and shrugs] (Kate)

Perhaps, though, there is more awareness now, not least because of increased attention to such issues in the media (including in books, on TV and on the internet) and through initiatives such as the National Infertility Awareness Campaign. Balen, Fraser and Fielding's (2006) research on understandings of 'infertility' among children aged 10 to 16 highlighted that although parenthood is certainly something they expect to achieve in their twenties or thirties, they are aware of both societal expectation of reproduction and the potential feelings surrounding childlessness. There is also evidence that these worries remain into early adulthood for those who decide to delay having children, as the following newspaper article extract suggests:

> It's not as if I want children yet. I am only 23 and don't even have a boyfriend. I like my life just the way it is, working hard, playing slightly harder. But having spent the past few years desperately worried that I

might get pregnant and downing contraceptive pills like sweeties, now it seems I might never get there.

I could unwittingly have caught chlamydia from a partner... I could have a partner with a low sperm count, a growing problem among European men. My (slightly excessive) alcohol intake could lower my chances of conceiving. I could halve my chances of motherhood just through passive smoking. Bizarrely (and controversially), it is being suggested that if I were to eat soya while trying to get pregnant, a compound in it, genistein, could prevent sperm from fertilising my eggs. Even worse, I could leave it too late and end up on the horrible IVF rollercoaster. (Seal 2005)

Goffman's (1963, p.15) notion of 'stigma' as an 'undesired differentness from what we have anticipated' and Becker's (1963, p.33) definition of a 'master status' as a status that 'overrides all other statuses' are both useful in understanding how individuals and couples experience 'involuntary childlessness'. As Pfeffer and Woollett (1983, p.82) suggest: '[It] seems that once you find yourself involuntarily childless, all other identifying marks are washed away. Of course such transformations are not unusual, they are the hallmark of a socially stigmatising condition'. With specific reference to 'infertility' and 'involuntary childlessness,' the discourses of social loss, biological identity and medical hope that predominate in contemporary academic and 'scientific' publications all operate to give us a picture that supports the dominant social order (Franklin 1990). Thus, it is possible to argue that the public exposure given to these issues over recent years has added to the stigma of the condition.

Not surprisingly, individuals experiencing 'infertility' and 'involuntary childlessness', and coping with an identity which is different and often discredited, engage in considerable amounts of emotional self-management (Exley and Letherby 2001). For the women in my study this was often related to both internal and external blame:

Emotionally, infertility is crushing... In a sense (to me) failure in this area becomes a failure in life. There is anger, shame, confusion, a feeling of helplessness. (Samantha)

I am now unemployed and registered as disabled. I have turned from an ordinary working woman into a nervous, incompetent wreck. My new GP thinks that my constant 'pain' is my own punishment of myself for being a failure as a woman. (Anon, by correspondence)

Similarly, female respondents in Throsby's (2004, pp.151, 152) research said:

Denise: I feel so tremendously guilty that I've deprived him [partner] of having children.

Mary: It's quite difficult [for my mother] because, you know, it kind of challenged her ideas of where she would be in terms of one day having grandchildren.

In Culley and Hudson's (2009) study of culture and 'infertility' in British South Asian communities, similar sentiments arose among males and females:

I want to be a mother. All women want to be a mother because we are born as mothers. If I don't have any children then I would feel very bad. (Focus group, older Bangladeshi Muslim woman, p.100)

What point in keeping this woman if she cannot provide children. (Focus group, Bangladeshi Muslim male, p.104)

Mason's (1993) study of male 'infertility' demonstrated that when men feel 'responsible' and express distress, this is often related to their sense of manhood and machismo. Thus, like women, they too feel that their sense of identity as a person – here a man – is affected. My research supported this:

The doctor puts it down to Rob's sperm really and I was thinking why can't it be something to do with me. I could have handled it more than he could. (Sarah)

I say, 'I can't have children.' It's not difficult to say but it used to be. It felt like a loss of manhood... I felt a lot less of a man. (Will)

In contemporary Western society, issues of kinship and the biological tie (Strathern 1992) and the fear of 'genetic death' (Houghton and Houghton 1984) are important: a fact demonstrated not least by the rise of surrogacy, the posthumous use of sperm to 'father' children and the purchasing of gametes. Biological (and, if at all possible, genetic) motherhood/father-hood go alongside dominant discourses of 'true' motherhood and father-hood and 'proper' families (Culley *et al.* 2009; Letherby 1999; Wegar 1997) and support the view that there are different measures of parental capital. In my own research, biological childlessness was often more of an issue for women than for men:

Andy does his best to be supportive, but it's not nearly such a vital issue for him, he'd like to have children 'but if we can't, we can't' – 'we can always adopt'. For me it's something that's central to my whole life and dominates my every waking moment. (Connie)

> I don't feel that Jim has suffered to the same extent as me emotion-
> ally... We were both so carefree four years ago – Jim still is, but infer-
> tility has had an effect on me. (G. Rogers, by correspondence, signed
> with initial and family name)

There was often tension over what treatment to have and when to stop:

> Before we split up he said 'If it doesn't work we'll buy a boat' and I
> said 'What am I going to do with all these feelings?' He said 'Nobody
> would put up with you.' That's what made me leave. I'd rather be on
> my own if that's how he felt. (Moira)

Conversely, in her study of UK migrant Turkish women's experience of
'involuntary childlessness' and 'infertility' treatment, Gurtin-Broadbent
(2009, p.126) found that many of her respondents reported that their husbands found the treatment more difficult because of the greater stigmati-
sation of male 'infertility' in their community:

> My husband entered a deep depression when he was told that he was
> infertile. He could not cope with this at all, he became very with-
> drawn. (Oya, 34).

Because of this Oya was prepared to bear the social burden of 'infertility'
even though the physiological problem lay with her husband.

Following treatment

The decision to stop treatment can sometimes bring relief, as my study
showed:

> It is now about 18 months since the last treatment. About six months
> ago we decided that we would call it a day and get on with the rest
> of our lives. Since we made that decision I have felt so much better.
> (Annette)

But following this there are other decisions for individuals and couples to
make, one of these being whether or not to attempt to adopt.[1] The young
respondents in Balen et al.'s (2006) research often referred to adoption as
an easy solution to 'involuntary childlessness', unaware of the difficulties
and delays involved in the process. In her research on IVF, Denny (1994)
argued that adoption is often regarded as a last resort after medical treatment has failed. Those of my respondents who had undertaken or were

---

1   I have considered experience beyond treatment, including the significance of remain-
    ing childless, elsewhere (see, for example, Letherby 2002a, 2002b).

planning 'infertility' treatment were keen to stress that they were trying everything they could to become biological parents:

> We haven't looked into adoption (I'm sure I'm too old anyway), but we wouldn't be interested. We would rather selfishly like our own child. (Pam)

> I have only fleetingly thought about adoption. We haven't exhausted all of the avenues open to us yet. (Moira)

Several women in my study told me that they would be willing to adopt but their husband/male partner would not. Two had been through the adoption interviews and had been accepted before they (as a couple) decided not to proceed. In both cases they reported that it was the husband who made the final decision. Reasons for not wanting to adopt were related to fear of the unknown:

> ...the thought that perhaps one's children may turn out to be a disappointment, especially adopted ones, as one doesn't know where they come from. (Steph)

Although there was awareness that having biological children can also lead to disappointment, Throsby (2004, p.77) similarly found that her respondents desired a biological child with their partners, were aware of 'horror' stories of adoption and, unlike my respondents, sometimes constructed adoption as indicative of desperation, the desire to have a baby 'at any cost'.

Some of the women in my research did in fact go on to adopt and, like some in Monach's (1993) study, continued to have a negative sense of themselves:

> One's infertility does not disappear in the face of happy parenthood. (Sheena)

> I have tremendous longing. Even though I have two terrific kids [adopted]. (Annie)

On the other hand, for some the social experience of mothering was more important than the biological experience of pregnancy and birth:

> I finally accepted that I wasn't going to give birth to a child and she's lovely [nodding to photo of adopted daughter on top of the television], lovely. Acceptance isn't easy but...no empty arms any more. The need to mother is different from the need to give birth. (May)

If parenthood is achieved in an unconventional way through, say, adoption or fertility treatment (particularly if the child is not genetically related to both parents) this not only disrupts the order of the expected individual life course whereby biological parenthood is viewed as an inevitable part of adulthood (Exley and Letherby 2001) but also the whole structure of family identity. As Strathern (1992) notes:

> Family life is held to be based on two separate but overlapping principles. On the one hand lies the social character of particular arrangements. Household composition, the extensiveness of kin networks, the conventions of marriage – these are socially variable. On the other hand lie the natural facts of life. Birth and procreation, the inheritance of genetic material, the development stages through which a child progresses – these are naturally immutable. (Strathern 1992, p.152)

With this in mind it is useful to draw on the work of Haimes (1990) who notes that, in cases of donor insemination and IVF where treatment uses the couple's own egg and/or sperm, all three elements of the 'normal' family are satisfied:

> the ideology of the family is not only demonstrated but also enhanced by efforts these couples are prepared to expend to become parents. The structure of the conventional form of 2-parents-plus-children is satisfied and the genetic composition begs no questions since the social, nurturing parents are also the genetic parents. So the resultant child is indubitably linked to her/his parents. (Haimes 1990, p.164)

In adoptive families (as in families formed through the use of donor gametes) only two out of the three key elements of 'normality' are satisfied, the child no longer being genetically linked to both or either parents. For some, cultural and religious beliefs may make some choices impossible or more challenging:

> Islam does not allow adoption, though Islamic texts are very positive about helping orphans… Also, in the Jewish tradition, adoption is condoned; however, ultra orthodox Jews stress the importance of a Jewish lineage of the child, and a conversion is needed. (van Balen 2009, p.42)

In addition to the adoption of particular cultural and religious practices in order to 'pass' (Goffman 1963) as 'normal', it is likely that, historically and to date, families sometimes kept or keep secrets (Abbott 2008). A brief look at internet adoption sites will show that the assumption is that prospective adoptive parents wish for a child that others will assume they are genetically connected to (Letherby and Marchbank 2003). This suggests that adoptive parents wish to hide/challenge the stranger status of themselves and their children that they fear that others will afford to them. Arguably, the recent rise in inter-racial celebrity adoptions could lead to greater acceptance of transracial adoptive families, despite the criticisms that they exploit less privileged individuals (Letherby and Marchbank 2003; Sandelowski and de Lacey 2002). However, the media coverage of such issues pays little attention to the complex assessment processes that prospective adopters experience, as the respondent experience reported on here suggests, and often involves a significant emotional transition (see also Abbott 2008; Daly 1988).

Many scholars report on the pressures that mothers and fathers feel to be perfect parents (Furedi 2001; Hays 1996). My research suggests that previous experience of 'infertility' and/or 'involuntary childlessness' adds a further dimension to self-perceived expectations:

> I…feel extremely inhibited about even moaning about them – especially to friends who are having problems having babies… Needless to say I do dote on my twins; but there are bad times as well as good, and it is difficult to acknowledge this. (Vicky)

> It worries me greatly that I might put…pressure on our children because of wanting them so much. (Samantha)

Throughout the 'infertility'/'involuntary childless' experience, the support of similar others via counselling, face-to-face support groups or internet support groups is valuable for some (Friedman 2009; Monach 1993) and the need for such support can continue into parenthood. Friedman (2009), for example, found support through blogging and argues that this helped her to understand her own experience and those of other adoptive mothers and of birth mothers. Similarly, the plethora of publications and websites devoted to the experience of parenting, including adoptive parenting, not only act as a supportive form of network capital (Urry 2007) but also highlight the ways in which individuals can positively define their experience and resist biological essentialism. For example:

Ed and Carrie's Story
When you first go through infertility, you think there's nothing like having your own. But if we had, we would have missed out on this opportunity. (Adoption Advocates)

Adoption provides a challenge to the self-identity and parental capital status of adoptive parents and also to the children within adoptive families, especially if 'positive self image is much more elusive in the absence of a clearly defined lineage' (Abbott 2008, p.82, drawing on Triseliotis). Research in the area suggests that both adoptive parents and adopted individuals (both as children and adults) find it difficult to talk about the experience, although, not surprisingly, people in situations where adoption is openly discussed felt much more comfortable in their adoption than those who feel uncomfortable asking their parents for information (Abbott 2008, p.82). Of course, though, there are sometimes some questions that adoptive parents may feel they cannot answer, as Annie, one of my respondents, said: 'How can I tell Tim about his birth? I wasn't there.' Again, support from others (including virtual support) in similar situations, for both parents and children, can help to challenge feelings of strangerhood.

Brief final reflections

Thinking sociologically about the experience of 'infertility', 'involuntary childlessness' and parenthood – both biological and social – is useful, not least because it highlights how dominant perceptions of what is 'natural', 'normal' and 'proper' can affect the sense of self, status and experience of those who do things differently. As this chapter highlights, the experiences of 'infertility', 'involuntary childlessness' and parenthood are complex and varied. Reflecting specifically on the experience of adoption, the perceived significance of kin and the (often) dominant view that the medical profession holds the solution can add to feelings of stigma and strangerhood. Yet, as Simmel (Wolff 1950) argues, because all relationships are characterised by attributes of nearness and distance and all individuals are linked into diverse networks and circles, all individuals experience being a 'stranger' at times, a person 'looking in'. In addition, dominant discourses do not remain static and the 'infertile', the 'involuntarily childless' and the 'voluntarily childless', alongside social and biological parents, use, reject and play a part in framing such discourses. Thus, in this situation as in others, it is important not to define individuals as passive dupes merely soaking up and/or accepting external definitions of themselves and their experiences. Rather, as a group, individuals within the discourse can be seen as constituting an alternative discourse; a challenge to more dominant and authoritative ones (Letherby 1999, 2002a). Legislative changes, shifting cultural norms and increased multiculturalism have led, in recent years, to a wide variety of family forms in the UK, with the so-called 'normal' nuclear family being increasingly less dominant. This suggests that although there remains some social stigma surrounding the experiences of non-parenthood and those who parent following assistance (either medical or social), the 'stranger' status of such individuals is less than it once was and may lessen further still.

References

Abbott, J. (2008) '"Someone Else's Child": A Personal View of Adoption.' In A.C. Sparkes (ed.) *Auto/ Biography Yearbook 2008*. Nottingham: Russell Press.

Adoption Advocates, *Ed and Carrie's Story*. Available at www.adoptionadvocates.net/adoptive_stories. html, accessed on 22 January 2010.

van Balen, F. (2009) 'Infertility and Culture: Explanations, Implications and Dilemmas.' In L. Culley, N. Hudson and F. van Rooij (eds) *Marginalized Reproduction: Ethnicity, Infertility and Reproductive Technologies*.[AQ] London: Earthscan.

van Balen, F. and Inhorn, M.C. (2002) 'Interpreting Infertility: A View from the Social Sciences.' In M.C. Inhorn and F. van Balen (eds) *Infertility around the Globe: New Thinking on Childlessness, Gender and Reproductive Technologies*. Berkeley and Los Angeles, CA: University of California Press.

Balen, R., Fraser, C. and Fielding, D. (2006) 'Children and Young People's Understanding of Infertility.' In R. Balen and M. Crawshaw (eds) *Sexuality and Fertility Issues in Ill Health and Disability: From Early Adolescence to Adulthood*. London: Jessica Kingsley Publishers.

Becker, H. (1963) *Outsiders*. New York, NY: Free Press.

Boivin, J. Bunting, L., Collins, J.A. and Nygren, K.G. (2007) 'International estimates of infertility prevalence and treatment-seeking: Potential need and demand for infertility medical care.' *Human Reproduction 22*, 6, 1506–1512.

Bourdieu, P. (1986) 'The Forms of Capital.' In J. Richardson (ed.) *Handbook of Theory and Research for the Sociology of Education*. New York, NY: Greenwood Press.

Coppock, V., Haydon, D. and Richter, I. (1995) *The Illusions of 'Post Feminism': New Women, Old Myths*. London: Taylor and Francis.

Culley, L. and Hudson, N. (2009) 'Commonalities, Differences and Possibilities: Culture and Infertility in British South Asian Communities.' In L. Culley, N. Hudson and F. van Rooij (eds) *Marginalized Reproduction: Ethnicity, Infertility and Reproductive Technologies*. London: Earthscan.

Culley, L., Hudson, N. and van Rooij, F. (2009) 'Introduction: Ethnicity, Infertility and Assisted Reproductive Technologies.' In L. Culley, N. Hudson and F. van Rooij (eds) *Marginalized Reproduction: Ethnicity, Infertility and Reproductive Technologies*. London: Earthscan.

Daly, K. (1988) 'The transition to adoptive parenthood.' *Journal of Contemporary Ethnography 17*, 1, 40–66.

Denny, E. (1994) 'Liberation or oppression? Radical feminism and in-vitro fertilization.' *Sociology of Health and Illness 16*, 1, 62–80.

Dermott, E. (2003) 'The intimate father: Defining paternal involvement.' *Sociological Research Online 8*, 4. Available at www.socresonline.org.uk/8/4/dermott.html, accessed on 22 January 2010.

Dermott, E. (2008) *Intimate Fatherhood*. London: Routledge.

Earle, S. and Letherby, G. (2003) 'Introducing Gender, Identity and Reproduction.' In S. Earle and G. Letherby (eds) *Gender, Identity and Reproduction: Social Perspectives*. London: Palgrave.

Exley, C. and Letherby, G. (2001) 'Managing a disrupted lifecourse: Issues of identity and emotion work.' *Health 5*, 1, 112–132.

Franklin, S. (1990) 'Deconstructing "Desperateness": The Social Construction of Infertility in Popular Representations of New Reproductive Technologies.' In M.V. McNeil, I. Varcoe and S. Yearley (eds) *The New Reproductive Technologies*. Hampshire and London: Macmillan.

Friedman, D. (2009) 'Someone Else's Shoes: How On-blog Discourse Changed a Real Life Adoption.' In M. Friedman and S.L. Calixte (eds) *Mothering and Blogging: The Radical Act of MommyBlog*. Toronto: Demeter Press.

Furedi, F. (2001) *Paranoid Parenting*. London: Allen Lane/Penguin.

Gillespie, R. (2000) 'When no means no: Disbelief, disregard and deviance as discourses of voluntary childlessness.' *Women's Studies International Forum 23*, 2, 223–234.

Goffman, E. (1963) *Stigma: Notes on the Management of Spoiled Identity.* Harmondsworth: Penguin.

Gurtin-Broadbent, Z. (2009) '"Anything to Become a Mother": Migrant Turkish Women's Experiences of Involuntary Childlessness and Assisted Reproductive Technologies in London.' In L. Culley, N. Hudson and F. van Rooij (eds) *Marginalized Reproduction: Ethnicity, Infertility and Reproductive Technologies.* London: Earthscan.

Haimes, E. (1990) 'Recreating the Family? Policy Considerations Relating to the New Reproductive Technologies.' In M.V. McNeil, I. Varcoe and S. Yearley (eds) *The New Reproductive Technologies.* Hampshire and London: Macmillan.

Hays, S. (1996) *The Cultural Contradictions of Motherhood.* New Haven, CT: Yale University Press.

Houghton, D. and Houghton, P. (1984) *Coping with Childlessness.* London: Unwin Hyman.

Katz Rothman, B. (1988) *The Tentative Pregnancy: Prenatal Diagnosis and the Future of Motherhood.* London: Pandora.

Letherby, G. (1994) 'Mother or not, mother or what? Problems of definition and identity.' *Women's Studies International Forum 17*, 5, 525–532.

Letherby, G. (1999) 'Other than mother and mothers as others: The experience of motherhood and non-motherhood in relation to "infertility" and "involuntary childlessness".' *Women's Studies International Forum 22*, 3, 359–372.

Letherby, G. (2002a) 'Challenging dominant discourses: Identity and change and the experience of "infertility" and "involuntary childlessness".' *Journal of Gender Studies 11*, 3, 277–288.

Letherby, G. (2002b) 'Childless and bereft? Stereotypes and realities in relation to "voluntary" and "involuntary" childlessness and womanhood.' *Sociological Inquiry 72*, 1, 7–21.

Letherby, G. and Marchbank, J. (2003) 'Cyber-chattels: Buying Brides and Babies on the Net.' In Y. Jewkes (ed.) *Dot.cons: Crime, Deviance and Identity on the Internet.* Cullompton: Willan.

Letherby, G. and Williams, C. (1999) 'Non-motherhood: Ambivalent autobiographies.' *Feminist Studies 25*, 3, 719–728.

Mason, M. (1993) *Male Infertility: Men Talking.* London: Routledge.

McAllister, F. and Clarke, L. (1998) *Choosing Childlessness.* London: Family Policy Studies Centre.

Monach, J.H. (1993) *Childless: No Choice – The Experience of Involuntary Childlessness.* London: Routledge.

Oakley, A. (1981) *Subject Women.* Oxford: Martin Robinson.

Petchesky, R.P. (1987) 'Foetal Images: The Power of Visual Culture in the Politics of Reproduction.' In M. Stanworth (ed.) *Reproductive Technologies.* Cambridge: Polity.

Pfeffer, N. and Woollett, A. (1983) *The Experience of Infertility.* London: Virago.

Sandelowski, M. and de Lacey, S. (2002) 'The Uses of a "Disease": Infertility as Rhetorical Vehicle.' In M.C. Inhorn and F. van Balen (eds) *Infertility around the Globe: New Thinking on Childlessness, Gender and Reproductive Technologies.* Berkeley and Los Angeles, CA: University of California Press.

Seal, R. (2005) 'Young, childless, anxious.' *The Observer*, 25 June. Available at www.guardian.co.uk/society/2005/jun/26/health.genderissues, accessed on 22 January 2010.

Strathern, M. (1992) 'The Meaning of Assisted Kinship.' In M. Stacey (ed.) *Changing Human Reproduction: Social Science Perspectives.* London: Sage.

Throsby, K. (2004) *When IVF Fails: Feminism, Infertility and the Negotiation of Normality.* London: Palgrave Macmillan.

Urry, J. (2007) *Mobilities.* Cambridge: Polity.

Walker, M. (1985) *Alone of All Her Sex: The Myth and Cult of the Virgin Mary.* London: Picador.

Wegar, K. (1997) 'In search of bad mothers: Social construction of birth and adoptive mothers.' *Women's Studies International Forum 20*, 1, 77–88.

Wolff, K.H. (1950) *The Sociology of Georg Simmel.* New York, NY: The Free Press.

CHAPTER 3

The Shift from Medical Treatment to Adoption: Exploring Family Building Options

Petra Thorn

Introduction

This chapter describes some of the issues to be addressed in infertility counselling when working with couples who consider adoption. I have written it from the perspective of an infertility counsellor with a background in family therapy who works in private practice and independently from an infertility clinic. This has implications for the setting and for the question of the stage of their infertility experience at which clients seek my service. I often work with couples, and when exploring family building options find it crucial to include both partners in the counselling process. Although occasionally couples come to see me before they start medical treatment, most do so after one or two failed medical treatments or when they consider ending treatment and voice a need to explore alternative options. They typically feel physically and emotionally exhausted while at the same time in a dilemma: although they acknowledge that they have a need to recuperate, they feel the ticking of their biological clocks and the pressure to tackle other options.

The following provides an overview of those counselling issues that I find pertinent to address with clients considering adoption. They include when to explore family building alternatives, understanding the importance of emotional resources, addressing the loss of control and the acceptance of social parenthood, managing the balance of giving and taking in a relationship and supporting couples in the development of their own rituals. I have chosen these issues because, from my experience, they represent the areas typically challenging for this group of clients. It goes without saying that couples' situations can be individual and distinct and they may therefore require support in areas not addressed in this chapter.

Given the clinical nature of this chapter I focus on practice issues rather than referring to research. In keeping with this, I have used quotes from couples themselves from time to time.

As I live and work in Germany, the chapter is written from the perspective of a German infertility counsellor, where the social, cultural and legal contexts in the area of infertility and adoption differ from those in Great Britain. In Germany, certain medical treatments for infertility, such as egg or embryo donation, are not available as they are prohibited. Although I am aware that it can be difficult to carry out egg donation in Great Britain as a result of the scarcity of egg donors and the long waiting time, British couples are more likely to consider this to be an acceptable family building alternative and have few reservations about travelling to other countries to have the treatment carried out. German couples are quite hesitant because of its illegal status and the need to travel abroad. Adoption may seem a solution for more couples in Germany than in Great Britain as a result of such legal restrictions but, as German federal statistics indicate, the number of adopted children has declined drastically over the last ten years. Whereas approximately 10,000 children were adopted in 1993, this number decreased to approximately 4500 in 2007 and about half of these children were adopted by relatives and step-parents rather than by couples experiencing infertility (Bundesamt 2008). For many years, couples willing to adopt have outnumbered children available for adoption. Currently, there are approximately ten times more couples waiting to adopt than there are children available for adoption. It is not surprising that the number of inter-country adoptions is rising, representing approximately one-third of all adoptions in Germany (Bundesamt 2008). These numbers indicate that adoption is not readily available and that couples have to be patient, prepared to wait and accept that their wish to adopt a child may not be feasible simply because there may not be children available for adoption. This aspect is likely to be very similar in both countries.

Raising alternatives

> We had four cycles of IVF and then just did not have the energy any more to go on. It was too straining. At the same time when thinking about ending treatment, I felt that there was a black hole. We had not given any thoughts to how life might go on, whether we would try and live without a child or whether we might go for adoption or something like that. This made ending treatment very difficult.

An issue I consider central in counselling infertile couples is the question of when is the best time to consider all available options. Often couples intuitively decide for or against certain options based – understandably – on their initial emotional reaction. However, such decisions need to be valid in the long run and the risk that couples reproach themselves for having taken hasty decisions that they have not thought through and may regret should ideally be minimal. Also, once a path has been decided upon, it may become difficult to stop because certain emotional and/or financial investments have been made. In many cases, couples start medical treatment without considering alternatives but hoping that treatment will be successful. Once treatment has failed or couples decide not to continue because it is emotionally, physically and financially exhausting, they may be in a state where developing alternatives presents yet another challenge which has to be tackled. Although not always possible, alternatives should ideally be raised and explored before a couple has decided to take a certain path.

In the first counselling sessions, quite independent from when couples seek counselling and where they are in their infertility journey, I invite them to brainstorm all alternatives: medical treatment including third-party reproduction, social solutions such as adoption or providing foster care, as well as life without children. Couples may intuitively feel drawn towards certain possibilities and opposed to others. However, in order to minimise the risk of later self-reproach, it is helpful to explore all options with the same degree of wholeheartedness. Counselling in this context has various tasks: in the first instance, it provides information about these options directly to clients, together with information about relevant educational literature and, if appropriate, it helps to establish contact with relevant professionals and institutions. In the second instance, it helps couples to reflect on the potential implications of certain decisions. One of these implications may be the insight that pursuing one option compromises other possibilities: for example, deciding to undergo a certain number of medical treatment cycles before starting the adoption process results in couples becoming older and this may affect their eligibility or suitability for adopting an infant. On a therapeutic level, counselling can explore the meanings attached to these alternatives. It can help couples to understand and, if necessary, to change such meanings by using skills such as reframing, using metaphors or challenging unspoken values or attitudes.

Exploring a life without children tends to be the most difficult issue for couples. It raises unease, if not anxiety, and couples tend to suppress this option and be reluctant to explore it. However, given that no family building alternative provides certainty of outcome, it is useful to be prepared emotionally for the possible 'worst' case scenario of not having a child. Reluctance can be addressed by assuring couples that exploring a life without children does not mean that they give up their wish to have children but that they develop a 'Plan B' should this not be possible; during many challenging situations in life people do not rely on their preferred outcome only but develop acceptable, or at least tolerable, alternatives. Developing such an alternative can help to counteract feelings of loss of control and helplessness, as couples can become proactive and decide if and when any of the ideas and strategies they may develop can be put into practice. However, the most important reason for considering life without children at an early stage of the infertility experience is to provide the couple with certainty that, even if all medical and social options fail, their life and their partnership have a meaning that transcends the wish to have a child and to become parents. This helps to decrease the pressure during medical treatment and during the vetting and waiting period prior to adoption.

Addressing emotional resources and self-care

> We both felt drained after three treatment failures yet felt time pressure to move on with adoption because we were in our late 30s. We felt we did not have the luxury of recuperating but had to start the next project straight away as, otherwise, we may be too old to adopt a child.

Many couples, especially the female partners, describe infertility to be one of the most severe crises in life. Medical treatment typically exacerbates feelings of exhaustion as it can be physically, financially and emotionally demanding. When ending treatment and considering adoption, it is helpful for couples to assess how much energy they have to pursue adoption. I often adapt Satir's (2008) concept of having a full or empty 'pot of self-esteem' and reframe this to a 'pot of energy' as this is something couples can relate to easily. Using a scaling question makes it easy and graspable, especially for the male partner who tends to be more comfortable with facts and figures, to indicate what level of energy both partners have. During or immediately after medical treatment, on average, such 'energy pots' are filled to about 50 per cent, rarely to 70 per cent or higher. Partners then need to assess individually, for themselves and as a couple, how much energy they need in order to pursue adoption and to explore what they need in order to fill their 'pot'. This might involve taking a break from pursuing any infertility-related activities, in a sense a 'holiday' from infertility, placing more value on his or her individual needs and the couple's relationship including (re)cultivating friendships.

When couples are younger, in their late twenties or mid-thirties, the suggestion of having a break from the pursuit of the wish for a child is relatively easy to introduce. With advancing age, however, such as in the above example, this becomes challenging. At the same time, as a result of the greater time pressure, it is even more important to find the right balance between self-care and the pursuit of a child. In these cases a helpful intervention can be to draw a time-line starting not from the current time but from a time in the future when the couple may have determined that this will be the final phase of infertility and that they will have to accept living without children. The time between this point in the future and now can be used to determine what infertility-related activities can be carried out and when, and during what stages breaks from infertility and other activities can be included. Even when such a time-span is very short, say one year, it is usually possible to explore one or two activities or themes that help to fill the 'energy pot' without necessarily slowing down the process. Helpful questions are: What can you do for yourself and for your partner so that your level of energy rises again? What can your partner do for you? By including questions about the partner and facilitating communication between the couple, this becomes an intervention that has the potential to strengthen the relationship and to increase a sense of team spirit.

Managing the loss of control and accepting the unknown

> Infertility leaves you helpless. Deciding to adopt a child is an even greater loss of control because you know nothing about the child and its background as often adoption agencies cannot tell you anything. It took us a long time to decide if we would be strong enough to accept such another loss of control.

Almost all couples describe the infertility experience as a loss of control over an issue that is central to their lives. Being diagnosed with infertility and undergoing treatment unsuccessfully leaves couples helpless, represents a significant loss and may temporarily impact on their level of self-esteem. When exploring adoption the sensation of 'losing control' can become even greater as couples need to decide if they can accept the unknown, that is, accept a child with whom they share no biological heritage and whose background they may know little about. A common fear is that the bond between an adopted child and his or her parents is not as strong and enduring as the love between parents and their biological offspring, and that by accepting social parenthood, the couple risks the loss of love between a child and themselves. Couples should explore this fear to understand what has caused them to think this. Often they are influenced by the strong cultural belief in many societies regarding the durability of biological ties and the fragility of social ones. It can be explained that parent–child bonding results from the love and nurture that parents provide and that biological connections do not necessarily make stronger families.

Not being able to pass on one's biological heritage and to experience pregnancy and the birth of the child are other losses when deciding to adopt. Each partner needs to assess his or her need to experience these and thus consider, separately, the issue of reproducing and of parenting a child. If the loss of not being able to pass on one's genes and of experiencing pregnancy and birth is too great for some individuals, adoption should not be pursued, or at least not at this stage in their lives. A further anticipated loss is that of the loss of love later in life if adopted children seek contact with their birth parents and perhaps develop a relationship with them. Couples worry that they will be rejected in favour of the birth parents, and they must be reassured that children are motivated to contact birth parents as a result of identity issues and the need to have information about their biological heritage but not in order to sever the bond to their adoptive parents.

Counselling at this stage serves several purposes: one task is to explore and understand the couple's reactions towards these different losses. These may be influenced by previous experiences of loss, by typical behaviour patterns of the family-of-origin of both partners and by the couple's current emotional stability. A second task is to explore the possibility of third-party conception versus adoption. This includes understanding the meanings attached to social and biological parenthood, to symmetrical (after adoption) and asymmetrical (after oocyte or sperm donation) parenthood, exploring the couple's confidence regarding a family composition that differs from the norm and discussing the implications, such as information sharing and the needs of children, teenagers and adults. A further task is to probe whether individual beliefs about the need for control and the ability to accept something unknown can be challenged and to see if couples are willing to transcend these beliefs, so that they have a greater spectrum of options to choose from. Exploring possibilities for support and (re)developing resources can facilitate such a change. Couples can be asked what support family members and friends can provide, what adoption agencies can do to facilitate their decision and whether contact with other adoptive families and learning from their experiences may be helpful. It can also be pointed out to couples that their willingness to make use of counselling at this stage of their infertility experience may be indicative that they will continue to be open to professional support once they have built their family. This signifies that they proactively manage challenges and problems and attempt to find solutions rather than passively accept the role of a victim of problems. Being confident enough to accept help in difficult times is a strong resource in itself.

Establishing and re-establishing a balance in the couple's relationship

> We were so out of sync, we had the impression that we could not agree on anything: I wanted to move on and get information about adoption, but my wife insisted on more medical treatment, and I found it so difficult to see her suffer through treatment. Managing these differences between us was almost more painful than infertility itself.

Infertility often results in an imbalance for couples: one is diagnosed with infertility and experiences feelings of guilt, the other is fertile; one partner suffers more from the inability to have children than the other; one undergoes treatment (often the female partner), the other can do little to alleviate the physical burden of treatment; one manages the emotional issues more easily than the other; one can accept infertility and/or family building alternatives more readily than the other. Many typical difficulties can be normalised and differences can be connoted positively: gender-specific reactions, such as the typically female need to share feelings and the typically male need to become proactive, can be suggested to be not only challenges but also resources; having both emotional and solution-focused perspectives present in a relationship is inherently enriching and provides for more problem-solving options. Couples often acknowledge the fact that it is helpful for one partner to have the strength to move on. At the same time, imbalances can challenge couples' functioning and can be a painful experience, especially if there are previous unresolved issues that re-emerge during the infertility experience, or if the imbalance becomes very polarised so that partners feel limited in their ways of managing problems.

One of the central questions in this respect is in what areas congruence is needed for couple functioning, or to put it in counselling terminology: what issues need to be resolved so that the couple as a 'team' is ready to move on? In some instances I have experienced couples who are reluctant to address differences because they fear that acknowledging them may exacerbate them. In others, one partner has the need to protect the other from his or her strong feelings, not knowing if such protection is desired or helpful. In yet others, one partner may dismiss the emotional reactions of their partner, considering them irrelevant, leaving the other partner feeling misunderstood. The latter is often the case with the feelings of guilt experienced by the partner diagnosed with infertility. Although 'guilt' as such may not be an appropriate concept, as infertility is not something deliberately brought about, this is often the terminology used by clients as it seems to best describe their feelings. Emotions that remain unexpressed may hinder the couple from finding adequate solutions and may subtly emerge as feelings of irritation in areas unrelated to infertility. Therefore, it is helpful to facilitate couples to express and share, rather than negate, feelings and to help couples resolve them. Couples can be encouraged to share with each other their different views and to explore resources for overcoming them. Helpful questions are: Would you explain to your partner your emotional reactions and your views? Can you explain what has contributed or influenced your reactions? What are you willing to give to your partner so that the two of you can overcome this difference? What do you need from your partner and/or from others? How have you resolved previous differences in your relationship? Who has determined the pace of decision-making so far and has this been helpful? Couples can also be made aware that giving and taking in some areas of their relationship may not be balanced in the short-term but in the long-term. They can be asked whether one partner can give and sustain an imbalance, feeling confident that, at some stage in the future, they will reach a balance again.

Other issues, such as discontinuing fertility treatment and considering adoption, may be more complex to resolve because they include accepting a family composition based on social rather than biological ties. In such cases it helps to explore the fears and fantasies both partners associate with certain options (in this case with adoption) and, where appropriate, to challenge any 'myths' such as believing that biological families have stronger bonds. I have found the following questions useful: What was your first reaction when you considered adoption? Do you know what led to this reaction? Do you know any adoptive families and how has this influenced your thinking?

Counselling should also serve to resolve differences or conflicts, in the sense of promoting understanding and acceptance. If a person feels emotionally validated because she or he has had the opportunity to share underlying reasons and their partner has expressed empathy and acceptance of these different views, it may become easier for each of them to accept differing views and to support them.

Understanding grief and developing rituals

> I did not know how I could show my feelings of loss. I cried a lot when I was on my own, but feared that my friends would not really understand why I was so sad – after all, I was never pregnant and thus did not really have to mourn the loss of a child.

Grief and loss related to infertility are emotionally difficult as they are not related to a concrete loss but to the loss of a potential, a wish. In most cultures there are no mourning rituals for this type of loss. Couples often report that family members and friends do not understand their profound feelings but expect them to move on with life quickly, suggesting that feelings of loss are considered to be unwarranted and hence remain unacknowledged. Infertility involves typical emotional reactions such as shock, disbelief and helplessness, anger and self-blame, shame, grief and loss. It can also include depressive reactions and low self esteem, especially after failed medical treatment. Gender differences are not only typical during the early phases of infertility but also prevalent when couples attempt to accept infertility and move on to different options: while women typically report a greater need to share their emotions and do so openly, men tend to distance themselves emotionally, do not voice a great need to communicate their feelings and concentrate on practical solutions. This lack of emotional and verbal expression by men may result in their loss being ignored and the focus being on the female partner only. It is therefore important to give men adequate opportunities to express or to manage their grief in ways appropriate for them. This may be by accepting a phase of withdrawal or by defining an appropriate time allocation for discussions concerning infertility between the couple and during the counselling process.

Once couples attempt to accept infertility, a mourning phase of many months is not uncommon, as are depressive reactions during this time, which are similar to mourning the loss of a significant other. Coming to terms with infertility, however, does not mean ceasing to think about it altogether but to accept it, to integrate it into one's identity and to find a way to value life without (biological) children while accepting that infertility-related thoughts may re-emerge at later stages in life.

Many infertility-related issues result in feelings of loss. Supporting couples in grieving these losses and in developing rituals appropriate for their circumstances can be a helpful way to find closure, to accept the unchangeable and to move on towards other options such as adoption. Grief can encompass the following issues:

- failure to conceive spontaneously and to require medical assistance

- (repeated) failure during medical treatment

- failure to conceive at all

- failure to give the partner a child

- failure to give parents a grandchild

- failure to fulfil the socially and culturally expected role of a parent

- loss of certainty and of being able to plan one's life.

Although couples can usually describe their losses very precisely, the suggestion of considering a mourning ritual is often greeted with reservation. As a result of the lack of a culturally accepted ritual and the invisibility of, as well as the taboo and stigma still associated with, infertility, couples may find it inappropriate or even shameful to develop a ritual. It can be helpful to give couples the explicit permission to feel and accept their profound feelings and to find appropriate ways to externalise their emotions. Although rituals are believed to be most powerful if others bear witness, the invisibility and the shame associated with infertility often result in couples preferring intimate rituals that they share between themselves only. Rituals can vary in complexity and couples themselves should decide what they find helpful. They can include:

- writing down and sharing with the partner the hopes and fantasies associated with the child they were not able to conceive

- finding an appropriate place for any medicine that may be left over from treatment and for any other objects symbolising medical treatment or the wish for a child; couples may initially decide to put them in a box for storage in a nearby location and later decide to change this location during the course of time, thus implying that infertility is becoming less significant for them

- preparing a box packed with all objects (books, magazine articles, etc.) that are a memory of the wish for a child and deciding the best place for this box; again, such a location may change over time and such a box can also be buried if this is appropriate for the couple

- participating in a support group dedicated to this issue; this signifies a semi-public ritual in a safe environment with professional guidance

- developing and sharing a ritual with family members and friends.

Some time ago, I was able to support clients who developed a very elaborate ritual that was shared with others. The couple invited their parents and close friends to gather near an old church which was not used any more. They had prepared cards with all their wishes and fantasies associated with children and tied these to balloons filled with helium. While the balloons were flying away, the husband read a text from the Bible that he and his wife had chosen earlier. After the balloons had flown away, the couple and their parents and friends prayed together and ended the day by sharing a meal. Initially, the couple were quite hesitant to show their emotions so openly and to risk so much vulnerability; they also feared that such a ritual may be exaggerated and not understood by their parents and friends. Afterwards, they recalled how powerful it was. It was a very sad and tearful occasion for everybody involved and, although parents and friends acknowledged some limitations in understanding the range of emotions for the couple, they fully accepted them and were able to empathise with the couple. The couple described this ritual as having had a very cathartic effect: the symbolic letting go of the wishes for a child and the sharing of intense feelings enabled them to find closure and to move on in their lives. It also provided them with a small network of significant others who appreciated their feelings of loss and with whom they created a strong bond as a result of the shared ritual.

Concluding comments

This chapter has provided some insight into counselling issues for couples experiencing infertility and considering adoption. Ideally, counselling should focus on clients' issues and needs and provide a supportive environment to explore these and to help clients move forward in their decision-making. Professionals providing counselling in this area not only require professional expertise and willingness for interdisciplinary care but also need to explore and understand their own emotional reactions and attitudes towards medical treatment for infertility and social and biological parenthood, as well as towards unusual and possibly controversial ways of building a family. They must be willing to update and integrate new knowledge in terms of medical and psychosocial developments regarding infertility. Over the last decade, professional organisations, such as the British Infertility Counselling Association, have been founded in many countries. They provide training and education in infertility counselling, as well as a platform to enable networking with other professional groups involved in infertility care. Such educational opportunities can contribute towards increasing or maintaining high professional standards so that up-to-date knowledge, skills and interventions can be applied in the area of infertility counselling.

References

Bundesamt für statistik (2008) *Statistiken der Kinder und Jugendhilfe*. Wiesbaden: Statistisches Bundesamt (from the German Federal Office for Statistics.).

Satir, V. (2008) *Peoplemaking*. (2nd edn). Palo Alto, CA: Science and Behavior Books.

Additional reading

Boden, J. (2007) 'When IVF treatment fails.' *Human Fertility 10*, 2, 93–98.

Brodzinsky, D. (1997) 'Infertility and Adoption Adjustment: Considerations and Clinical Issues.' In S.R. Leiblum (ed.) *Infertility: Psychological Issues and Counselling Strategies*. New York, NY: John Wiley & Sons.

Covington, S.N. and Burns, L.H. (2006) *Infertility Counseling: A Comprehensive Handbook for Clinicians* (2nd edn). Cambridge: Cambridge University Press.

Salzer, L.P. (2006) 'Adoption after Infertility.' In S.N. Covington and L.H. Burns (eds) *Infertility Counseling: A Comprehensive Handbook for Clinicians* (2nd edn). Cambridge: Cambridge University Press.

Sewall, G. and Burns, L. (2006) 'Involuntary Childlessness.' In S.N. Covington and L.H. Burns (eds) *Infertility Counseling: A Comprehensive Handbook for Clinicians* (2nd edn). Cambridge: Cambridge University Press.

Throsby, K. and Gill, R. (2004) '"It's different for men": Masculinity and IVF.' *Men and Masculinities 6*, 4, 330–348.

CHAPTER 4

Where Infertility Arises from a Prior Health Condition – Fit to Adopt?

Marilyn Crawshaw and Rachel Balen

Introduction

Although the majority of UK adoptive parents have fertility difficulties, there is no national data about how many were aware of them *ahead* of trying to conceive. It is likely that most will have presumed themselves fertile until found otherwise. For some, though, knowledge of fertility impairment – or its probability – will have come much earlier. Some cancer survivors, for example, are advised that the treatment is likely to have damaged their chances of ever becoming a biological parent. Other medical treatments, including some for rheumatoid conditions, can carry a similar legacy. And then there are health conditions which themselves can lead to impaired fertility such as Turner's syndrome (TS) for females or cystic fibrosis (CF) for males. As medical treatments improve, so the numbers of survivors who look to adoption as their route to parenthood will increase. Adoption agencies need to ensure that they do not discriminate against such applicants either through the use of blanket 'one size fits all' policies or through disablist attitudes such as seeing disabled applicants as 'only fit' to adopt disabled children.

This chapter considers issues unique to this group, drawing on the limited evidence base and focusing in particular on cancer survivors (acquired health condition) and those living with CF and TS (congenital health conditions) alongside discussing the experiences of disabled parents. In the case of cancer survivors, findings will also be drawn on from a study led by one of the authors (Crawshaw and Sloper 2006, hereafter called the 2006 study) into the experiences of 38 male and female teenage cancer survivors aged 16 to 30 growing up with possible fertility impairment.

To avoid clumsy terminology, 'health condition' will be used to denote both health conditions and physical impairments unless specified otherwise.

When health conditions meet infertility

Coping with the onset of an acquired or a congenital health condition is typically characterised by its day-to-day consequences. Managing symptoms, treatments and appointments with health and social care services can dominate the experience, exacerbated by being in a society geared primarily to its non-disabled members. This only abates as symptoms ease, coping skills increase or societal barriers are lowered. For some, this is a part of childhood experience, while for others there are clear 'before' and 'after' lines in adult life. Many will not be in a permanent adult relationship when fertility impairment becomes known or threatened.

Knowledge of the physical impact of a health condition does not always extend to understanding its impact on the reproductive system, among health professionals (Balen and Glaser 2006; Pacey 2007) or those directly affected (Blacklay, Eiser and Ellis 1998; Crawshaw *et al.* 2009; Zebrack *et al.* 2004). As well as uncertain or incomplete information, some receive incorrect information. Professionals also report being unsure when and how to inform people of their fertility status, especially when impairment occurs during childhood or from birth. Sometimes parents withhold information in the belief that it is 'better' for their child not to know until 'ready'; some young people avoid seeking information for fear of upsetting their parents (Loughlin 2006). The potential for obstetric complications or genetic risk may lead some to avoid pregnancy altogether (Davies, Greenfield and Ledger 2003). Whereas some do not wish to become parents either biologically or through adoption (just as in the non-disabled population), others feel that fertility damage leads to a 'double jeopardy':

> It's one more bad thing about CF. (Sawyer *et al.* 1998, p.228)

> Maybe Richard won't want to get married if we can't have kids. Maybe we won't be able to cope with having a big hole in our life together where our kids should be. It just doesn't seem fair that cancer has taken my fertility away as well as my leg. (Self 2006, p.238)

Although the evidence is not conclusive, some studies have shown that those with fertility-limiting health conditions may delay or avoid intimate and/or permanent relationships (Farrant and Sawyer 2006; Langeveld *et al.* 2003; Puukko *et al.* 1997; Stam, Grootenhuis and Last 2005). Sawyer *et al.* (1998) in their study of 50 males with CF concluded that, unlike situations where the diagnosis of infertility occurs within the context of a relationship, men with CF have to form relationships with the knowledge or expectation of infertility and for some this 'really got in the way' (p.230):

> I love children. I'm very sad about it. There's no point now in getting married. (24-year-old male with CF Sawyer *et al.* 1998, p.228).

Some may look back and see how their health condition, together with fertility difficulties, influenced their growing up especially when both carry stigma.

> I knew they [friends at school] weren't doing it to be upsetting but secretly I actually thought 'God, if they're making these jokes [about infertile people], you know, there's a possibility that I can't and this is what we all think of people that can't have them'. Then that sort of was quite difficult at 16, 17...although on the outside I was probably laughing, on the inside I was actually quite upset. I think it just sort of brought it home that, actually, that would mean I was different and having already been different cos of having no hair and being in a wheelchair. (Male aged 28, 2006 study)

There is a danger, however, in seeing the impact as inevitably negative. There is also evidence to suggest that some individuals gain considerable strength through coping with adversity. Personal relationships can be enhanced as can positive awareness of interdependency (Woodgate 2006); social skills and awareness of others can be enhanced through managing contact with professionals and other patients from a range of backgrounds (Hinds 1997; Kelly, Pearce and Mulhall 2004). Parry and Chesler (2005) in their study with cancer survivors aged 17 to 29 years reported that those who thrived saw themselves as survivors not victims. They viewed themselves as having self-reliance, resilience, optimism, happiness and belief in their ability to deal with whatever life had to throw at them, while remaining aware of their vulnerability and the uncertainty of life – a view echoed by some in the 2006 study:

> I think that was the determination and the desire to achieve things that had come out of having cancer. The determination to, to make it happen... And so in some ways, yes I'm glad I had cancer. You know it sounds bizarre, a bizarre thing to say, you know, it prepared me with a lot more worldly experiences than I probably would have got. (Male aged 26, 2006 study)

It's probably made me grow up as well…just grown up in a way that like you have to accept that you can't really get everything you want, but then that kind of makes you think well you can get through things and whatever you do want you have to work at it…it's made me strong as well, so like if I have to cope with other things in my life, well I can get through that as well. (Female aged 21, 2006 study)

It is clearly relevant and important for adoption services to know how long the person affected has been aware of their fertility impairment and to understand the extent of their factual knowledge, its impact and the reasons for adoption becoming their preferred route to parenthood.

Timing of fertility analysis

Where there is uncertainty about fertility damage (which is not unusual), one option is to seek fertility testing. Again, this is neither scientifically nor emotionally straightforward and is not offered routinely (for fuller information see Pacey 2006; Picton 2006). Hence, adoption social workers or others should not assume that any delay in seeking testing is a result of avoidance or denial.

There is some evidence, albeit limited, that both genders may delay being tested until ready to actively pursue parenthood, on the basis that uncertainty is preferable to confirmation of infertility (Green, Galvin and Horne 2003), especially where there are no stored sperm or eggs to fall back on:

I think postponing dealing with something isn't denial, I think you're just putting it to a time when you can deal with it when you're at a stage that you feel you can deal with it. (Male aged 28, 2006 study)

It is one thing over the last couple of years that has started niggling me just thinking like, do I want to know, do I, don't I? Obviously I don't at the moment but it's like I want to know just in case if I can or I can't… And it's like…it's one of those things if I find out I can, brilliant, if I find that I can't, how is it gonna…I don't know but it's like, just one of these things, do I, don't I? (Male aged 23, 2006 study)

And initially it was something that I thought about and didn't want the tests. I wasn't…ready to have a family and I felt that it would be more difficult to know that I couldn't have children than it was to not know at that point. I think for every appointment after that it's one of the things that comes up and they talk to you about and I think in the first appointment [husband] came to, it came up again and we again at that point made the decision that it's something that we'd go to the clinic when we were, when we wanted to have a family, when we'd got to the stage when it was the right time. (Female aged 25, 2006 study)

This is to be viewed within a context in which there are virtually no pre- or post-testing psychosocial services available. In addition, the lack of discussion with and help with strategy building about fertility and sex from professionals, family members and friends is reported frequently among those living with health conditions (Sawyer *et al.* 1998) making it unsurprising that many feel ill prepared to proactively choose to be tested.

Interest in parenthood

Research has shown that children and young people think about becoming parents from an early age (Fraser, Balen and Fielding 2006). There is no reason to think that those living with a health condition are any different. A majority (76%) of cancer survivors in Schover *et al.*'s (1999) mixed gender and age study were interested in having children and very few (6%) reported their desire had decreased following treatment. Similarly, teenagers in two later studies by one of the authors believed prior to their cancer diagnosis that they would be 'free' to exercise reproductive choice as adults (Crawshaw and Sloper 2006; Crawshaw *et al.* 2003):

> that would be the normal thing to do – get married, have house, have kids, have car, have a job, the normal nuclear family or whatever it is… I just kind of assumed I would have children, but I never really thought that much of it. (Female aged 21, 2006 study)

For some, (in)fertility may not become an issue until they hit their late teens or twenties. Among young people with TS attending a creative therapy group, one said: 'I don't think about the future, like fertility, too much'; another declared: 'It doesn't mean a lot to me yet' (Loughlin 2006, p.167). One young man with CF in Sawyer *et al.*'s (1998) study held similar views when hearing at age 15 that he was probably infertile: 'I didn't really think about it much. At the time I wasn't upset' (p.228).

Most (80%) respondents in one study thought that their cancer experience would make them better parents and just over half wanted children in the future rising to just over three-quarters (77%) among those childless at diagnosis (Schover *et al.* 2002a). In a later study, also with cancer survivors, many reported that their cancer experience made them feel more confident in their skills as existing or future parents, even if their cancer returned and shortened their life expectancy (Zebrack *et al.* 2004).

Disclosing infertility

Those wishing to adopt who were not in permanent relationships at the time they learnt of their fertility impairment, or whose relationship subsequently breaks down, either have to (re)enter such a relationship or move towards adoption as a single person.

It can be a considerable challenge to decide how and when to disclose fertility status, including to romantic partners (Orten and Orten 1994). For example, in the 2006 study there were those who believed it better to disclose early on:

> Yeah, he knew from the beginning when we first – I mean, when we got together, you know, I told him. I thought I'm going to tell him straight from [the] start, because if he finds out further down [the] line, if he's like 'Oh why didn't you tell me?' So I told him everything he needed to know at [the] beginning. (Female aged 25, 2006 study)

Others were more cautious, only sharing information once the relationship was becoming serious:

> It was obvious that I'd had chemo…cos I used to always say when I had long hair or when I was bald or make little jokes about when I was bald and there was photographs of me with like a skinhead virtually, just like no hair. So he sort of clicked that I'd had cancer and things and then I was forced into telling him cos I had to have another operation… And it wasn't about the fertility stuff at that point. I didn't bring that up with him until I realised how serious it was. And how important it was that he realised that there was a possibility that he might never be able to have kids with me which I thought was a bigger issue than it was…he doesn't mind, he knows about it and he says that if we have to adopt, we have to adopt, and we'll think about it then. (Female aged 20, 2006 study)

Adoption services may find it important to consider how disclosure was effected (if a couple) and how the potentially long-standing existence of fertility impairment of one partner has been managed within the relationship. For a single person it will be important to find out who else is aware of the person's fertility status, as complete lack of disclosure, for example, may not bode well for the potential adopter being able to cope with openness in relation to adoption.

Views about alternative routes to parenthood

There is little research about how differently, if at all, those living with health conditions fare within alternative routes to parenthood, how they view such routes and how they choose between adoption and fertility treatments. What there is suggests that adoption may appear more attractive than fertility treatments, especially where adoption is viewed more favourably within the wider society. In one US study, less than 5 per cent of those with cancer-related fertility difficulties had sought fertility treatment, almost two-thirds (61%) said that they would consider adoption if they were unsuccessful at becoming biological parents and less than a quarter (23%) would consider donor insemination (Schover *et al.* 2002a). We have not, however, been able to find any other research measuring *actual* take-up.

Not all will have the choice of trying for biological parenthood through fertility treatments. Despite increased awareness of the relative ease of sperm banking, for example, not all males are offered such an opportunity for a host of reasons, including clinician gate-keeping and severity of onset of ill health (Achille *et al.* 2006; Schover *et al.* 2002b). Among those with less high-profile health conditions and among females in general (where fertility preservation is more experimental and carries greater health risks), access to fertility preservation is even more limited. Financial constraints over accessing assisted conception treatments may also limit take-up (Achille *et al.* 2006; Zebrack *et al.* 2004), especially given the impoverishment associated with cancer survivorship and/or living with health conditions, and the fact that fertility treatments are predominantly provided through private health care. In such situations, adoption services need to be alert to any significant residual feelings of frustration, distress or stress.

There are other gender differences to consider. Some health conditions and/or treatments (Marsden and Hacker 2003) can lead to early menopause and may prompt preoccupation with motherhood at an earlier age than peers. Life and career planning can be affected by having such a narrow window in which to find a permanent partner and start a family, as might later feelings if their relationship came 'too late'.

Even among those with adequate time in which to contemplate the alternatives, lack of accurate information about adoption (Zebrack *et al.* 2004) may mean that their attitudes require as significant a revision as those of many mainstream prospective adopters. In the 2006 study, adoption was frequently seen as holding the potential to reward through 'doing good' or, more altruistically and in keeping with resilience through adversity, through 'giving something back':

> But it's like now right I can't have kids, but you can adopt, you can do loads of other things, like just because one option's closed, the others are all open, so it's like it's easy to dwell on that and say 'Oh I can't have kids, I can't do this, can't do that' but…it could be good is if you're adopting you're giving other kids a chance, you know, and that can be just rewarding in itself. (Female aged 21, 2006 study)

Underpinning such attitudes are beliefs about the relative importance of biological and social parenthood, some of which appear gendered. A number of females in the 2006 study had received offers of egg donation or surrogacy from other females (and some were open to the idea). In contrast, no males had been offered sperm, perhaps reflecting a stronger social taboo on 'gifting' among men and more limited social and verbal male discourses about alternative routes to parenthood.

Views about using donor sperm or eggs appeared influenced by the competing tensions of sexual 'ownership' and biological connectedness – and this may have bearings on capacity to manage adoptive relationships. For example, in the 2006 study one woman felt that the fact that her partner and the egg donor would be the resulting child's *biological* parents would lead her to feeling as if he had 'slept' with the egg donor and that the child was 'theirs'. On the other hand, another described her *preference* for egg donation over adoption as resulting in part from her belief that it might relieve her feelings of guilt at not being able to 'give' her husband a child:

> That yeh, we needed a bit of help to get going but then it would still be ours, I suppose, whereas fostering and adopting bring up a lot more other, a lot different issues that it's not your child, it's somebody else's child and actually how we'd feel about that… I think maybe from my point of view that, one thing that has always concerned me was that I might not be able to give [husband] his children – and egg donation would still be [husband's] children – so I think maybe I'd feel a little bit less guilty about that in a way. (Female aged 25, 2006 study)

Some males felt repelled at the thought of their partner being impregnated with another man's sperm through donor insemination (and some *fertile* women have elsewhere reported feeling that donor insemination was akin to adultery). There was no parallel feeling expressed by women about receiving another woman's eggs into their bodies.

One young man summed up well the sentiments of those who were able to separate parenthood from biological connection alone and feel comfortable – so crucial for adopters:

> I think you can be a biological father and not be someone's dad, you know...personally I think the two things are completely different. (Male aged 23, 2006 study)

Whatever the reasons for turning to adoption, adoption services need to assess whether associated feelings have been sufficiently processed to avoid them adversely affecting readiness to adopt – or, where the intervention is in the adoptive family's later life, whether associated feelings have re-emerged – and whether coping with adversity has led to the development of resilience.

Parenting with a health condition

Although the non-disabled population may assume that disabled people are 'unfit' to become parents (Campion 1995), this is not borne out by research. Indeed some have argued that the experience of coping with health conditions can enhance parenting:

> some of the skills acquired in the course of our experience as disabled people – adaptability, resourcefulness, patience – actually make us particularly well suited to the task of parenting!... Disabled parents have qualities and offer experiences that children value. Examples are the tendency to move at a slower pace and in some cases at a lower level, the willingness to spend more time sitting down and rather less time rushing about, and a certain flexibility around the number of different approaches that can be taken towards reaching a goal. (Wates 2002, p.53)

> Being able to live with what comes, adapt to what happens and to accommodate a wide range of possibilities is part of being disabled but is essential to being a parent. (O'Toole and Doe 2002, p.93)

> For those wishing to adopt children also living with a health condition, they argue that they can provide a model of resilience and acceptance that the children could integrate into their own lives: 'offering what they see as the best gift a child can have: a parent who will love them in their wholeness'. (Wates 2002, p.93)

What is crucial for adoption social workers and other professionals is to be alert to their potential to discriminate. There is evidence from disabled non-adoptive parents seeking help that professionals assume their *capacity* to parent is limited before even considering whether appropriate *support* is in place – that is, whether disabled parents are coping on a level playing field with others (for a fuller discussion see Crawshaw 2008; Morris and Wates 2006). The use of such a medical/individual/tragedy model approach may explain what Wates (2002) points out:

> If concerns are identified up front, then they can be discussed and any resource issues addressed. When, however, they remain on the level of unvoiced assumptions and fears on the part of professionals they easily become a discriminatory barrier...support needs are seen as evidence of parental inadequacy rather than as an indication of the need to provide appropriate community care services. Some of those who have got through the [adoption] selection process report that they themselves had to educate and reassure their assessors as part of the process, teaching them to recognise the social, environmental and structural context of disability rather than seeing it purely in terms of the specifics of an individual's medical condition. (Wates 2002, p.53)

Drawing on the experiences of another socially marginalised group, Hicks (2005) stressed the need to move from 'sameness models' in assessments of gay and lesbian potential adopters towards an acknowledgement of difference and an appreciation of strengths, a move equally applicable to disabled people:

> Social workers are beginning to acknowledge that many lesbian and gay men are skilled at dealing with prejudice and discrimination in positive ways and that such skills are important attributes for foster carers and adopters that can be passed on to children. (Hicks 2005, p.52)

Summary: Implications for adoption

In this chapter we have tried to reflect the experience of living with a health condition, both acquired and congenital, through which fertility has been affected. Adoption social workers and other professionals work primarily with adopters who realise their fertility difficulties in adulthood when they are already with a lifetime partner. Assessing and supporting those who have become aware much earlier that biological parenthood was not possible, and who are continuing to live with the health condition that caused this, requires additional levels of knowledge and, most importantly, awareness. We have suggested that professionals need to consider the unique aspects of this group through looking for their particular strengths and resilience, rather than taking an assumed pathology standpoint.

It has been suggested that the emphasis in adoption to date has been on finding appropriate adoptive parents for disabled children rather than considering the adoptive parenting potential of disabled adults (Wates 2002). More research is needed to test anecdotal experience that disabled people are less likely to be approved or to have children placed, if approved (especially non-disabled children). (Interestingly the same point is made by Saffron (2006) in her discussion of the (lack of) placements with lesbian and gay adopters.) If this is indeed the case, and if appropriate support is unavailable or limited (i.e. a systems and services failing), or if professionals see the need for support as indicating inadequate parenting capacity (individual model approach), then children needing permanent families may be being deprived of a very important parenting resource.

References

Achille, M.A., Rosberger, Z., Robitaille, R. *et al.* Lebel, S. (2006) 'Facilitators and obstacles to sperm banking in young men receiving gonadotoxic chemotherapy for cancer: The perspective of survivors and health care professionals.' *Human Reproduction 21*, 12, 3206–3216.

Balen, A. and Glaser, A.W. (2006) 'Health Conditions and Treatments Affecting Fertility in Childhood and Teenage Years.' In R. Balen and M. Crawshaw (eds) *Sexuality and Fertility Issues in Ill Health and Disability: From Early Adolescence to Adulthood.* London: Jessica Kingsley Publishers.

Blacklay, A., Eiser, C. and Ellis, A. (1998) 'Development and evaluation of an information booklet for adult survivors of cancer in childhood.' *Archives of Diseases in Childhood 78*, April, 340–344.

Campion, M.J. (1995) *Who's Fit to be a Parent?* London: Routledge.

Crawshaw, M. and Sloper, P. (2006) *A Qualitative Study of the Experiences of Teenagers and Young Adults when Faced with Possible or Actual Fertility Impairment Following Cancer Treatment.* York: University of York, SPSW Publications.

Crawshaw, M., Glaser, A., Hale, J. and Sloper, P. (2009) 'Male and female experiences of having fertility matters raised alongside a cancer diagnosis during the teenage and adult years.' *European Journal of Cancer Care 18*, 4, 381–390.

Crawshaw, M.A. (2008) '"What about My 'Right' to Choose?" Young People with Physical Impairments Exercising Reproductive Choice.' In G. Bockenheimer-Lucius, P. Thorn and C. Wendehorst (eds) *Umwege Reproduktionsmedizin 30 Jahre nach Louise Brown [The Long Way to Having an Own Child: Ethical and Legal Problems 30 Years after Louise Brown].* Göttingen: Göttingen University Publishers.

Crawshaw, M.A., Glaser, A.W., Hale, J.K., Phelan, L. and Sloper, P. (2003) *A Study of the Decision Making Process Surrounding Sperm Storage for Adolescent Minors within Paediatric Oncology.* Available from the Department of Social Policy and Social Work, University of York, York YO10 5DD, UK.

Davies, H., Greenfield, D. and Ledger, W. (2003) 'Reproductive medicine in a late effects cancer clinic.' *Human Fertility 6*, 1, 9–12.

Farrant, B. and Sawyer, S. (2006) 'Sexual and Reproductive Health in Young People with Cystic Fibrosis: Hard to Talk About but Too Important to Ignore.' In R. Balen and M. Crawshaw (eds) *Sexuality and Fertility Issues in Ill Health and Disability: From Early Adolescence to Adulthood.* London: Jessica Kingsley Publishers.

Fraser, C., Balen, R. and Fielding, D. (2006) 'The Views of the Next Generation: An Exploration of Priorities for Adulthood and the Meaning of Parenthood amongst 10–16 Year Olds.' In R. Balen and M. Crawshaw (eds) *Sexuality and Fertility Issues in Ill Health and Disability: From Early Adolescence to Adulthood*. London: Jessica Kingsley Publishers.

Green, D., Galvin, H. and Horne, B. (2003) 'The psycho-social impact of infertility on young male cancer survivors: A qualitative investigation.' *Psycho-Oncology 12*, 2, 141–152.

Hicks, S. (2005) 'Lesbian and gay foster care and adoption: A brief UK history.' *Adoption & Fostering 29*, 42–56.

Hinds, P. (1997) 'Revising theories on adolescent development through observations by nurses.' *Journal of Pediatric Oncology Nursing 14*, 1, 1–2.

Kelly, D., Pearce, S. and Mulhall, A. (2004) '"Being in the same boat": Ethnographic insights into an adolescent cancer unit.' *International Journal of Nursing Studies 41*, 8, 847–857.

Langeveld, N.E., Ubbink, M.C., Last, B.F., Grootenhuis, M.A., Voute, P.A. and De Haan, R.J. (2003) 'Educational achievement, employment and living situation in long term young adult survivors of childhood cancer in The Netherlands.' *Psycho-Oncology 12*, 3, 213–225.

Loughlin, E. (2006) 'Infertility: An Unspoken Presence in the Lives of Teens and Young Women with Turner Syndrome.' In R. Balen and M. Crawshaw (eds) *Sexuality and Fertility Issues in Ill Health and Disability: From Early Adolescence to Adulthood*. London: Jessica Kingsley Publishers.

Marsden, D. and Hacker, N. (2003) 'Fertility effects of cancer treatment.' *Australian Family Physician 32*, 1/2, 9–13, cited in M. Self (2006) 'Becoming a Parent – The Transition to Parenthood Where There is Pre-existing Fertility Impairment.' In R. Balen and M. Crawshaw (eds) *Sexuality and Fertility Issues in Disability and Ill Health: From Early Adolescence to Adulthood*. London: Jessica Kingsley Publishers.

Morris, J. and Wates, M. (2006) *Supporting Disabled Parents and Parents with Additional Support Needs: Adult Services Knowledge Review 11*. London: Social Care Institute for Excellence. Available from www.scie. org.uk/publications/knowledgereviews/kr11.pdf, accessed on 23 January 2010.

Orten, J.L. and Orten, J.D. (1994) 'Women with Turner's Syndrome: Helping Them Reach Their Full Potential', cited in E. Loughlin (2006) 'Infertility: An Unspoken Presence in the Lives of Trees and Young Women with Turner Syndrome.' In R. Balen and M. Crawshaw (eds) *Sexuality and Fertility Issues in Ill Health and Disability: From Early Adolescence to Adulthood*. London: Jessica Kingsley Publishers.

O'Toole, C.J. and Doe, T. (2002) 'Sexuality and disabled parents with disabled children.' *Sexuality and Disability 20*, 1, 89–101.

Pacey, A.A. (2006) 'Fertility Preservation Methods and Treatments for Males.' In R. Balen and M. Crawshaw (eds) *Sexuality and Fertility Issues in Ill Health and Disability: From Early Adolescence to Adulthood*. London: Jessica Kingsley Publishers.

Pacey, A.A. (2007) 'Fertility issues in survivors from adolescent cancers.' *Cancer Treatment Reviews 33*, 7, 646–655.

Parry, C. and Chesler, M.A. (2005) 'Thematic evidence of psychosocial thriving in childhood cancer survivors.' *Qualitative Health Research 15*, 8, 1055–1073.

Picton, H. (2006) 'Fertility Preservation Methods and Treatments for Females.' In R. Balen and M. Crawshaw (eds) *Sexuality and Fertility Issues in Ill Health and Disability: From Adolescence to Adulthood*. London: Jessica Kingsley Publishers.

Puukko, L-R.M., Hirvonen, E., Aalberg, V., Hovi, L., Rautonen, J. and Siimes, M.A. (1997) 'Sexuality of young women surviving leukaemia.' *Archives of Disease in Childhood 76*, 3, 197–202.

Saffron, L. (2006) 'Challenging preconceptions of lesbian parenting: Victoria Clarke in conversation with Lisa Saffron.' *Lesbian and Gay Psychology Review 7*, 1, 78–84.

Sawyer, S.M., Tully, M.M., Dovey, M.E. and Colin, A.A. (1998) 'Reproductive health in males with cystic fibrosis: Knowledge, attitudes and experiences of patients and parents.' *Pediatric Pulmonology 25*, 226–230.

Schover, L.R., Brey, K., Lichtin, A., Lipshultz, L.I. and Jeha, S. (2002a) 'Knowledge and experience regarding cancer, infertility and sperm banking in younger male cancer survivors.' *Journal of Clinical Oncology 20*, 7, 1880–1889.

Schover, L.R., Brey, K., Lichtin, A., Lipshultz, L.I. and Jeha, S. (2002b) 'Oncologists' attitudes and practices regarding banking sperm before cancer treatment.' *Journal of Clinical Oncology 20*, 7, 1890–1897.

Schover, L.R., Rybicki, L.A., Martin, B.A. and Bringelson, K.S. (1999) 'Having children after cancer: A pilot survey of survivors' attitudes and experiences.' *Cancer 86*, 4, 697–709.

Self, M. (2006) 'Becoming a Parent: The Transition to Parenthood Where There is Pre-existing Fertility Impairment.' In R. Balen and M. Crawshaw (eds) *Sexuality and Fertility Issues in Disability and Ill Health: From Early Adolescence to Adulthood.* London: Jessica Kingsley Publishers.

Stam, H., Grootenhuis, M.A. and Last, B.F. (2005) 'The course of life of survivors of childhood cancer.' *Psycho-Oncology 14,* 3, 227–238.

Wates, M. (2002) 'Disability and adoption: How unexamined attitudes discriminate against disabled people as parents.' *Adoption & Fostering 26,* 2, 49–56.

Woodgate, R.L. (2006) 'The importance of being there: Perspectives of social support by adolescents with cancer.' *Journal of Pediatric Oncology Nursing 23,* 3, 122–134.

Zebrack, B.J., Casillas, J., Nohr, L., Adams, H. and Zeltzer, L.K. (2004) 'Fertility issues for young adult cancer survivors of childhood cancer.' *Psycho-Oncology 13,* 689–699.

CHAPTER 5

Assessing Infertile Couples for Adoption: Just What Does 'Coming to Terms with Infertility' Mean?

Marilyn Crawshaw

Introduction

The majority of people turning to adoption in the UK are heterosexual couples where one or both partners are subfertile.[1] Many have used assisted conception services with their adult-centred focus and now have to adapt to the adoption services' focus on finding parents for children in care. Their task is to develop sufficient knowledge and self-awareness to be sure that adoptive parenthood is now their first choice. The task of the adoption services is to assess couples' readiness by providing appropriate information (including through preparation sessions), the opportunity to discuss adoption with social workers and other prospective adopters, and assessments that draw on theoretical and research evidence as well as practice wisdom.

This chapter does not provide the procedural or legal detail of the assessment process (see Beesley *et al.* 2002). Instead, it considers the challenges of assessing how far one aspect of many prospective adopters' experiences – their infertility history – helps or hinders their ability to adopt successfully. While its main focus is Western heterosexual couples, much can be adapted for use with infertile single people, gay couples and those from different cultural contexts.

---

1   Although the term 'infertility' is in common usage – and indeed is in the title of this book – most people are assessed clinically to be subfertile. Given its more common usage, the term 'infertility' will be used in the remainder of the chapter.

Where does attention to infertility fit?

The purpose of considering the impact of infertility is expressed most simply as 'What risks might it pose to an adopted child?' These can include:

- compromising the child's ability to bond with infertile adopters and vice versa

- compromising the ability to meet the child's lifetime needs.

In other words, this is not about taking a voyeuristic interest in someone's inability to conceive but is instead about assessing the current meaning to them of not being able to become biological parents and its impact on their emotional and social well-being; how far the 'here and now' reflects the 'there and then'. Assessments need to take account of changes to that dynamic over time in order to consider the likelihood of any previously 'risky' reactions being reactivated in the future. While social workers may approach assessments in terms of risk, prospective adopters are more likely to use terms such as loss, coping and stress to describe their experiences. It is the social worker's task to transfer these to a risk framework. Considering infertility-related experiences solely within a risk framework, however, runs the danger of omitting applicants' problem-solving strategies and how far they have developed strengths and resilience as a result of their adversity. Particular care, therefore, needs to be taken to ensure that these important aspects are not marginalised.

Social workers also need to take account of the social and stigmatising context of involuntary childlessness (Throsby 2004). Assumptions of reproductive choice, social approval of parenthood, expectations of motherhood and fatherhood and the significance of genetic relatedness in parent–child relationships, for example, are shaped and reinforced by the wider context in which prospective adopters have been brought up, mediated by gender, ethnicity, age and disability.

In this chapter, I will outline key theoretical frameworks associated with coping with traumatic personal experiences and consider how to use a combined strengths and risks approach to assessment and preparation. In doing so, I will introduce possible intervention tools that may assist during both home study work and in preparation groups.

Assessing loss reactions associated with infertility

Those turning to adoption through infertility do so having lost their primary goal of having their own biological child(ren).[2] Their experience of reproductive medicine services (for a useful summary see Millar and Paulson-Ellis 2009) might influence their preparedness for adoption, including:

- undergoing infertility investigations but not seeking treatment

- being diagnosed with 'unexplained infertility', male factor infertility, female factor infertility or reproductive 'incompatibility'

- having miscarriages

- trying medical treatment with their own gametes (eggs and sperm)

- having treatment using donated gametes (sperm, eggs or embryos).

While all have now decided to pursue parenthood outside the medical arena, only the latter group have already pursued actively the formation of a family without full genetic links.

Whether feelings of loss are accommodated in ways that will not impact negatively on future parent–child relationships can be a challenge for prospective adopters to evidence and for social workers to assess, especially with the growing awareness that managing infertility is a lifelong task. I turn first to what adoption social workers might consider a 'good-enough' stage of resolution for now.

Theories and experiences of loss and trauma

Experiences of infertility-related loss differ between individuals and among couples, as they are affected by the individual and social meanings that the loss of a planned-for biological child holds in the past, present and future. This can include loss of:

- control over destiny

- control of body function

- genetic continuity

---

2   A small number turn to adoption as a result of secondary infertility, i.e. where they have a biological child/ren but fertility difficulties have prevented them being able to complete their family naturally.

- future as a biological mother or father
- future as a biological parent with partner
- physical experience of pregnancy, birth and early infancy
- fertile identity as an individual and/or as a couple
- providing a biological child for one's kinship system.

Losses can impact on the individual's sense of themselves (including as male or female) and decisions to do with work, training, home and so on may prove increasingly difficult to keep 'on hold' as time goes on. Losses can also impact on a couple's sense of themselves as a couple. This can be heightened where there is a history of other significant losses even where coping had previously been satisfactory (for example, death of loved ones, miscarriage), where pre-existing levels of self-esteem are low, where there is a reproductive/parenting history that carries social disapproval (for example, promiscuity, abortion, 'relinquishment' of previous children), where there are pre-existing tensions in the adult relationship and where the achievement of biological parenthood is especially highly valued within the family and social networks of those affected. For some, becoming a parent may feel more a route to self-actualisation and 'coming of age' within one's community or extended family than a life choice. Feelings towards self can also affect those towards other people (especially those who are parents or pregnant) or other events. Reactions across a number of spheres may spiral out of proportion if coping levels become too stretched (Cooper-Hilbert 1998).

Theoretical approaches to loss have been developed primarily in order to understand human responses to death (of others or self). So-called 'stage' theories adopt a pathway approach that culminates in a point at which those affected are able to 'move on'. Typically this includes initial stages of shock and disbelief through, variously, stages of denial, bargaining, anger, guilt, loneliness and sadness to a point at which the individual starts to reorder their lives in ways that take account of the loss (Parkes, Laungani with Young 2003; Worden 1991). Although such theories were never intended prescriptively – in other words, they allowed for movement backwards and forwards within an overall progression – that is often how they have been viewed in practice. More recently, an alternative, 'dual process' theory has gained favour, based on research that suggests that most people cope with grief through a combination of 'loss-oriented' and 'restoration-oriented' coping from the start (Stroebe et al. 2001). In other words, rather than a pathway process, grieving is thought to involve oscillation between discharging feelings of grief *alongside* getting on with rebuilding life. Where people appear stuck, attention therefore needs to be paid to assessing whether it is the balance between the two arms that is proving dysfunctional rather than progression through stages.

Where the loss arises from fertility difficulties and is of a hoped-for state, rather than of a person, it has been suggested that this causes 'unfocused grief' and mourning for the 'death' of one's genetic continuity (Houghton and Houghton 1984) and unfolds across time and context. The subjective meaning of infertility thus requires ongoing renegotiation whenever triggered anew by relevant life experiences (Cooper-Hilbert 1998). Moreover, unlike death the loss of one's fertility does not usually start with a single event but only becomes clear over time *and* the opportunity to 'overcome' it through treatment or a 'miracle' conception remains tantalisingly present.

Coping styles
Alongside theories of loss, the adoption social worker can draw on theories and research into coping styles. Two broad strands of coping – emotion-focused (processing/managing feelings to lower the strain/threat) and problem-focused (devising actions to lower the strain/threat) – are likely to be employed in varying combinations. Within these strands, patterns can be defensive or active.

Where emotions or actions are defensive, individuals or couples become 'stuck' – for example, displaying relentless distress, anger or rumination; adopting 'busy-ness' or 'manic repair' modes; refusing to discuss alternatives. Here, reflective coping or decision-making is inhibited, as are feelings of compassion or awareness towards others. Where family members, friends or professionals find it difficult to tolerate the thought that conception may never happen (and/or that adoption is the way forward), they can unwittingly reinforce any tendency towards such defensiveness – what Cudmore (2005) has called the 'conspiracy of silence or inappropriate reassurance' (p.7).

Where active coping is employed, feelings are discharged *alongside* taking actions – in a similar vein to the dual-process model of grieving. Those affected can tolerate the possibility of treatment failure and can occasionally stand back from personal experience to see infertility in its wider perspective. Some may have been contemplating adoption for some time while acknowledging their sadness at not achieving biological parenthood. Here, the ability to reflect and to empathise with others (so crucial for successful adoption) is present.

It is simplistic to suggest that coping styles are essentially gendered but there is evidence to suggest that women are more likely to use predominantly emotion-focused approaches and men those that are problem-focused (Greil 1997; Martin and Doka 2000; Sydsjö *et al.* 2005). Thus, women appear to react to infertility with more emotional affect and for longer than men, to look to a wider range of others for support and to favour talking about their feelings more than (only) using activities as a way of coping.

Given that most adoption social workers are female, it is crucial to be alert to any tendency to see problem-focused coping styles as necessarily defensive. Looking instead for signs of a dual-process approach, even where one side is more dominant, may be an important antidote. If female applicants have strong networks of confidantes but are unable to engage in reflective discussion of the needs of adopted children to be put first, then this is as much of concern as male applicants who have acquired detailed knowledge of adoption processes but fail to understand their purpose.

Most theories concentrate on individual coping but the adoption social worker needs to also understand the couple dynamic and how this too affects coping.

Understanding the couple context

A couple is more than two individuals: simple but true. Unlike one-to-one work, adoption social workers are working within a triad. They need to be clear about when they expect the couple to use their *relationship* to work on a task and when they are gathering information that requires them to shift backwards and forwards between individual and couple roles. Some activities straddle both of course – for example, in taking the social history the social worker will be (i) gathering information about their lives as individuals, (ii) gathering information about their life as a couple and (iii) encouraging active reflection at individual and couple levels.

Most Western heterosexual adults choose a partner with a very similar age and social profile to themselves, with a shared outlook on key issues (say, approach to family life) and shared interests (say, music, films, sport). Couples expect a comfortable psychological proximity to each other – a 'marital fit' or 'dynamic equilibrium' – that makes them feel safe and at ease and helps them contain their painful selves as well as nourish their happy selves (Cooper-Hilbert 1998; Howe 1995). Because mature adult behaviours are constantly interfered with by 'inner infant' reactions, the couple's relationship will include 'care-giving' and 'care-receiving'. When their equilibrium is threatened, they will together seek to restore it. Thus, each individual may have their own reaction but this will in turn influence and be influenced by their reaction as a couple. As interactive systems, adult partnerships cannot be fully understood without taking into account the roles and reactions of both partners, and the stance they adopt *as a couple.*

How do couples cope with stress?

When stresses become too great for *giving* as well as *receiving* enough care from each other (and sources of outside support prove insufficient to compensate), the potential for the relationship to become dysfunctional is heightened. In their work with couples undergoing fertility treatments, Pengelly, Inglis and Cudmore (1995) found this could manifest in four main approaches to communication:

1. **Unilateral refusal to discuss or negotiate** – where one partner refuses to discuss anything with the other.

2. **Coercive negotiation** – where one or both only engage in discussion under duress, taking measures to avoid it such as staying at work late/refusing to switch the television off/claiming the other is cruel or unreasonable by expecting discussion.

3. **Mutual reassurance** – where both seek constant reassurance from the other but avoid problem-solving.

4. **Mutual avoidance** – where talking is kept to a minimum by both, or only involves arguments, ostensibly for fear of upsetting each other.

Attachment theory can offer helpful insights into such patterns. When our wants, desires or yearnings are unmet as infants, we experience rage or deep distress and set up defences against the resulting pain. We go on to develop internal working models for organising our responses that are influenced by the extent to which we have reliable, 'good enough' caregivers on hand. Internal working models are then used to manage future experiences, including in adult partnerships, and are shaped further by life experiences and relationships (Howe 1995; for a discussion of the use of the Attachment Style Interview with prospective adopters see Bifulco *et al.* 2008).

Where individuals feel emotionally fragile or stressed and have an insecure attachment history, they are more likely to cope defensively (see above) by splitting into 'good and bad' those events or people (including adult partners) that threaten them. The more rigid the split, the less likely that mixed feelings towards others (including partners) can be expressed and the less able is the couple's relationship to handle problem-solving and constructive dialogue. Couples can also use splitting *as a couple* to defend against mutually experienced stressors.

From their research and professional practice with adult couples under stress, Mattinson and Sinclair (1981) produced a theoretically informed typology of four dysfunctional relationship patterns that fits well with the above communication patterns. They suggested that each partner experiences feelings of want/yearning and anger/rejection towards the other, with only one operating consciously as a result of 'splitting':

Babes in the wood: where both partners defend against their anger by only expressing want/yearning between them, clinging together in the face of adversity.

Cat and dog: where both partners defend against their feelings of want/yearning by only expressing anger and rejection towards each other. They may nevertheless stay together and idealise the rest of the world.

In these two groups above, couples will mainly use 'mutual reassurance' or 'mutual avoidance' communication styles.

Net and sword[3] *(1):* where the male partner casts the net by expressing feelings of anger/rejection and uses the sword to deny any feelings of want/yearning for the other, and vice versa for the female partner.

Net and sword (2): where it is the female partner who expresses anger (and hence casts the net and uses the sword), and vice versa for the male partner.

In both the above, it is the expression and impact of difference in their conscious and unconscious feelings that keeps the couple together, mainly using 'unilateral refusal to discuss or negotiate' or 'coercive negotiation' communication styles.

These four relationship patterns are set out in Table 5.1.

---

3   Net and sword describes the gladiatorial combats of old in which the gladiator strove to encompass another with a net while wielding a sword.

Table 5.1: Dysfunctional relationship patterns

	Male partner	Female partner
Babes in the wood	Conscious want/yearning Unconscious anger/rejection	Conscious want/yearning Unconscious anger/rejection
Net and sword (1)	Conscious want/yearning Unconscious anger/rejection	Conscious anger/rejection Unconscious want/yearning
Net and sword (2)	Conscious anger/rejection Unconscious want/yearning	Conscious want/yearning Unconscious anger/rejection
Cat and dog	Conscious anger/rejection Unconscious want/yearning	Conscious anger/rejection Unconscious want/yearning

Note: Yearning can also be experienced as wanting; rejection can also be experienced as anger.
Source: Mattinson and Sinclair (1981).

In contrast, those who have developed the capacity as a couple to register, tolerate and think about what is painful and difficult (including in the relationship itself) will demonstrate open communication and be more likely to cope well with adoption, including being able to feel empathy towards, rather than threatened by, birth parents. They will be better placed to interpret and respond more accurately to each other's feelings, to communicate more openly and be more willing to compromise, recognising and affirming their resourcefulness as a couple. This will be supported or reinforced where the couple also has good extended support networks and where their desire to adopt is socially acceptable within their key reference communities. Such typologies may aid adoption social workers to look behind the impression that couples present on the surface.

Hearing from the couple about what they have been through, how they coped with infertility, especially when under stress, and what were their communication patterns can provide valuable information about their potential to solve problems, process feelings and tolerate any differences in coping styles. Inviting them to tell their story as a demonstration of the success of their journey may aid social workers' assessments and enable couples to see themselves as resourceful and resilient. I shall return later to ways of capturing transferable elements to take forward into adoption. For now, paying attention to whether their mourning is advanced sufficiently is a priority.

With this theoretical backdrop, it might be helpful to consider the different stages that couples may have been through before arriving at the adoption agency's door.

Assessing the impact of involvement in medical interventions

When it becomes clear that conception is not straightforward, the involvement of health services turns this private matter into a more public affair and the 'patient' role begins. Those affected have to manage their emotional reactions under professional scrutiny, feeling a loss of control as appointment times, test results and so on take over. Physical investigations can be physically and emotionally intrusive, lengthy and gender specific. Once a diagnosis is arrived at and treatment starts, hope and some return of control may defend against the fear of involuntary childlessness. However, the impact of the diagnosis on their couple identity, as well as on their individual identities and future, has to be managed.

Were their reactions to the diagnosis complementary or did they have to manage differences? Were their reactions 'in character' or not? How far did any patterns continue? What similarities are there in seeking professional involvement in forming their families through adoption and have any feelings been reactivated?

Even if tests reveal a male impairment, the female body is usually the treatment 'site'. Social exchange theory tells us that people take considerable risks in order to attain socially valued positions such as parenthood.[4] Many embark on assisted conception treatments despite their low success rate and high risk (when viewed with cognitive-instrumental rationality) because the social gains are high and risks low (when viewed with subjective-expressive rationality). Treatments, including those involving donated gametes, may start while one or both partners are still processing the impact of diagnosis and not yet fully signed up to treatment. Of particular concern is if one is unaware or disregarding of this in the other and if health professionals do not consider it appropriate to intervene.

Treatments also bring uncertainty and losses, including:

- waiting for each stage to begin

- limited contact with professional support between treatment cycles

- cycles abandoned if ovaries are over- or under-stimulated

---

4   Social exchange theory proposes that social behaviour is the result of an exchange process. The purpose of this exchange is to maximise benefits and minimise costs. According to this theory, people weigh the potential benefits and risks of social relationships. When the risks outweigh the rewards, people will terminate or abandon that relationship.

- eggs failing to be fertilised in the laboratory

- previously frozen embryos or sperm not thawing successfully for treatment

- fertilised embryos failing to implant following transfer from the laboratory.

And, of course, life on the 'outside' continues.

Here again, some well-chosen questions by social workers need to be asked within the context of understanding and assessing couples' abilities to manage the stress, differences and decisions that may arise in the adoption journey: How did applicants handle their feelings of loss and tolerate any painful reactions or differences to treatment or outside events, individually and as a couple? What are their retrospective reflections on the effectiveness of their coping approaches and the history of their decision-making patterns? Have they been able to acknowledge any difficulties to each other? What did they learn about themselves as individuals and as a couple that they can take forward into adoption?

Assessing the impact of leaving medical interventions

Clearly adoption social workers need to know how far adoption remains a 'second best' choice. Reasons for leaving medical intervention can be helpful to ascertain as they may carry different legacies for the shift from the need to be pregnant to the need to be a parent:

- medical advice – sometimes with the caveat that new treatments may come on-stream in the future

- too emotionally or physically demanding

- unacceptable for religious or cultural reasons

- financial – the majority of fertility treatments are only available in the private healthcare sector in the UK

- adoption seen as more likely to achieve the goal of parenthood.

Couples have to cope with any feelings of being a medical 'failure' alongside managing the loss of health professionals and treatment regimes with which they may have formed strong attachments. Where one partner is fertile, now is also a time for them to look afresh at whether they wish to remain together knowing that biological parenthood remains possible for one. For those who ended treatment reluctantly, for example because of financial reasons, leaving it behind may prove especially fraught. Unresolved difficulties that were masked by immersion in treatment can resurface here with the risk that they are avoided again by too rapid an entry into adoption.

For some, there may be considerable turbulence at crossing into the 'coming to terms' stage that marks 'grief work' from the 'anticipation of grief'. Gradually people realise that they are more often feeling sad about not becoming a biological parent than yearning for conception to happen or aggrieved that it did not – what I have elsewhere called a 'necessary sadness' (Crawshaw 1995). This is rarely a linear process but more one achieved after oscillating backwards and forwards. Acknowledging the possibility that they may never conceive is a different pain to that with which they are already familiar. Their previous pain is looking for a resting place from which it may periodically come to visit with an intensity as of old but where recovery will be more rapid and easier to negotiate. 'Moving on' is not pain-free but is a differently experienced pain.

Unlike other moves into grief work, such as a funeral, there is rarely a ritual to accompany this stage *and* the possibility of further treatment or a 'miracle' conception remains. Individuals within a relationship may also, of course, be at different stages which may cause conflict, loneliness or a sense of dislocation.

As the couple move on, emotional and physical energy that was previously expended on managing treatment is now available to manage the transition out of it. People know when they are ready to move on, though may need several rehearsals and become angry or tearful when others raise it. Externalising the internal is an important step; others may take the step alongside, but only the couple can decide whether to keep up the pace or stay put for now.

Where couples are able to see how resourceful they have become through treading the path of infertility, they can start to see how that can be harnessed into becoming adoptive parents. They can feel more in control again, drawing on the added resources acquired individually and as a couple through adversity. Decisions over the way forward are reclaimed from the medical arena and transferred into that of adoption. This switch in the locus of control may prove difficult. Couples feeling good about regaining control may resent losing even part of it again (to the adoption process), even though this represents a step on the way to family life. Cudmore (2005), in her work with adopters, found that assessment often brought a renewed loss of privacy, especially where the professional approach used dialogue that was more inquisitorial than reflective.

For adoption social workers, knowledge about couples' engagement with professional services within the context of their infertility can provide helpful information. Unlike in adoption, some health professionals encourage the belief that maintaining secrecy about a child's origins is beneficial to healthy family life, downplaying any significance of genetic forces or biographical identity (Daniels 2004; Lorbach 2003). Couples will have had the 'choice' as to whether to disclose their medical involvement to others and, as face-to-face support groups are rarely available, there is limited opportunity to come together with others even if desired. In other words, they may have retained their privacy, especially if sensitive to the stigma of infertility. In adoption, openness with the child is paramount, others must be informed of the adoption application and group work is invariably a requirement (although privacy over infertility outside the service context can usually be retained). Although some may welcome the opportunity to come together with others who share their infertility experience as well as their desire to adopt, others will be apprehensive or resistant. Those disclosing infertility in their family, social or work networks for the first time will have to learn how to manage others' reactions; for those who have already been open, the task will be to manage reactions to the decision to adopt.

As well as encouraging couples to tell their story, adoption social workers can use tools to facilitate those who feel less comfortable in sharing thoughts and feelings. The loss exercise (see Exercise 5.1) can be used either in preparation groups or within home studies. It is designed to (i) encourage individuals and couples to self assess their current feelings of losses, including their relative weighting, (ii) generate discussion between partners and (iii) enable adoption social workers to see how far their assessment matches the self assessments.

Exercise 5.1: Loss
· · · · · · · · · · · · ·

Patricia Johnston, an adoptive parent, identified six main areas of loss that people need to have thought about and assessed themselves on before entering into adoption. It can also be used to work out where you might need some extra support or where you may need to pay attention to yourself (or your partner, or yourselves as a couple if you are a couple), at any stage in the adoption process, including after placement. You could also complete this exercise from time to time and see what changes have taken place. I have laid out a table based on her ideas:

1. Consider the following question: If I had had the power to avoid personally experiencing one or more of these losses, which would I have chosen to avoid? – i.e. which are the most significant losses to me and which are the least?

2. Rank the statements from 1 to 6, with number 1 being the most significant loss to you and number 6 the least.

3. Next, look at each loss and give it a weighting on a scale of 0 to 3 according to the following:

    0   experiencing the finality of this loss means little or nothing to me

    1   this loss bothers me somewhat, but other losses bother me more

    2   this loss is relatively important for me

    3   experiencing this loss is very painful for me

Loss	Ranking 1–6	Weighting 0–3
Loss of control over many aspects of your life		
Loss of individual genetic continuity linking past and future		
Loss of a jointly conceived child with your life partner		
Loss of the physical experience of pregnancy (including getting your partner pregnant if a man), birth and early infancy		
Loss of the emotional experience of pregnancy (including getting your partner pregnant if a man), birth and early infancy		
Loss of the opportunity to parent		

Assessing transferable strengths in managing uncertainty and difference

Assessing adjustment to losses alone misses important dimensions of infertility experiences that can introduce risk or resourcefulness into adoption, namely coping with uncertainty and/or difference.

Infertility-related losses unfold over time, fuelled by uncertainty at each step. Many people describe themselves as 'living on the edge' – waiting for the next appointment or test result, the next menstrual cycle and so on. The only certainty is that conception has not yet occurred. There is uncertainty too for prospective adopters at each step, including whether they will get approved, whether a match will be found, whether strong-enough attachments will be formed, whether the adoption order will be made, whether the family will remain intact over its lifetime and whether their adopted child will later wish to seek birth relatives.

With the realisation of fertility difficulties, those affected become alert to feeling different. Given that such difference is an unwelcome, socially devalued identity, it is frequently a source of stress. The more protracted this period, the more that couples can feel isolated from prior social networks as well as dislocated from their preferred approach to life planning. This can be exacerbated where they have little access to others who share their experiences, as referred to above. As couples relinquish their quest for biological parenthood they start to feel reintegrated and see more similarities with those around them. However, managing difference is part and parcel of the adoption experience and can re-stimulate earlier feelings.

Those who have contemplated forming a family through the use of donated gametes have already considered how to manage genetic difference. For those coming to this for the first time, it can be helpful for adoption social workers to normalise fears – such as that they will not bond with an adopted child; that they will fall short of what it takes to be a successful adoptive parent – so that these fears can be discussed constructively, while also assessing coping potential in the light of past and present experiences.

Although biological and adoptive parents' tasks have more similarities than differences, the latter's handling of the differences[5] – including their accommodation of the possible influence of genetic-relatedness – will contribute significantly to successful outcomes (Johnston 1992; Waterman 2003). Where adoption-related differences are experienced as deficient,

---

5   In this chapter, I have not discussed the impact of ethnic differences between parent and child or between adult partners as this is covered more fully in Chapter 9.

shameful and threatening, this may be manifest by prospective adopters denying that they exist, downplaying them or overstating their significance. Kirk (1964), in his seminal text, suggested that a productive way into such discussions is to explore whether prospective adopters feel an *entitlement* to parenthood (rather than a right), to claim an adopted child as their own and believe that they deserve and belong to each other.

Although attachment building (between adoptive parent and child) and entitlement building are different, they are also inextricably woven: one could not happen without the other. They require alertness to, and dealing with, any ongoing feelings about infertility; recognition and acceptance of differences with minimal feelings of threat; and skill in handling the *societal* view of adoption as a second-best alternative – as one adoptive father put it:

> Being an adoptive parent can seem a mark of biological imperfection...
> All adoptive parents are vulnerable to feelings of regret about their lack
> of a blood tie with the children they love, but it is possible to note and
> accept these feelings without being dismayed or undermined by them.
> (May 2005, pp.64–65)

While many only turn to adoption as a result of infertility, entitlement requires couples to embrace it as an active choice. It is nevertheless unsurprising that studies suggest that grieving emerges afresh alongside the myriad of other emotions at placement and from time to time thereafter and needs to be anticipated, acknowledged and normalised by social workers (Ludlum 2008; Millar and Paulson-Ellis 2009; Tollemache 1998).

Adoption social workers need to garner information about past and present ways of coping with uncertainty and difference to see whether increasing resourcefulness is evident. It is not the job of adoption social workers to offer therapeutic help but it is appropriate (indeed vital to a therapeutic outcome) to invite couples to reflect on and identify how they can transfer their strengths and resourcefulness into their adoption experience – including helping their adopted child cope with losses and uncertainties – at the same time as identifying potential sources of stress. The use of a transferability exercise, such as Exercise 5.2 below, can usefully augment conversational approaches.

Exercise 5.2: Transferability – Part I
. . . .

	What made me/us feel stressed or vulnerable during infertility investigations or treatment?	Ways of coping that worked for me as an individual	(For couples only) Ways of coping that worked for us as a couple
In relation to the health professionals and treatment centre			
In relation to what was happening at home or in my/our wider family or support network			
In relation to what was happening at work, socially and so on			

Exercise 5.2: Transferability – Part 2

	What might make me/us feel stressed or vulnerable during the adoption assessment and preparation?	What might make me/us feel stressed or vulnerable between approval and placement?	What might make me/us feel stressed or vulnerable after placement?
In relation to professionals and the agency	And what might ease that:	And what might ease that:	And what might ease that:
In relation to what might happen at home or in my/our wider family or support network	And what might ease that:	And what might ease that:	And what might ease that:
In relation to what might happen at work, socially and so on	And what might ease that:	And what might ease that:	And what might ease that:

Summary

In this chapter, I have explored a range of theoretical perspectives and suggested prompts and tools to aid assessment of the risks and strengths posed by the infertility experiences of prospective adopters. These should be considered integrally with other influences – childhood experiences, support networks, parenthood expectations and so on – on suitability to adopt.

The pathway through assessment invariably starts with a shared vision of a hopeful outcome. Prospective adopters are eager to get started on their journey; social workers are keen to find committed and reflective adopters. As contact develops, difficult and painful issues have to be explored – their infertility, their relationship, the potential for challenging behaviours in adopted children – and the strains associated with going through the scrutiny of assessment and preparation emerge. Where this engenders strong reactions, the temptation for social workers is to back off, especially in areas such as infertility where they may feel less confident about the appropriateness of their approach. In fact, adoption social workers can usefully provide the 'container' to allow feelings to be worked through actively rather than defensively, hence aiding preparation for adoption as well as gathering important assessment evidence. The arousal of strong feelings should not be seen as an automatic negative indicator but more as an opportunity to gauge how individuals and couples make meaning of, and process, feelings, or get 'stuck'.

There will (always) be invisible parties in the room where infertility is present – the child/ren originally planned for and the child/ren that they may adopt. Prospective adopters have to manage their relationship with both 'children' in order for neither to adversely affect the other. Social workers too need to feel confident enough to discuss this dynamic and model the importance of expressing any mixed feelings. Lousada (2000) has written movingly from his therapeutic work with adult adopted people that 'not only is it the absent birth mother who has to be kept in mind for the adopted child, but also the experience of infertility for the adopting couple' (p.55).

Adoption assessments involve giving factual information, asking questions in a transparent and respectful way and engaging in discussion with a warm, confident manner. Encouraging the disclosure and exploration of important information, including of feelings and experiences about infertility, can be achieved without threatening autonomy, especially when the identification of strengths and resilience is being sought. Prospective adopters often want to put their infertility behind them but experienced social workers know that it will not always stay there. Assessments that see strengths coming out of adversity can both encourage adopters to harness those strengths and set the scene for enabling adopters to journey reflectively throughout their adoption experience.

References

Beesley, P., Hutchinson, B., Millar, I. and de Sousa, S. (2002) *Preparing to Adopt: A Training Pack for Professionals.* London: British Association for Adoption and Fostering.

Bifulco, A., Jacobs, C., Bunn, A., Thomas, G. and Irving, K. (2008) 'The Attachment Style Interview (ASI): A support-based adult assessment tool for adoption and fostering practice.' *Adoption & Fostering 32,* 3, 33–45.

Cooper-Hilbert, B. (1998) *Infertility and Involuntary Childlessness: Helping Couples Cope.* New York, NY: Norton.

Crawshaw, M.A. (1995) 'Offering Woman-centred Counselling in Reproductive Medicine.' In S.E. Jennings (ed.) *Infertility Counselling.* Oxford: Blackwell.

Cudmore, L. (2005) 'Becoming parents in the context of loss.' *Sexual and Relationship Therapy 20,* 3, 299–308.

Daniels, K.D. (2004) *Building a Family with the Assistance of Donor Insemination.* Palmerston North, New Zealand: Dunmore Press.

Greil, A.L. (1997) 'Infertility and psychological distress: A critical review of the literature.' *Social Science and Medicine 45,* 11, 1679–1704.

Houghton, D. and Houghton, P. (1984) *The Gift of a Child: Coping with Childlessness.* London: Unwin Hyman.

Howe, D. (1995) *Attachment Theory for Social Work Practice.* Basingstoke: Macmillan.

Johnston, P.I. (1992) *Adopting after Infertility.* Indianapolis, IN: Perspectives Press.

Kirk, D. (1964) *Shared Fate.* New York, NY: Free Press.

Lorbach, C. (2003) *Experiences of Donor Conception.* London: Jessica Kingsley Publishers.

Lousada, J. (2000) 'Infertility and the "Bureaucratic" Child: Some Thoughts on the Treatment of Two Adopted Patients.' In A. Treacher and I. Katz (eds) *The Psychology of Adoption.* London: Jessica Kingsley Publishers.

Ludlum, M. (2008) 'The Longing to Become a Family. Support for the Parental Couple.' In D. Hindle and G. Shulman (eds) *The Emotional Experience of Adoption: A Psychoanalytical Perspective.* London: Routledge.

Martin, T.L. and Doka, K.J. (2000) *Men Don't Cry: Women Do. Transcending Gender Stereotypes of Grief.* Philadelphia, PA: George H. Buchanan.

Mattinson, J. and Sinclair, I. (1981) *Mate and Stalemate.* London: Tavistock Institute of Marital Studies.

May, P. (2005) *Approaching Fatherhood: A Guide for Adoptive Dads and Others.* London: British Association for Adoption and Fostering.

Millar, I. and Paulson-Ellis, C. (2009) *Exploring Infertility Issues in Adoption.* London: British Association for Adoption and Fostering.

Parkes, C.M., Laungani, P. with Young, B. (2003) *Death and Bereavement Across Cultures.* Hove: Brunner-Routledge.

Pengelly, P., Inglis, M. and Cudmore, L. (1995) 'Infertility: Couples' experiences and the use of counselling in treatment centres.' *Psychodynamic Counselling 1,* 4, 507–525.

Stroebe, M.S., Hanson, R.O., Stroebe, W.S. and Schut, H. (eds) (2001) *Handbook of Bereavement Research.* Washington, DC: The American Psychological Association.

Sydsjö, G., Ekholm, K., Wadsby, M., Kjellberg, S. and Sydsjö, A. (2005) 'Relationships in couples after failed IVF treatment: A prospective follow-up study.' *Human Reproduction 20,* 7, 1952–1957.

Throsby, K. (2004) *When IVF Fails – Feminism, Infertility and the Negotiation of Normality.* Basingstoke: Palgrave Macmillan.

Tollemache, L. (1998) 'The perspective of adoptive parents.' *Journal of Social Work Practice 12*, 1, 27–30.

Waterman, B. (2003) *The Birth of an Adoptive, Foster or Stepmother: Beyond Biological Mothering Attachments.* London: Jessica Kingsley Publishers.

Worden, J.W. (1991) *Grief Counselling and Grief Therapy.* London: Routledge.

CHAPTER 6

Adoption and Infertility: The Role of the Adoption Panel

Jenny Gwilt

This chapter will consider infertility and adoption from the point of view of adoption panels in England and Wales. It will review their legal powers and duties and those of adoption agencies in relation to infertility and adoption. It will consider statutory and good practice guidance and how adoption agencies have interpreted and used these. Finally, it will look at the panel's role in quality assuring the work of the agency, the key issues that it needs to know about, how to manage and learn from couples attending panel meetings and how panels formulate their recommendations and advice to agencies.

Adoption law

Adoption law in England and Wales has gone through a lengthy evolution since the first legislation in 1926 (1926 Adoption Act), often falling behind social needs, public opinion and practice issues. The 1926 Act was designed primarily to regularise the adoption arrangements for illegitimate babies. Numbers rose rapidly until their peak in 1967, comprising almost wholly so-called 'relinquished babies' rather than children from public care. Improved and more widely available contraception, legalised abortion, improved welfare benefits and changing social mores then resulted in a gradual decline in numbers of relinquished babies. At the same time, the study *Children Who Wait* showed large numbers drifting in the care system without a clear plan for their future (Rowe and Lambert 1973). The Children Act 1975 gave social workers more powers to provide permanent adoptive homes for these 'hard-to-place' children.

Despite such developments, changes were still slow. The 1976 Adoption Act took 12 years to implement, by which time its provisions were already out of date (Ball 2005). The children now in need of adoption were increasingly older, with a history of abuse, neglect or physical or learning disabilities, all of which would challenge any adoptive family. A review of adoption law also recognised that, for some, continuing contact with birth families might be appropriate as might other forms of legal permanence. However, legislation did not follow until a change of government in 1997 refocused attention with the issue of the statutory guidance, *Adoption: Achieving the Right Balance* (Department of Health 1998). This challenged the view held by many practitioners that the Children Act 1989 required children in care to be rehabilitated to their birth families without limit of time. It emphasised the importance of timely decision-making to avoid delay in achieving permanent arrangements through the formation of secure relationships within a new family.

A period of intense public debate about adoption and other forms of permanence followed, together with further inquiries and publications, culminating in the Adoption and Children Act 2002. This represented a complete and radical reform of domestic and inter-country adoption law across both statutory and voluntary agencies,[1] and an alignment of adoption law with the Children Act 1989 to ensure that the child's welfare is the paramount consideration in all decisions. By modernising adoption services, incorporating 'good practice' developments, improving country-wide consistency and providing a clearer framework within which barriers to the adoption of older and more challenging children would be removed, it was hoped that more people would come forward to adopt.

The Act itself has nothing specific to say about infertility and adoption, although it allows, for the first time, both partners of an unmarried couple to apply jointly to adopt, whether heterosexual or not, providing that 'proper regard is had to the need for stability and permanence in their relationship' (Section 45). The Adoption Agencies Regulations 2005 specified in detail what should be taken into account in determining suitability to adopt.

The adoption panel
During the drafting of the new adoption regulations, there was detailed discussion with a range of stakeholders about whether adoption panels bring added value to the process. There was widespread agreement

---

1   In England and Wales it is only local authority adoption agencies or licensed voluntary adoption agencies that can provide adoption services; private profit-making adoption agencies are illegal.

confirming their value as a body independent of the adoption agency and able to bring a degree of scrutiny and challenge to actions proposed by agency staff – is adoption the right plan for a child, should individuals and couples be approved as suitable to adopt, should a child be placed with a specific family for adoption? The panel makes recommendations and offers advice to the adoption agency; it is the agency that makes the final decision, although there is now an independent review mechanism in cases of dispute about suitability to adopt.

The adoption panel, with a maximum of ten members and a quorum of five, is made up of professional and lay members, including an independent chair (a role the author has occupied many times), two social workers with relevant experience, a medical adviser and three independent members, the latter including at least two with personal experience of adoption. Most panels include an adoptive parent and an adopted adult and some are fortunate to include a birth parent of an adopted child, ensuring that all key personal perspectives are represented. Lay members bring a variety of personal backgrounds and are often able to ask straightforward, jargon-free questions derived from their own experience.

The work of the panel is supported by a legal adviser and a professional adviser who is a senior social worker or social work manager with specialist knowledge of adoption. As personal details are rarely shared, neither panel members nor those attending panel will know whether anyone on the panel has personal experience of infertility that may influence their views.

Regulations and guidance

As well as the Act and Regulations, there is statutory and good practice guidance about adoption, including the assessment of prospective adopters. Statutory guidance explains in layperson's language what the regulations mean and how to meet their requirements. It must be followed, unless adoption agencies have a very good reason not to do so in specific circumstances and can show that they can meet the requirements in another way. The guidance sets out clearly what must be done from the moment when prospective adopters first approach the adoption agency for information, to the time when a child placed with them is adopted. This includes the duty to:

- provide information and counselling

- invite enquirers to information meetings where they can meet other prospective adopters and adoptive families

- check eligibility (applicants must be over the age of 21 and living permanently in this country)

- undertake checks and seek references

- provide preparation courses

- undertake a home study

- assess applicants' suitability to adopt in the light of information gathered.

When the panel meets to discuss an approval application, the information which must be made available is set down in regulation and includes criminal record enquiries, a written report about their health, personal references, information from the records of the local council where they live and the prospective adopters report (PAR) written by the assessing social worker. The PAR's content is extensive but is, in essence, the assessment of suitability to adopt in the light of their history, characteristics and present circumstances.

The potential for mismatch

Most infertile couples arrive at the adoption agency after a long and frustrating journey through infertility treatment. It has often carried high emotional and financial costs and they look forward to a speedy adoption process resulting in them becoming the parents of a young baby with a straightforward history. Despite extensive publicity, many remain unaware that there are few 'relinquished' babies available and that adoption agencies have stringent approval requirements. Many couples approach the adoption agency either before or immediately after their infertility treatment is complete. Given the agency's paramount duty to the child, it will want to consider the extent to which such couples have resolved their feelings about their infertility and whether adoption is a positive choice. This is the first of a number of stages where there can be a mismatch between the hopes of the couple, the needs of children awaiting permanent families and the expectations of adoption agencies.

Agency policies in relation to infertility

Prior to the 2002 Act, adoption agencies – both voluntary and statutory – had a range of inflexible policies about those whom they would not consider as prospective adopters; groups most commonly targeted were smokers, those who were overweight or considered too old and couples who had not been together for 'long enough'. Many agencies set arbitrary limits requiring couples to have completed infertility treatment for, say, six months or a year before applying.

During the consultation process on the regulations and guidance there was unanimous professional agreement that before making an application infertile couples needed time to grieve for the fact that they would not have birth children and to adjust to the idea of adoption. However, in order to increase the chances of children from the care system being adopted, one government aim for the 2002 Act was to broaden the range and increase the number of people coming forward. Applicants were therefore no longer to be automatically excluded, except for certain criminal convictions. In other words, there should be no 'blanket bans', with every case considered on its merits, which is also a requirement of human rights legislation. Infertile couples might therefore now expect to be able to approach agencies as soon as they feel ready. Anecdotal evidence is, however, that practice has not changed, blanket bans are still in force and couples have to wait a specified amount of time after ending treatment before agencies will accept their application.

With many couples initially hoping to adopt a young and, as they see it, 'straightforward' baby, and adoption agencies with a long list of older children, sibling groups, children with disabilities and children with attachment difficulties awaiting placement, the difficulty is obvious. Given workload demands on qualified, experienced social workers, agencies prioritise the assessments of those most likely to provide a home for children in those categories. Infertile couples may face a long wait even before their assessment can begin; very disheartening for people who have already waited so long to become parents and who have seen literature advertising the need for more adoptive parents.

Infertility and inter-country adoption

For those for whom the prospect of adopting an older child from the care system is too daunting, inter-country adoption (ICA) can seem like the answer. After all, it appears to them that there are many unwanted babies in developing countries whose parents are too poor or too ill to care for them, as well as babies orphaned by illness and war. The 'one child only' policy in China has led to significant numbers of girl babies being abandoned. Prospective adopters may hold the view that such babies 'deserve' to be rescued and will have a better life in the UK; many professionals hold the view that it is wrong to remove children from their homeland and culture, wrong to take away a country's future and better to support children in their country of origin.

Whatever the range of political views, the 2002 Act recognised that ICA is here to stay and overhauled the legislation in order to provide more safeguards for birth parents, children and adopters. Infertile couples who want to go down this route have to satisfy the adoption agency that they are 'suitable' to the same standard as those pursuing domestic adoption, as well as demonstrating understanding of and empathy with the culture of the country of origin that they have chosen. Local authority adoption agencies can deal with ICA applications as long as they have someone with specialist knowledge on the panel; voluntary agencies must be specially licensed to do inter-country work.

Brief reports

In circumstances where the agency receives information early in the process that people are unlikely to be 'suitable' – for example, where an applicant has a serious health condition – the Act allows it to take a brief report to panel before a preparation course and home study are offered. The panel can recommend either that the couple are not suitable or that a full assessment should go ahead. This very useful provision means that such cases can be dealt with before the couple have to invest further in the process and it enables the agency to make best use of precious social work resources, although some who are turned down this way can feel cheated.

What is the role of the panel?

The core adoption decisions are: whether the plan for a child should be adoption, whether an individual or couple are suitable to adopt and whether a child should be matched with a particular family. The scrutiny and challenge role of the panel is a vital part of the quality assurance process of ensuring that the evidence for these decisions is comprehensive and strong. The panel wants to know that key issues have been explored thoroughly, that there is a clear 'audit trail' showing how the assessing social worker's conclusions and recommendations have been arrived at and that couples have been appropriately engaged in the process.

Inevitably, in such a complex process of gathering and testing evidence, contradictions will appear, but as long as these have been explored and the worker has presented an informed, professional judgement in their report, then this is acceptable. However, in the author's experience, many home study reports are incomplete or too descriptive with little attempt to answer the 'so what?' question: What does this evidence tell the panel about the suitability of the couple to adopt? Where this occurs, the chair must liaise with the agency to ensure that the work is redone or rewritten so that the panel can make their recommendations based on evidence of a good standard. While it is helpful and appropriate for the couple to be asked to contribute to the report – an account of their lifestyle, their motivation to adopt and what they think they have to offer would be typical topics – it is the social worker who is assessing their suitability and the panel which is making recommendations to the agency based on that assessment.

Key issues for the panel to consider

While it may seem obvious to many infertile couples that adoption is the way forward if they cannot have birth children, the differences between the two processes are great. Some infertile couples can and do choose not to become adoptive parents, acknowledging that adoption would always be 'second best' as they could never feel the same about an adopted child as a birth child. However, many approach adoption agencies thinking that adoption is the obvious choice and only then begin the journey of discovering what it really involves. It is only when information, advice and counselling are offered that the real iterative process of deciding, with the agency, whether adoption is the right path can begin.

A couple seen recently at panel told us that they started out seeing adoption as a means for them to become parents – what children could do for them – but as time went on and they met others, read and talked to their social worker and each other, they came to the point of understanding what *they* could give to a child. They realised that being given the opportunity to parent a child whose early life had been difficult was a privilege. For the panel, this was a good illustration of a couple who were on an emotional journey from infertility and despair to a point where adoption was embraced as a positive choice; they were ready to become adoptive parents, seeing the child as the centre of the process rather than themselves.

The examination by the panel (and the agency) of adoption motivation is fraught with difficulty, beset as it is by social, cultural, religious and other expectations. Panel members, as well as social workers, bring their own set of values and beliefs about parenthood and adoption. It is vital that they recognise how these impact on their judgements about applicants' suitability. The panel chair has a key role here in getting to know individual members, understanding their points of view and helping to ensure that applications are considered on merit.

Motives can be varied – for example, 'rescuing' abused and neglected children, giving children from 'poor' backgrounds a better life, following religious tenets, not being able to have birth children or providing legal permanence for an existing placement or relationship. Panel members may hold differing views as to which motives are more or less acceptable. However, any may be acceptable as a *starting point*, as long as the information-giving, assessment and preparation processes are successful in moving applicants to a point where they are able to meet the needs of the adoptive child in the context of their history in their birth family. People who are resilient, able to see how the world might look through the eyes of the child and can provide empathetic parenting may be suitable to adopt – whatever their starting point. Infertile couples not at this stage and without these qualities are not suitable, however sad the panel might feel on their behalf.

A key issue for the panel is whether commitment is equally strong for both partners; it is common for the idea of adoption to come from one, with the other initially more reluctant, less willing to give up the mental picture of the birth child they would have had, perhaps afraid of the reaction of family, friends and colleagues and worried about the stigma of adoption. This part of the couple's history is usually well described in the PAR, together with details of how it has been resolved. The panel will be vigilant, questioning the assessing social worker and (perhaps) asking the couple face to face about whether there is now an equal commitment, even if the journey each has taken to reach that point is different. The way this issue has been resolved may also provide clues as to how well developed are the couple's problem-solving and dispute-resolution skills.

The question of unresolved infertility issues is perhaps the most difficult area for the panel. Some issues may be still unresolved when applications are considered, some are the subject of disagreement between the partners, between the couple and others or between the couple and their assessing social worker. Unresolved issues about practical matters – such as who (if anyone) will give up work to care for children, what other childcare arrangements will be made, what hobbies and interests will no longer be possible – may seem comparatively trivial. However, sometimes the unpicking of these 'on the surface' matters reveals that they mask more difficult issues about the extent to which infertile couples have resolved the question of which partner (if not both) had 'responsibility' for the fact that they cannot have birth children. Where it was one partner's medical condition that led to infertility, then at least they can focus on and discuss a clear and identifiable problem. Where this was known from the start of their relationship the non-affected partner will (usually) have made a commitment to their relationship with that in mind. However, the reality of not being able to have children together can resurface at the time when the couple would have been ready to try to start a pregnancy. The content of the PAR should show clearly what discussions they have had and how they arrived at a point where the issue of 'responsibility' was resolved sufficiently for them to move forward to adoption.

Where fertility difficulties came to light as a result of trying to conceive, discussions may be fresh in the couple's mind during assessment. For those with unexplained infertility, some might take the view that this is easier to deal with as it is not one partner's 'fault'. For those who have achieved pregnancies only to see them end in miscarriages, coming so near to their ideal of 'ordinary' parenthood may present particular difficulties. For all couples, the panel will want to see evidence that *both* partners have jointly accepted responsibility for not being able to have children together and are equally committed to adoption as the way forward. The panel will also want to know how far secret hopes for a future pregnancy remain, as for a significant minority the possibility of having birth children never really goes away. Some panel members, including the author, know couples where approval as adoptive parents or having a child placed for adoption is closely followed by a successful conception. Couples may find themselves in the bizarre (to them) position of being told by their social worker that they must use contraception after a placement is made, at least until the adoptive child has settled in.

There are various assessment tools and research messages available to help the social worker decide, with the couple, whether they are 'ready' to adopt. Although some social workers might disagree, it is the author's view that this is a professional judgement rather than a science and there is no guarantee of success, abundantly evidenced by couples who are approved but never matched with the 'right child', couples who split up while waiting for a match and couples where it becomes obvious after placement that too many infertility issues remain unresolved.

Of course, some complicated feelings and emotions that are part of infertility – particularly the anger about 'why me?' – may never be completely resolved. Infertility can have a profound impact on personal identity and self-esteem and the panel will want to see evidence in the PAR of applicants' self-awareness in discussions and interactions between themselves as a couple and with others. Both partners as individuals, and together as a couple, have ongoing resiliencies and vulnerabilities. The assessing social worker should have identified these so that the panel can understand how they might build on and harness their resiliencies to help them through the challenges of empathetic parenting at the same time as having strategies in place to deal with their infertility-related vulnerabilities – any feelings of failure, loss of dreams and hopes, perceived lower social standing and stigma – whenever these vulnerabilities come to the fore.

Adoption is a lifelong journey for adoptive parents and children. Feelings about being infertile can be triggered by events, behaviours, anniversaries and so on across their life cycle as adoptive parents. For example, when their adoptive child suddenly asks why they do not have birth children or when the anniversary of the day they discovered they could not have birth children coincides with a particularly difficult period in their adoptive parenting, prompting reflection on how family life might have been different. The panel want to know that the couple understand and accept these future challenges.

The question for the panel then is whether the couple have demonstrated their ability to resolve any internal differences sufficiently to have the potential, with training and support, to meet the parenting needs of an adoptive child. The panel is not there to *assess* the couple as suitable to adopt or not, but rather to ensure that the *agency* has made a rigorous assessment and to decide whether or not to accept the agency's view about the couple's suitability.

Birth families and infertile adopters

The adoption triangle – child, birth family, adoptive family – is at the centre of adoption. The birth family aspect may pose particular difficulties for infertile couples. All adoptive parents have mixed feelings about birth families: why have they 'given a child up for adoption', how could anyone be cruel to or neglect a child? Even though adoptive parents are aware of the circumstances, difficulties and history that many birth parents have faced, nevertheless it is often hard to accept that a child has suffered. For some infertile couples, the strength of feeling may be almost unbearable. Unable to have birth children themselves, it can be hard to accept that others do not treasure and care for their children properly, a factor that is even more crucial now that most adoptions are of children removed from birth parents because of neglect and abuse. Such feelings will have been acknowledged during preparation and assessment (including, sometimes, through meeting birth parents) and will need to be revisited when an 'actual' match is proposed. By being able to 'walk in others' shoes', adoptive parents may be better able to become attuned to the needs and feelings of the child, including (often) their ambivalence towards the birth parents. If adopters themselves cannot give 'positive enough' pictures of birth parents to a child, then the child may find it more difficult to accept their own history and take any positives into their new life. The panel will want to be reassured that the couple can empathise sufficiently with birth parents to help an adoptive child understand and value their history.

There is no room in this chapter to explore in any detail the complex subject of post-adoption contact with a birth family – parents, siblings, grandparents, significant others. Infertile couples often have greater difficulty around contact issues than those who are already parents when they adopt. Many couples have said that what helped most with contact issues was to meet birth parents face to face – in preparation courses or before or after a match with an adoptive child. Seeing birth parents in person can destroy myths, lay fears to rest, help them help the child to feel they 'have permission' to move to a new home and enable them to integrate the meeting into the history to be told later to their child. Where prospective adopters show significant reluctance around contact issues – except where there is the threat of violence or abduction – then the panel will be concerned that the vital link between the child's past and their future will not be made.

Infertile couples and their own families

As well as their own feelings and wishes, infertile couples must also deal with the expectations and feelings of their own extended families, including wishes and dreams about grandchildren and so on. Many grandparents are as key a support for adoptive children as for birth children. Others find it more difficult to feel the same about a child who is not part of their family's genetic inheritance. Prospective adopters do not always tell their own families that they have applied to adopt for fear of not being approved or of receiving a negative reaction. If this is still the case by the time the application comes to panel, there would be serious concern that the couple are not ready to acquire and be proud of the status of adoptive parents.

Applicants attending the panel

In the past it was seen as good practice to invite prospective adopters to attend at least part of the panel meeting that considers their application. Current regulations *require* agencies to do so, but the panel must not hold it against applicants any decision not to attend. There is anecdotal evidence that some agencies do not make this clear and take a dim view of non-attendance.

Having been part of the first trials of this practice in a voluntary adoption agency and having introduced attendance in a number of agencies before the advent of the new regulations, the author is very committed to it. Attendance is not a test or exam but for many it is 'natural justice', the chance to make their case in person to the panel rather than to a group of – as they may see it – faceless, nameless bureaucrats. Whether or not they have got on well with their assessing social worker, it is their chance to say things in their own way. For the panel, it is the chance to let the couple 'leap off the page' and become real, to test imagined persona against reality, to find the answers to unanswered questions and, most important, to observe at first-hand how the couple work together.

For infertile couples, there are two extra dimensions. First, 'will they ask us about our infertility?', to which the answer is 'probably not'. It would be invidious to ask personal and intimate questions in a room full of strangers. Second, although the legal position will have been explained, most applicants have not understood that the panel is making a *recommendation* to the agency, not the final decision. Many see the panel meeting as a 'decision-making meeting', maybe their last chance to convince others that they are suitable to adopt – perhaps their last chance to become parents. It is therefore invested with frightening powers and can be a daunting experience.

How to make it better? The working of the panel should be explained in advance, they should see a book with pictures of panel members and their roles, the chair should take personal responsibility for welcoming and looking after applicants' welfare and questions should be carefully crafted so they are searching but not too difficult. Finally, prospective adopters should always be given the opportunity to tell the panel anything they think panel needs to know and to put their case to be approved.

The panel's job is to help those attending to give of their best, remembering that they are with panel members for perhaps half an hour or less while their assessing social worker has been working with them over many months. The weight to be attached to evidence from attendance is therefore light compared to the rest.

To sum up: What the panel is looking for in considering suitability to adopt

- Are there any unresolved issues in their history as individuals and as a couple – how significant to adoption, how many, how capable of resolution – especially their infertility?

- What are their resiliencies and vulnerabilities?

- How strong is their relationship?

- Can they be empathetic parents, responding to the needs of the child, as well as or in spite of their own needs?

- Can they see the world through the eyes of the child and respond accordingly?

- How do they resolve differences?

- Can they make secure attachments?

- Can they confide in others and do they have others in whom to confide?

- Do they have a strong support system – at home, in the wider family, friends, the community, the agency – and are they willing to seek help?

- If they have been together a long time, can they adjust their lifestyle and is there 'emotional space' for someone else in their lives?

- Do they understand the lifelong nature of adoption?

- Can they help the child to understand and value their history?

- Do they understand the primacy of what they have to give as adoptive parents over what a child will give to them?

In relation to prospective adopters who are infertile, the key risk for the panel to be aware of is that the child of their wishes and dreams and the child who may be available to adopt are so different that the couple may not be able to accept and deal with the challenge in a positive, hopeful and constructive way.

Bringing the approval process together

Having read all the papers, identified and discussed the issues, questioned the social worker and, probably, met the couple, the panel must come to a view about suitability to adopt and make a recommendation to the agency. The panel may also offer advice to the agency about which children might benefit from adoptive parenting by this couple, taking into account their strengths, vulnerabilities, views and wishes. The minutes must be a detailed record so that the rationale and evidence for the panel's recommendations is clear to the agency's decision-maker and (possibly) to the court. The panel will benefit from regular feedback from those attending – social workers, team leaders, foster carers, family support workers, prospective adopters – about what the experience was like, as well as hearing how those approved or not approved have progressed.

What next?

After the seemingly endless process of becoming approved, couples feel exhilarated – 'finally we will become parents'. The next stage can often come as an unwelcome surprise because it may consist of…nothing. Once having added them to the list available for matching, some adoption agencies do not maintain regular contact and couples talk of their bewilderment and intense anxiety when they do not hear anything, sometimes for months. Couples' details will be circulated to child and family social work teams locally but discussions about their suitability to parent particular children are not always conveyed to the couple themselves.

So what would good practice look like? The most important element from the point of view of an approved couple is to know they are not forgotten and to be kept aware of efforts to match them. Regular phone calls and visits from their support worker, newsletters, opportunities to continue their training and development, and workshops (including alongside social workers and foster carers) where they can meet others in the same boat will all help to sustain them as well as increasing their understanding of the backgrounds of children with whom they may be matched.

Matching practice

Matching prospective adopters to children is an art not a science. Because so little is understood about what makes for a successful match, the government is currently funding research on this subject as part of its Adoption Research Initiative, details of which can be found at www.adoptionresearchinitiative.org.uk. Before the 2005 Act, adopters were approved in very limited, specific terms, for example for one girl aged three to five years or a sibling group of two children under five. This reflected the wishes of prospective adopters and the judgement of the agency about their capabilities. However, it had many disadvantages and, if a possible match was identified of a child outside their approval criteria or the couple themselves wanted to change their approval terms, this required a formal panel reconsideration. This crude system did not reflect the complexities of matching, the fact that nearly all children in the care system function well below their chronological age before placement with an adoptive family nor the fact that most approved adopters are flexible.

The 2005 regulations and guidance allowed matching to reflect better the child's specific parenting needs and adopters' specific parenting skills, strengths and vulnerabilities. Couples are now recommended by the panel and approved by the agency only as 'suitable to adopt' and the panel will then offer advice to the agency about the type of home, parenting skills and parenting style on offer, as well as the ages, numbers and gender of children who might be well matched.

Local authority adoption agencies generally start the matching process by considering whether the couple can meet the needs of local children awaiting placement. The exception is where authorities are so small geographically that a local placement might carry a high risk of accidental encounters with birth family members. However, all local authorities in England and Wales and some voluntary adoption agencies now belong to regional adoption consortia among which details of prospective adopters are circulated. Placements can take place on a reciprocal, no-fee or fixed-fee basis, though there is currently hot debate as to whether the latter is a disincentive and should be replaced by national funding arrangements. Finally, there is also a national adoption register, run by a voluntary agency on behalf of the government, which provides a computerised matching service for children waiting and available adopters who have yet to be matched through other routes.

The above systems are all 'worker led' and hence take no account of the fact that sometimes in adoption, as can happen when adults meet their 'partner for life', the unexpected occurs and a couple see or hear about a child who is unlike the one they imagined but there is 'just something about that child…'. Hence, many local authorities now also use 'adopter-led' matching methods. At one event the author attended, all approved adopters on one agency's list, plus some whose applications were almost complete and adopters approved by local voluntary agencies, were invited to a matching evening. The room was filled with posters designed by children waiting for homes and videos were shown of them in their foster homes. The evening began with an inspirational address by a couple who had adopted two older girls whom they had heard about through a previous event. They had come along with a fixed idea of adopting a young boy but then were attracted by a video of their (now) daughters. Much careful work followed before and after placement (which was not problem free) but finally the girls had settled happily, showing the potential for successful 'adopter-led' matching.

In similar vein, the British Association for Adoption and Fostering (BAAF) produces the newspaper *Be My Parent*, to which prospective adopters can subscribe and in which agencies 'advertise' children awaiting placement. For children where all these methods have failed or where this is anticipated then the child's agency may run a specific local or regional media recruitment campaign.

Once a possible match has been identified, meetings are held between the child's social worker, the adopters' support worker and, later, the prospective adopters themselves, to consider whether they can, with placement-specific training and support, meet the child's needs. This is a very difficult time for the couple who may not be the only family being considered and who may not know how the final choice will be made. Their hopes may be raised only to be told that the child's social worker does not think they are right for the child or that another family is a 'better match'. For an infertile couple, this process may have sad and unfortunate echoes of their repeated attempts to achieve conception or to maintain a pregnancy to term.

Once initial agreement has been reached that a match is possible, then reports about the child (child permanence report or CPR) and the adopters (prospective adopters report or PAR), a matching report and a plan for adoption support for the proposed placement will go to the adoption panel of the agency responsible for the child. The required documentation and process are set down in regulation and guidance and may take some considerable time. Whereas previously more than one set of prospective adopters may have been presented to the panel, current statutory guidance is that there should be only one. The responsibility for choosing which adopters and making the case to the panel lies with the social worker(s).

The prospective adopters may be invited to attend the matching panel but this is not currently a requirement. The panel will study the papers with the workers for both the child and the potential adopters present and consider the primary issue of whether the couple can meet the child's specific parenting needs. The panel will also look closely at an infertile couple's identified strengths and vulnerabilities to try to judge whether and when the child's history and characteristics are likely to trigger unhappy memories or echoes of their infertility and what strategies have been identified to deal with these. If the panel is satisfied that this is a 'good match' then it makes such a recommendation to the agency, giving advice about the proposals for adoption support, about how the parental responsibility for the child will be shared between the adoptive family and the agency until an adoption order is made and about proposed contact arrangements. The agency decision-maker will then make the final decision.

For an infertile couple, hearing a positive decision from the agency must (again) seem like the end of a very long journey – they will at last get to meet the child to whom they will become parents. But, of course, this is only the beginning of the most exciting and challenging journey of their lives. If the path to that point seems very long and complicated, they must remember that the process is designed to find families for children and not children for families.

References

Ball, C. (2005) 'The Adoption and Children Act 2002; A critical examination.' *Adoption and Fostering* 29, 2, 6–7.

Department of Health (1998) *Adoption: Achieving the Right Balance* (LAC(98)20). London: Department of Health.

Rowe, J. and Lambert, L. (1973) *Children Who Wait: A Study of Children Needing Substitute Families*. London: Association of British Adoption Agencies.

CHAPTER 7

'For Him, It's Got to Be Your Own Son': Adoption and Infertility in British South Asian Communities

Lorraine Culley and Nicky Hudson

Introduction

This chapter addresses the issue of how ethnicity and culture might shape the perception of adoption in the context of infertility. Most work on infertility and adoption has concerned itself with the needs, interests and experiences of dominant social groups and white couples in the West in particular. The experience of adoption after infertility in minority ethnic communities remains largely invisible to social scientists, practitioners and policy makers.

Few studies have explored the availability or needs of adopters from minority communities generally (Frazer and Selwyn 2005). However, a MORI poll showed that those from 'Black' (Black-Caribbean, Black-African and Other Black people) communities were twice as likely to express an interest in adoption than white respondents (MORI 2001 in Frazer and Selwyn 2005, p.136). Despite this apparent interest in adoption, a number of sources suggest that children from 'minority communities' wait longer to be placed than white children and that there is generally a shortage of adopters from minority ethnic groups, with agencies needing to recruit more diverse families for adoption (Frazer and Selwyn 2005; Selwyn *et al.* 2008).

Generalised statements about minority ethnic communities, however, mask a more complex picture of diverse experiences. For South Asian communities, for example, figures from 2003 suggested that there were more 'Asian' adopters than there were 'Asian' children waiting to be adopted (Frazer and Selwyn 2005). The availability of adopters, therefore, is not necessarily the same for all minority ethnic groups and this highlights the inappropriate use of homogenising terms such as 'Black', BME (Black and minority ethnic) or 'minority ethnic' in this context.

Given the lack of work on diverse perceptions of adoption after infertility, this chapter aims to open up areas of debate and discussion rather than provide a definitive overview. Much of the literature that discusses ethnicity, 'race' and adoption to date has focused on the complex and highly contested issue of 'transracial adoption' (Barn 2000; Kirton 2000). This set of debates, while clearly of consequence to wider debates about the welfare of adoptive children from minority communities, is not the central focus of this chapter. Instead, this chapter contributes to the understanding of the ways in which adoption, as a means to overcome childlessness, is perceived among members of British South Asian communities.

Ethnicity and perceptions of adoption

Some commentators have suggested that the adoption process may be perceived as 'closed' to particular groups, including those from minority backgrounds (Sunmonu 2000), and that negative perceptions of social workers may exist in some minority communities (Millar and Paulson-Ellis 2009; Selwyn, Frazer and Fitzgerald 2004). It is argued that the need for culturally appropriate recruitment and assessment of minority families is therefore of central significance in increasing the numbers of appropriate adopters (Selwyn et al. 2008; Singh 1997).

A small number of international studies have addressed the phenomenon of adoption among childless couples in the Indian sub-continent. In an Indian study of infertile couples, 10 per cent of participants had adopted and 12 per cent reported future intention to adopt (Unisa 1999). However, the process of adoption was generally informal in that the child was usually a child of a close relative. Bharadwaj (2003), however, found negative feelings associated with adoption in a study of Hindu couples in India, suggesting that:

> It is an open and public declaration of failed fertility, not to mention the fears of failed sexuality. Most significantly, an adopted child breaks the link between the body and the progeny and becomes a visible 'third party' in a way that makes it impossible for family groups to collude in a conspiracy of silence. (Bharadwaj 2003, p.75)

Couples in Bharadwaj's study were therefore more likely to opt for donor treatment (in secrecy) rather than adoption. In India, adoption leaves the child and family open to stigma, especially since most available children

are those abandoned by mothers because they were born outside marriage. These international studies help to illustrate some of the cultural
specificities of adoption; however, extrapolating from these findings to
Indian communities in the UK is problematic. The relatively small samples involved also suggest the need for caution in generalising to a wider
context.

In order to address this absence in the current literature, the rest of
this chapter explores the perceptions of adoption in the context of infertility among men and women from British South Asian communities.
We approach the issue using examples from a programme of work which
has explored the social context of infertility and the experience of assisted conception within British South Asian communities.[1] This work
has involved three research projects with a range of South Asian communities.[2] The first, ASFERT, explored perceptions of infertility and experiences of infertility services in the NHS (Culley *et al.* 2006b). The second,
GAMDON, examined public perceptions of gamete donation in these ra-
cialised and sometimes marginalised communities (Culley *et al.* 2006a).
The third was a doctoral study which explored the experiences of using
assisted reproductive technologies (ARTs) within South Asian communities (Hudson 2008). It is important to point out that none of these studies
were directly concerned with adoption. However, in the course of discussing and exploring infertility and its consequences, many participants in
these studies raised (often spontaneously) the issue of adoption, and it is
insights from these discussions which we draw on in this chapter.

We begin from the premise that infertility is not simply a medically
diagnosed reproductive impairment, but a socially constructed reality
(Greil 1991). The most important decisions which people make – to define
themselves as infertile, to seek treatment (or not), to decide between forms
of treatment, to consider adoption or other alternatives and so on – are all
part of a fundamentally social process. Therefore, in order to understand
the socio-cultural context of adoption and infertility, we first of all need
to understand the social meaning of infertility and the impact of childlessness within diverse communities. In what follows, we first discuss the
'public' perceptions of infertility in South Asian communities and the way
in which our focus group participants characterised cultural and religious
norms around infertility and adoption. We then go on to discuss how
adoption was perceived by some of the individual participants who had
direct experience of infertility and its treatment.

Involuntary childlessness in British South Asian communities

Evidence from our research clearly demonstrates that British South Asian communities are highly pronatalist. Children are highly desired, parenthood is culturally mandatory and childlessness is socially unacceptable (Culley and Hudson 2006; Culley et al. 2006b). Children are seen as essential for 'normal' adult existence and thus infertility or involuntary childlessness is a highly stigmatised condition, although there is evidence of a growing acceptance of delayed childbearing and a trend for smaller families in some South Asian communities (Beishon, Modood and Virdee 1998). The impact of the 'parenthood mandate' varies to some extent between communities and between socio-economic groups within communities and there is some resistance to the imperative of early childbearing among some younger women. However, voluntary childlessness is almost unheard of (Culley and Hudson 2006).

In pronatalist communities, infertility is highly visible and childless couples are subjected to social scrutiny. Women, in particular, bear the burden of infertility. Participants in all our studies made the point that women are 'blamed' for childlessness and many examples were given, in our focus groups in particular, of negative reactions to childless women from wider family and community. For some married women, a secure place in their new family was not achieved until they had produced a child. Focus group participants in the ASFERT study reported that infertility would be considered 'good grounds' for divorce or, in some communities, for taking a second wife.

The desire for children is multi-faceted. Data from the focus groups and key informant interviews in the ASFERT and GAMDON studies revealed a number of reasons why children were seen as vital. Social, economic, religious and emotional reasons were advanced for having children and these issues may all impact in some way on how the 'alternatives' to family building are perceived. The continuation of the lineage of the family name and the extended 'clan' were common themes in the ASFERT study. Considerations of the meaning of 'relatedness' and the significance of biological relatedness were also central to the discussions of third-party assisted conception in the GAMDON study.

Relatedness, infertility and adoption

Several authors have explored how applications of ARTs impact on forms of relatedness (Carsten 2003; Franklin and McKinnon 2002; Franklin and

Ragone 1998; Ginsburg and Rapp 1995; Konrad 2005; Strathern 1992; Thompson 2005). These are, however, commonly discussed in the context of white 'majority' communities. Within the GAMDON study, despite the high emotional and social costs of infertility, third-party assisted conception was perceived as highly problematic, with many emotional and relational risks (Culley and Hudson 2009a; Culley *et al.* 2006a). While some of these risks were specific to the use of donated gametes, two of the concerns raised by participants were possibly of considerable significance in perceptions of adoption.

First, a major concern for all communities was the importance of a specifically genetic link between father and child. While this was discussed in the context of assisted reproduction using third-party gametes rather than adoption, it nevertheless points to the central role of genetic fatherhood, which has possible implications for the contemplation of adoption. The significance of genetic fatherhood would seem to confirm the view that biological paternity is of paramount significance for male identity, authority and power (Nash 2004). Culturally this was seen as important, as the child (especially a male child) would share the substance of the wider kin via the genetic link to the male and would, therefore, continue the 'family line', which is highly culturally significant in communities with patrilineal systems of inheritance (Lessor *et al.* 1990). Interestingly, the use of donated eggs was seen as less socially threatening. The use of donated eggs was considered to be an inclusive technique which allowed both parents to have 'ownership' over the process of conception and for the child to be 'connected' to both parents. Pregnancy and birth established a 'connectedness' of mother–foetus/child, irrespective of any genetic link. The father maintains what was viewed as a more crucial genetic link with the child, which would ensure both his relationship to the child *and* the continuation of the family 'line' (especially with male offspring) (Bharadwaj 2003). In both cases, however, 'biological' connectedness between parent and child was seen as paramount.

The centrality of genetic fatherhood (and gestational motherhood), then, is an important aspect of the context for beginning to think about the issue of adoption in South Asian communities. In this context, adoption, like third-party assisted conception, is also likely to be seen as relationally 'risky' and a potential threat to social continuity. Not only is it a threat to patrilineal descent, it is, as Bharadwaj has argued, a highly visible admission of a 'failure' of highly valorised fertility, with masculinity also potentially threatened in this process (Bharadwaj 2003; also see Inhorn 2003).

A second issue which emerged in the GAMDON focus groups, with women in particular, also has potential importance for attitudes to adoption. This concerns the perception, which many women in the focus groups referred to, that men would be unable to parent effectively a non-related child. This was related to what women saw as fundamental male attributes. Men were not seen as emotionally in need of a child but as primarily fulfilling a social need for fatherhood:

> Sometimes I get the feeling that – do they have children because they love, they want to have a child and they want to develop that child, or it is just the cultural thing that, let's follow the protocol here and let's have a child. (Indian Hindu woman)

Whereas women were seen as nurturing, emotionally strong and mentally adaptive to non-related children, men were seen as lacking in instinctual parenting desires. It was felt that men were less able to 'father' children who were not biologically related to them. As evidence of this, some women drew analogies between stepchildren and adopted children, arguing that men had difficulty in parenting in this context. The only way that men could be motivated to 'father' a child was if they were unquestionably biologically connected to that child.

> Because if it's not their child, then, at the end of the day they'll never love it. (Indian Hindu woman)

Formal and informal adoption

Although exploring attitudes to adoption was not a central concern of the projects, nevertheless, as we have seen, this was raised as a topic in all three studies. Our focus group participants in ASFERT and GAMDON often discussed this in response to questions about the acceptability of infertility treatments, the desirability of own gametes rather than donated gametes in ART and as an alternative 'solution' for couples who were unable to have their own child, with or without donated gametes. The most common way in which the issue of adoption was raised was in relation to processes of informal adoption within families. Several groups in the ASFERT study and all the focus groups in the GAMDON study gave examples where one family member, usually a brother of the husband, would offer one of their children to a childless couple or, indeed, offer to specifically conceive a child with his wife to 'give' to the childless couple. These, alongside divorce and the possibility of taking an additional wife, were regarded as alternative 'solutions' to infertility. It was not always clear, however, whether intra-family 'adoption' of this kind was primarily a practice common in the sub-continent, or whether it also took place in British South Asian communities, and, if so, to what extent.

In all communities, *formal* adoption was reported as uncommon practice, although an Asian adoption worker interviewed as part of the ASFERT project did inform us that, after much hard work in the community, this was slowly becoming more acceptable and more Asian families were seeking to formally adopt a child. This seemed to be primarily confined to the Indian Hindu and Sikh communities, rather than the Bangladeshi and Pakistani Muslim communities. This latter point may relate to the status of adoption in Islam. As part of the ASFERT project we interviewed a local imam, a well-respected Islamic scholar, whose view was that formal adoption (*tabanni*) was not permissible in Islam. This is also the view of most Sunni authorities (Fortier 2007). A similar prohibition exists against the use of third-party gametes in infertility treatment.[3] As Inhorn (2005) explains, Islam is a religion that can be said to privilege, or even mandate, biological inheritance; preserving the '*nasab*' or known biological origins of a child is a moral imperative:

> The Islamic scriptures, including the Qur'an, encourage the kin fostering of orphans but do not allow legal adoption as it is known in the West, whereby a child takes its adoptive parents' surname and is treated as one's own child. (Inhorn 2005, p.441)

Third-party donation and adoption are thus regarded as confusing issues of kinship, descent and inheritance, which are central to Islam. However, if one takes care of a child as a custodian or guardian, then adoption is permitted as long as the child retains the name of the biological father. Such a child cannot inherit in the traditional Islamic form, although they can be left money from that proportion of the estate (one-third) which a Muslim is allowed to give to a charity or to anyone who would not automatically receive a share of the inheritance (Fortier 2007). While there is no specific religious objection to formal adoption within the Hindu or Sikh faiths, it would still appear to be the case that this is a practice that is seen to be culturally 'deviant' in Indian society (Bharadwaj 2003).

The views of infertile couples

The perceptions of adoption reported above are the 'public' perceptions of those who are not necessarily faced with the reality of childlessness. The ASFERT study also included 37 interviews with 50 participants who had been defined as, or defined themselves as, having difficulty conceiving a child and the doctoral research involved interviews with 15 infertile participants. Most were undergoing, or had undergone, assisted conception treatment of various kinds. In general, these interviews confirmed the findings of the focus group study: the pronatalist context; the stigmatising impact of infertility; the difficult emotional impact of infertility; the sometimes negative family response to infertility; the need for confidentiality about their fertility problem and their treatment; and the unfavourable cultural attitudes towards formal adoption.

Adoption was not being actively considered by most interviewees, probably primarily because they were mostly still engaged in treatment and did not want to consider the implications of not being able to have a biologically related child. The impressions which emerge from the interviews suggest that adoption might be considered by some couples as a 'last resort' option (in common with literature on the white community – see Becker 2000; Franklin 1997; Throsby 2004). Most others, at the point of interview at least, did not think this was something they would consider.

Four participants in the ASFERT study said categorically that they would not consider adoption (these were people who already had one child). One Pakistani woman suggested that, for her, adoption was unlikely to be an option since there was a more culturally sanctioned alternative available:

> Erm, don't think, not in the culture. I mean, even though things have changed, you know, we probably could adopt, but I think it would be, in our culture, that, my husband would get married again. (Pakistani Muslim woman)

Of the five participants who reported that they would have considered adoption if treatment was unsuccessful, four were women. In each case, however, they described how the main reason for not having pursued this further was because their husbands were not willing to adopt:

> I tried to get him to watch this video but he wasn't having it. He's just not interested in adoption and fostering. He just isn't interested. But it's something I'd love to do. I'd love to do it straight away if I could – if he would agree with it, but he just doesn't want it. (Indian Hindu woman)

> For him, it's got to be your own son. I just, but I find a lot of Asians like that, as well, I think. Adoption's never talked about... But I don't

> think my partner would, unless he surprises me, I don't think he'd ever consider adoption at all. (Indian Sikh woman)

The men found it difficult to articulate their objection to adoption:

> I, for some reason, have been…against adoption, for some reason, I don't know, it's just me. It's just the way I, I feel about adoption. She was, she was pretty keen on it, but, er, I said no. I'd rather try, you know, for our own, own child rather than, erm, go for, for adoption. (Indian Muslim man)

This general view expressed in the interviews, that men were less positive about the possibility of adoption than women, confirms the focus group perspective that non-genetic fatherhood is more problematic than non-genetic motherhood. Several interviewees mentioned the cultural acceptability of adoption within their communities. Feelings here were somewhat mixed, but the general view was that formal adoption was not considered a desirable practice within Asian cultures, though few could articulate why. Again, however, the possibility and acceptability of informal or intra-family adoption was raised in several accounts.

> I mean, I don't know how other people would take it…[laughs]…cos, er, a lot of the time, none of our relatives have sort of adopted, a lot of the time, just say for example I didn't have any children of my own, I would sort of get, not get, but probably have one of his brother's children. Obviously they'd go back and forth as they wished, but nobody in the family has ever sort of adopted so I don't know how people would react to it. I don't see them reacting to it positively. (Pakistani Muslim woman)

A distinction was therefore made between official routes of adoption (through social services or from overseas countries) and informal, unofficial adoption, which may take place within families. This finding was also echoed in the 'public perceptions' of adoption which emerged in the community-based research.

The notion of 'formal' adoption was clearly not something which had been considered in any depth by the participants in our work with infertile couples. For many, the desire for a biologically related child, coupled with the need to be perceived by the wider community as achieving parenthood via socially sanctioned routes, may account for their reluctance to consider adoption, at least until all options for achieving pregnancy had been exhausted.

Conclusion

Our lack of understanding of the complex relationship between ethnicity and adoption is compounded by poor ethnic conceptualisation and descriptors, both within adoption work (Selwyn *et al.* 2004) and more broadly within the research literature (Kirton 2000). We need to recognise the diversity within the broad categories which are often used to describe the 'other than white' population. As we argue in this chapter, even the term 'Asian' or 'South Asian' is itself problematic and represents a diverse set of communities which may have different attitudes towards adoption. There is, however, a lack of research which is sensitive to this complexity.

This chapter has not attempted to 'explain' a failure to recruit and retain South Asian adopters in culturalist terms. Research has suggested that this issue is multi-faceted and relates on the one hand to a younger age profile, family composition, income, unemployment, poverty and language barriers within Asian and other minority ethnic communities and, on the other hand, to the failure of authorities to put in place appropriate policies, planning and training (Frazer and Selwyn 2005; Selwyn *et al.* 2008). In this chapter, we have sought to present some findings from our work on infertility which seem particularly pertinent to how adoption is *perceived* in British South Asian communities and which may inform future research and professional practice.

As we have seen, there is limited research which explores the impact of diverse ethnicities, religious identities and cultural contexts on the experience and resolution of infertility within the West. We have presented some of the perceptions of adoption constructed by British South Asian communities in the course of three research projects exploring infertility. We have described a highly pronatalist social context, in which infertility is highly stigmatised and at the same time formal adoption is also regarded as socially problematic. We have suggested that these perceptions may relate to the significance of biological relatedness, especially biological fatherhood, and in some cases to concerns about the religious acceptability of formal adoption, particularly in Muslim communities. Intra-family adoption, however, seems to be both more acceptable and possibly more common within South Asian communities, though this requires much more research.

While we have discussed the perception of adoption with South Asian communities, it is nevertheless important to avoid essentialism. We would not argue that there is an 'essential' South Asian attitude to either infertility or adoption. Our work on infertility suggests that there are diverse interpretations of infertility which are constructed differently by different generations, genders and social classes and that such discourses are dynamic (Culley and Hudson 2009b). This is also likely to be the case for adoption and it is not helpful to see cultural and religious meanings as prescriptive codes for action (Phillips 2007). It is important, therefore, that social workers and other practitioners do not fall into the trap of assuming that South Asian families are *inevitably* unlikely to consider adoption because of 'cultural' concerns or fail to address the structural and political issues which hinder effective adoption practice in a diverse society. Certainly formal adoption is an uncommon practice within South Asian communities and few infertile couples will have experience of family or friends who have been through this process. This means, therefore, that considerable efforts need to be made to inform potential parents and the wider community about the possibilities and opportunities of making families by adoption.

In conclusion, although more research on this issue is badly needed, our limited exploration nevertheless suggests some possible ways in which professional practice may move forward on this issue. First, social workers need to be aware of the potential importance of the cultural specificity of kinship and parenthood in South Asian communities, as demonstrated by our study of public perceptions of childlessness and infertility treatment. The additional stigma experienced by childless couples and the potentially restricted options for treatment need to be recognised and reflected sensitively in the adoption process. Second, adoption services should be alert to the significance of a lack of exposure to the practice of 'formal' adoption among members of South Asian communities. Childless couples may be less likely to have come into contact with other South Asian adults who have adopted and will potentially be less familiar with the practice and mechanisms of adoption. Finally, social workers may also need to think specifically about how to enable South Asian adopters (pre- and post-placement) to manage any pressures from family or community members who may have less positive attitudes to adoption.

Notes

1. The term 'South Asian' is used to refer to members of those communities, including East African Asians, whose ancestral roots can be traced to India, Pakistan or Bangladesh. Although they share common geographical origins in the sub-continent, South Asian communities in Britain are of diverse regional, linguistic, religious, caste and class origins (Culley and Hudson 2009b; Peach 2006). According to the 2001 census, the size of the minority ethnic population was 4.6 million or 7.9 per cent of the total population

of the United Kingdom. Of these, over 2.3 million people described their ethnic origin as Indian, Pakistani, Bangladeshi or 'Other Asian'.

2. The NHS-funded ASFERT study (2002–2004) explored experiences of involuntary childlessness among four South Asian communities: Pakistani and Bangladeshi Muslim communities, the Indian (Punjabi) Sikh community, and the Indian (Gujarati) Hindu community. Phase 1 explored 'community' perceptions of this issue, consisting of 14 single-sex focus groups carried out with South Asian community members (n=93) who were not necessarily childless themselves, and interviews with 21 key informants. Phase 2 consisted of in-depth, semi-structured interviews with a non-probability, purposive sample of 50 people of South Asian origin experiencing infertility (37 women and 13 men).

   The ESRC-funded GAMDON study (2005–2006) explored public understandings of gamete donation among British South Asian communities. This comprised 14 focus groups (10 female, 4 male) with a total of 100 participants who were not themselves affected by infertility, drawn from British Indian, Pakistani and Bangladeshi communities.

   The third study (Hudson 2008) was the doctoral research of one of the authors and explored the importance of community, context and identity on the infertility experience. This included in-depth interviews with 15 individuals (14 women and 1 man) from Indian, Pakistani and Bangladeshi communities.

3. The position on adoption in the Shi'a branch of Islam is less certain, with some evidence of a tolerance of gamete donation, surrogacy and adoption as legitimate ways to 'save infertile marriages' in countries such as Iran (Inhorn 2005).

References

Barn, R. (2000) 'Race, Ethnicity and Transracial Adoption.' In I. Katz and A. Treacher (eds) *The Dynamics of Adoption*. London: Jessica Kingsley Publishers.

Becker, G. (2000) *The Elusive Embryo: How Women and Men Approach New Reproductive Technologies*. Berkeley, CA: University of California Press.

Beishon, S., Modood, T. and Virdee, S. (1998) *Ethnic Minority Families*. London: Policy Studies Institute.

Bharadwaj, A. (2003) 'Why adoption is not an option in India: The visibility of infertility, the secrecy of donor insemination, and other cultural complexities.' *Social Science and Medicine 56*, 9, 1867–1880.

Carsten, J. (2003) *After Kinship: New Departures in Anthropology*. Cambridge: Cambridge University Press.

Culley, L. and Hudson, N. (2006) 'Diverse bodies and disrupted reproduction: Infertility and minority ethnic communities in the UK.' *International Journal of Diversity in Organisations, Communities and Nations 5*, 2, 117–126.

Culley, L. and Hudson, N. (2009a) 'Constructing relatedness: Ethnicity, gender and third party assisted conception in the UK.' *Current Sociology 57*, 2, Monograph 1, 257–275.

Culley, L. and Hudson, N. (2009b) 'Commonalities, Differences and Possibilities: Culture and Infertility in British South Asian Communities.' In L. Culley, N. Hudson and F. van Rooij (eds) *Marginalized Reproduction: Ethnicity, Infertility and Reproductive Technologies*. London: Earthscan.

Culley, L., Hudson, N., Rapport, F., Johnson, M. and Bharadwaj, A. (2006a) *Public Perceptions of Gamete Donation amongst British South Asian Communities*. Final Report to the ESRC. Grant no. RES-160-25-0044. Available at www.esrcsocietytoday.ac.uk, accessed on 26 April 2010.

Culley, L.A., Hudson, N., Rapport, F.L., Katbamna, S. and Johnson, M.R.D. (2006b) 'British South Asian communities and infertility services.' *Human Fertility 9*, 1, 37–45.

Fortier, C. (2007) 'Blood, sperm and the embryo in Sunni Islam and in Mauritania: Milk kinship, descent and medically assisted procreation.' *Body and Society 13*, 3, 15–36.

Franklin, S. (1997) *Embodied Progress: A Cultural Account of Assisted Conception.* London: Routledge.

Franklin, S. and McKinnon, S. (2002) *Relative Values: Reconfiguring Kinship Studies.* Durham and London: Duke University Press.

Franklin, S. and Ragone, H. (1998) *Reproducing Reproduction: Kinship, Power and Technological Innovation.* Philadelphia, PA: University of Pennsylvania Press.

Frazer, J. and Selwyn, J. (2005) 'Why are we waiting? The demography of adoption for children of black, Asian and black mixed parentage in England.' *Child and Family Social Work 10*, 2, 135–147.

Ginsburg, F. and Rapp, R. (1995) *Conceiving the New World Order: The Global Politics of Reproduction.* Berkeley, CA: University of California Press.

Greil, A.L. (1991) *Not Yet Pregnant: Infertile Couples in Contemporary America.* New Brunswick, NJ: Rutgers University Press.

Hudson, N. (2008) 'Infertility in British South Asian Communities: Negotiating the Community and the Clinic.' Unpublished PhD thesis. Leicester: De Montfort University.

Inhorn, M. (2005) 'Fatwas and ARTS: IVF and gamete donation in Sunni v. Shi'a Islam.' *Journal of Gender, Race and Justice 9*, 2, 291–318.

Inhorn, M.C. (2003) '"The worms are weak": Male infertility and patriarchal paradoxes in Egypt.' *Men and Masculinities 5*, 3, 236–256.

Kirton, D. (2000) *'Race', Ethnicity and Adoption.* Buckingham: Open University Press.

Konrad, M. (2005) *Nameless Relations: Anonymity, Melanesia, and Reproductive Gift Exchange Between British Ova Donors and Recipients.* Oxford and New York: Berghahn Books.

Lessor, R., Reitz, K., Balamaceda, J. and Asch, R. (1990) 'A survey of public attitudes toward oocyte donation between sisters.' *Human Reproduction 5*, 7, 889–892.

Millar, I. and Paulson-Ellis, C. (2009) *Exploring Infertility Issues in Adoption.* London: British Association for Adoption and Fostering.

Nash, C. (2004) 'Genetic kinship.' *Cultural Studies 18*, 1, 1–33.

Peach, C. (2006) 'Demographics of BrAsian Settlement, 1951–2001.' In N. Ali, V.S. Kalra and S, Sayyid (eds) *A Poscolonial People: South Asians in Britain.* London: C. Hurst & Co.

Phillips, A. (2007) *Multiculturalism without Culture.* Princeton, NJ: Princeton University Press.

Selwyn, J., Frazer, L. and Fitzgerald, S. (2004) *Finding Adoptive Families for Black, Asian and Black Mixed-parentage Children: Agency Policy and Practice.* Executive Summary. Bristol: National Children's Home and Hadley Centre for Adoption and Foster Care Studies. Available at www.bris.ac.uk/sps/research/projects/completed/2004/rj4058/rj4058execsumm.pdf, accessed on 26 January 2010.

Selwyn, J., Harris, P., Quinton, D., Nawaz, S., Wijedasa, D. and Wood, M. (2008) *Pathways to Permanence for Black, Asian and Mixed Ethnicity Children: Dilemmas, Decision-making and Outcomes.* Research Brief. London: Department for Children, Schools and Families. Available at http://publications.dcsf.gov.uk/eOrderingDownload/DCSF-RBX-13-08.pdf, accessed on 26 January 2010.

Singh, S. (1997) 'Assessing Asian families in Scotland: A discussion.' *Adoption and Fostering 21*, 3, 35–39.

Strathern, M. (1992) *Reproducing the Future: Essays on Anthropology, Kinship and the New Reproductive Technologies.* Manchester: Manchester University Press.

Sunmonu, Y. (2000) 'Why black carers are deterred from adoption.' *Adoption and Fostering 24*, 1, 59–60.

Thompson, C. (2005) *Making Parents: The Ontological Choreography of Reproductive Technologies.* Cambridge, MA: MIT Press.

Throsby, K. (2004) *When IVF Fails: Feminism, Infertility and the Negotiation of Normality.* Basingstoke: Palgrave Macmillan.

Unisa, S. (1999) 'Childlessness in Andhra Pradesh, India: Treatment-seeking and consequences.' *Reproductive Health Matters 7*, 13, 54–64.

CHAPTER 8

'A Sense of Belonging':
The Experience of a Black Adopter

Sally Baffour

I am writing as a Ghanaian woman who adopted within the UK, draw-ing on my knowledge and understanding of cultural, religious and family aspects of infertility and adoption within some African families, which comes from my own experience and that of many other Africans with whom I have had contact over the years.

Cultural background and attitudes

I was born in Ghana in the late 1950s; my parents were a housewife/seamstress with six children and a very accomplished and learned man who was prolific in many ways, including having 19 children. Fertility was part of our make-up, at least that is how families like ours were per-ceived, and this added to our appeal as suitable marriage partners.

Many African countries share the value that a family's wealth is mea-sured by the number of children. Polygamy in Ghana enabled men to sire many children, providing hands for the farms, sons for fishing and daughters to sell the produce. Chiefs shared out land to families accord-ing to their size so children became the most important reason for mar-riage, rendering it pointless without. This put great and unfair demands on women who were held responsible for everything to do with fertility in the marriage. Somehow it was never considered that men could be at fault, until perhaps a woman who had been forced to leave the marital home ended up having children with her next husband. In West Africa, in extreme cases, an 'infertile' woman was sent back to her father's home and her dowry returned, bringing shame and disgrace on her family and limiting her chances of future marriage as well as considerably reducing the dowries of other, younger girls in that family.

What infertility does to an African woman is to fundamentally erode the basis on which she is defined. This is also applicable to men. Most would rather live in denial than admit it. Men are relegated to the status of a 'eunuch', lose their status, dignity and respect and have been known to be the butt of many cruel jokes. Traditionally, a man's status and chance to hold any office of responsibility is determined by his ability to 'prove' his manhood through having many children and taking good care of them. The qualities displayed by acquiring wisdom and knowledge through the experience of caring for so many children are seen to qualify him for higher office. Eunuchs have a role in the village too: primarily to take care of the Queen and Queen Mother, both as bodyguards and by waiting on them. That is the extent of the responsibility. Mothers of infertile men, and, in particular, some of the men themselves, will go as far as encouraging their wives to go and get pregnant discreetly and bring children back home as a way of covering up their inadequacy. It is so demeaning for a man to be exposed as infertile that it remains a family secret. Children who may have been sired by other men are never told the truth about their paternity.

For my family, infertility was not altogether alien. For ten years after marriage, my paternal grandmother was unable to have children. In Ghana, female members of the couple's families traditionally meet and discuss their concerns regarding the wife's apparent infertility. A new bride will be recommended, traditionally a relative from the wife's side of the family (to keep it in the family), before it is officially discussed, first with the wife then the husband. The wife's female relations discuss the matter sensitively with her, putting forward the recommended new bride, before moving her into their home. A cousin of my maternal grandmother was brought in as a second wife to my paternal grandfather and they all lived together. After she had the first two children for my grandfather, my grandmother then became pregnant with my father and then gave birth to five more children.

The beginning

In my late teens, I came to London in 1974 to study interior architecture and worked for 12 years in the field after qualifying. My career in the City took precedence over everything so I was in my early thirties when I got married in 1986. Childbearing was a given. So, after two years without children I went to check things out medically 'just to be sure', when a friend suggested it, and found that, due to extensive fibroids, I only had a 5 per cent chance of conceiving. My husband and I were amazed and disbelieving. We told no one except my mother and, with her support, quietly considered the option of IVF which was recommended to us immediately. We believed it would work and were further shocked when, six weeks after successfully conceiving, I miscarried. We gave up after the same thing happened with the second attempt.

My mother has always been my rock. The grief that I would have suffered through this time was considerably lessened by her tremendous empathy and support, even though it was done by telephone as she was in America. The two miscarriages gave a clear indication of the very minuscule chance I had of successfully carrying a pregnancy. My mother finally asked me one of the most important and profound questions that every woman who finds herself in this situation should consider: 'What is it about having children that motivates you most? Is it the experience of childbirth or the opportunity to be a mother?'

Mama insisted that I give her an answer after my husband and I had discussed it and slept on it. After contemplating it in deep discussions into the night, both my husband and I agreed that even if the opportunity to experience childbirth had eluded me (which of course is what I would have loved to experience in its entirety) I could still be a mother. It was after sharing our thoughts with her that my mother told me that, at the age of ten, I had told her I would adopt children from around the world. She added, 'Well here is your opportunity.'

We had never thought about adoption but a seed had been planted; the more we thought about it, the more the idea grew on us. But the question now was, 'How and where does one begin to embark on adopting?' We knew no one who had adopted as it was very unusual in the UK Ghanaian community. Our immediate thought was to see how we could adopt a child from Ghana; after all there are many orphans in the children's homes in Accra that we could happily parent. We had no idea what the process was or where to begin.

Our initial idea of going down the inter-country adoption route came naturally to us and we would have eventually done so if we had not found out that our friends Jane and Kwami (not their real names) were adopters who had been assessed and approved here in the UK.

Deciding to become an adopter

In our lines of work, my husband and I knew very little about social services. As we were oblivious to their activities, we would never have known to contact them. It was at one of our traditional summer barbeques that we spotted our friends' two children, who were the best behaved children at the party. Their Scottish mother later confided in me that she and her Ghanaian husband had adopted them separately and they were not even siblings. I was shocked and remember thinking how incredible that they were actually 'normal' children.

Jane was kind enough to show me the ropes. She gave me the contact number of my local social services adoption team which, by sheer coincidence, was the same team they had dealt with. My first phone call to the department was met with rejection when, after establishing my ethnicity, I was told they had closed their books. Jane said that was nonsense and called them herself. Interestingly, she was told that their books were open. So, using her as my lead, I called back and my persistence paid off. I was later to discover that they could not have closed their books because they were inundated with looked-after Black children with hardly any Black families to place them with.

This was my first encounter with the typical barriers that (I was later to discover) inhibit most African and Caribbean people when applying to be adopters in the UK. Through the work that I have since been involved in with the British Association for Adoption and Fostering (BAAF) adoption panels and the General Social Care Council (GSCC), and as an advocate for children in care, I was later to learn about many other barriers.

Understanding the barriers that Black Africans and Caribbean people face

The 1960s had been a particularly difficult time for many Caribbean families after being encouraged to come to the UK to work. The lack of understanding of the traditional child-rearing practices of Black African and Caribbean people led to misunderstandings by social services, which resulted in children being taken into care for reasons that the community perceived to be erroneous and spurious. Rooted in this uncomfortable history – which caused great disruptions in many homes – a deep schism resulted between the Black community and social services that continues to this day.

The over-representation in care of Black and, in particular, dual heritage children of Caribbean and African origin in many parts of the country is, I believe, a direct outcome of the Black minority ethnic (BME) community's disinterest in engaging with social services. Since there were not enough families capable of caring for African and Caribbean looked-after children coming forward to offer permanent homes, they continued to languish in care as their numbers rose.

The nature of our families back in Africa and the Caribbean is to care for children within the extended family whenever the need arises, either through permanent illness of parents, being orphaned or parents developing mental health problems. Thus, the African saying, 'it takes a village to raise a child'. Although done unofficially, this practice is recognised and accepted by the entire community. Until the death of Victoria Climbié in 2000, many African families brought children to Britain from within their extended families or communities in the Caribbean or Africa to care for them unofficially 'as their own'. Alternatively, they finalised the adoption abroad then returned to Britain, instead of going through the humiliation of dealing with social services (as they had no confidence that they would be dealt with fairly).

The confidence of many infertile Africans is so low that any rejection and unhelpfulness only serves to compound their loss, stripping them of the energy needed to go back and try again. I know that if Jane had not been around to insist on my getting back to my local authority, the initial rejection I got on my first call would most certainly have ended my enquiry and put me off adoption permanently. Enough resistance had been experienced by African and Caribbean families when making adoption applications for the bad news to be spread among the community; people were warned not to venture into dealing with social services because they would be met with racist rejection.

Why our naivety worked for us

Our naivety worked for us because we had not been privy to the historical discourse between social services and the Black community described above; I was to discover this later. That is why we were so easily persuaded by Jane to persist in our application. My husband had been sent to boarding school in England from the age of six while my father had sent me straight to university in England. Therefore, coming from privileged backgrounds, our lives had been sheltered from the social problems that became the pathway for children in care, and so we approached the process with a very open mind.

Once the local authority had agreed to assess us, our allocated link worker turned out to be the same one that Jane and Kwami had when they adopted their children a few years previously. One of the first questions she asked was whether we had any problem with being assessed by a white social worker. We saw no reason why we would and told her so. It was much later, when faced with real issues of racism, that I recognised, with hindsight, the relevance of that question. Fortunately, our link worker was a very experienced social worker who was not defensive about racism, which we found very helpful. However, when later dealing with racism at the children's schools, we found that we had to rely on our own networks and resources to deal with the issue because social services were ill-equipped to help.

Our approach to dealing with racism has always been constructive, with the aim of educating the bully to understand, in real terms, the negative impact of their behaviour on young adopted children and the devastating lifelong damage that it could cause. Purely from a humanitarian point of view, we have found this approach very effective in turning many people into anti-racist advocates who end up looking out for Black children.

Being mentored throughout our assessment by both Jane and Kwami was crucial to our success. Whenever we felt uneasy about some of the questions being asked, they were the people we turned to for further explanation. Although it was an informal arrangement between us, it was invaluable and it encouraged and guided us. What helped more than anything – especially for my husband – was the impact of seeing another Black person (Kwami) who had successfully adopted and was very comfortable with it.

Sharing information

Knowing how our community perceived infertility and having previously failed in our attempts at IVF, we decided not to discuss adoption with anyone until we were absolutely sure of our success. We were very careful who we told in our community for fear of ridicule or being discouraged by 'well-meaning' people who would more than likely remind us of the 'difficult and impossible-to-manage looked-after children' that would probably be placed with us. Discussing with friends on a need-to-know basis limited it to those who were our adoption referees.

My family were younger and more broad-minded than my husband's family who were older and more traditional. Since I had the issue of infertility, we told my siblings, knowing that they, like my mother, would support us absolutely. My in-laws were informed once the match had been agreed and they, surprisingly, did not object.

Our twins (of Caribbean origin) were placed at age two. We quarantined ourselves for about a month working out ways to manage their extremely challenging behaviour, settling them and bonding. This proved especially difficult for me as the children viewed me with suspicion and kept their distance. At the beginning, we were determined not to broadcast our adoption and after two months went to a very close friend's barbeque to test the water. Our friends were naturally shocked to see us with two-year-olds, never having seen me go through pregnancy. I cannot imagine whatever made me think they would believe that the twins were our birth children and felt ridiculed when one of them derided us with a comment to that effect. I was very embarrassed. By the time we left, we had decided to be open about the adoption and build our children's confidence to avoid giving people the chance to ridicule them.

Years later, those family friends became foster carers once they had been educated out of their ignorance. This affirms the power of taking a confident stance about adoption from the point of view of educating others. We soon realised that speaking boldly about adopting because of my infertility, as I began to do, had a liberating effect on many women in our community and we soon found people coming to us discreetly to find out more. They, like us, needed to see that someone in the community had succeeded against all the odds and they were greatly encouraged to try it too.

The motivation to adopt

My initial motivation to adopt was because I wanted to be a mother. I believed at that stage that it had to be of children who were orphans so that we would not have to deal with any relatives. We could pass them off successfully as our own birth children, hiding the truth about their heritage and adoptive status, purportedly to protect them from embarrassment and ridicule.

Our adoption preparation training opened our understanding in ways that forced us to rethink many of our attitudes. First was the realisation that there were actually no orphans in the care system. The reality of the reasons why children come into care in the UK was new and shocking to both of us. We had no idea that parents could be alive and yet incapable of bringing up their children. Our sheltered upbringing had not prepared us for this. While we could understand it in the case of parents with mental health issues, the effects of drugs and alcohol on parenting ability completely threw me. What I learnt in that preparation programme was so new to anything that I had ever known or could have imagined that it changed our lives completely.

Once we realised that there were no orphans and, with great difficulty, accepted that the only way forward would have to be with children with the types of backgrounds described above, the possibility of contact with birth parents, the dysfunctional family history of many of the children (which in my mind was worse than fiction in some cases) and the descriptions of children's behaviour that were alien to my experience and background proved a real challenge. I had had no idea how judgemental and intolerant we were of anything that was different from our own experiences. Adoption soon changed all that.

The description of the challenging behaviour of such tiny children put me off and I actually decided that my life experience had not provided me with the tools to manage such behaviour. I felt inadequate and fearful. The prospect of attempting to bring such behaviours into my home was frankly frightening, because it was too unfamiliar, and I knew there was no way that any of my siblings would stand for it or accommodate it. Being a close-knit family, I would be bringing children not only into our nuclear family but also into the wider family and, therefore, the children would have to 'fit in'. I was to realise later that what was more important was for the children to gradually work through the baggage they unknowingly came with, and that they began to fit in as we all got used to each other's ways.

My husband had experienced racism at school, having been at boarding school in the UK from the age of six, so he understood its nuances in a way that I did not. He was able to point out to me that some of the children's issues and behaviours were a clear indication that they were experiencing racism. At that point my motivation switched to the need to protect these tiny children from such wickedness and I decided to go ahead and adopt. This time it was with unwavering determination and conviction. I was ready for whatever this journey would throw at me. Admittedly, some of the issues have taken me to places and along paths that I would not have pictured in my wildest dreams but the journey has enriched my life and made me a better and stronger human being. I had always planned to go back to work once the children settled down but this appeared to take forever, so I decided to play it by ear and go at their pace.

Bonding with the children

Bonding with the children was the next phase. No amount of training could have prepared us for the role of adoptive parents. The extremes of challenging behaviour that came with the twins, although they were only two years old, baffled us. Nothing until then had prepared us or armed us with the tools to manage. This was also a constant reminder of the birth children we would never have. Birth children, we felt, would have behaved more like our nieces and nephews: they had predictable behaviours that we were familiar with. My son could not relate to me at all and expressed his mistrust, rejection and dislike of me openly, coming to me for food alone. He only went to my husband. That was difficult, extremely difficult, because I had naively thought that children in care would automatically attach to anyone who offered them a home and that I would automatically love them instantly.

Every day brought new challenges. The attitude that I discovered helped was simply that we would use our creativity and all our resources to find solutions one day at a time. While their behaviour remained alien, and I spent all my time trying creative ways to deal with it, I just could not feel any love for them. The greatest help was from understanding why their behaviour was so difficult. They had been let down by every adult in their lives, including the foster carer (who had also abused them), and had no sense of trust, not even for themselves. The concept of trust, which forms the basis of respect for oneself, of order and of reasonable behaviour, was completely lacking in their experience. The sadness of that reality drew enough compassion in me to enable me to care for their needs as best as I could and focus on helping them to settle. The struggle to find love in my heart for them was a real worry, because it felt like my role as a mother was false and dishonest, and this left me feeling quite guilty. What I was to learn was the need to allow the love to grow between us, from me to them and from them to me. And it would not necessarily happen at the same time. It was like forcing my way through bushy cornfields of challenging behaviour to find that elusive clear patch of love.

My love for them came before theirs for me. That was important to me personally, as I imagine it would have been even sadder the other way round: if the child loved me desperately and I was unable to reciprocate. Playing in the garden one afternoon as I watched them from the window, I saw my daughter had run off with my son's tricycle. He was livid and screamed, cried, threw every tantrum possible, just trying to get her to give it back. After a few minutes of really rubbing it in, she jumped off his bike and back onto hers and carried on casually, as if nothing had happened. He rushed to rescue his tricycle before she changed her mind and, before the last tear had dropped down his cheek, he turned to his sister and gently invited her to come onto his tricycle to ride with him. I broke down in tears of compassion. That was when the children provided me with the hook to hang my coat of love on.

It was months later, with not a hint of improvement in my son's relationship towards me, that my mother decided to visit from America to see how she could help. The minute he laid eyes on her, my son ran into her arms as if he had known her all his life and he never left her side. He loved my mother. It was instant love. What transpired after that was an eye-opener for me. Seeing the great relationship I had with my mother (who he loved so much) gave my son the permission and confidence to gradually begin to build a relationship with me. I had to go at his pace and today we are inseparable.

Support

The children's challenging behaviour was a problem for everyone; for us, for friends and, especially, for family. We lost many friends who could not tolerate their behaviour but all came back on board once their behaviour settled. Family was the hardest, but I stood my ground and stuck up for the children by correcting their behaviour but never rejecting them, and eventually they all came round. The children and I always presented as one unit and I decided to be strong for them. They could not help being that way but I had every confidence that with perseverance they would be OK. Plus, I had my mother's indomitable strength, support and assurance to back me.

On one of my days of great despair, my mother said to me:

> Bringing up children who have come through the care system can be likened to the gold we used to collect along the river beds in Ghana when it was known as the Gold Coast when I was young. Open to the elements, it was covered in soot and filth from being tossed about aimlessly by the flowing water. Yet when the goldsmith puts that filthy stone through the kiln which burns off all the impurities, the most beautiful shiny gold is what remains. The kiln is the parenting that you provide for the child.

Whenever I am tested to the limit by my children I hear my late mother's words.

I was acutely aware of the intensity of scrutiny and investigation that traditionally goes into eliminating suitors before marrying into any family, and I knew the same would be expected of a child coming into the family. A child whose background was such that they would be able to 'fit in' to the family culture and identity was obviously what was desired by all. Mental health, kleptomania, drugs, alcohol and other diseases would disqualify any suitor. The same applied to children for adoption. Most families – who pride themselves on a family heritage of dignity, honour and integrity acquired over generations – guard their names jealously. Therefore, whoever acquires that name is expected to respect the privilege and order their lives in such a way as to maintain the good name of the family. There was an innate fear that children's propensity for the problematic behaviours that might be present in their family of birth would bring shame on the adoptive family, thus ruining the family's name and reputation.

Initially some members of our family attempted to distance themselves from the twins because of their challenging behaviour. I became more determined to stick up for them and stand by them. I knew then that it was my duty to help find solutions to their issues if they were going to grow to be happy in my family, which also acted as a social mirror against which I could determine their progress. My family was important to my twins because they loved being part of a large family with many cousins that they got on well with. It is one thing feeling you belong to a group but another if the group accepts you as one of them. Knowing that the only barrier to becoming fully integrated was their behaviour intensified my determination to work with my children. Their future depended on that too, because in the real world they would be judged by their behaviour.

The more relaxed way in which we were brought up (which is how I see my nieces and nephews bring brought up by my siblings) did not work for our twins initially. Instead, we instituted a strict and orderly routine which soon started to settle them because, for the first time, they could predict the next step – time for food, bath, sleep, tea, park time and playtime – and this made them feel secure.

The family support on the whole was great, especially in terms of their facilitating the 'rites of passage' that are traditional to claiming and settling a new child into the family. One of the main such rites for a birth child in Ghanaian families is the 'naming ceremony' and 'out-dooring' which takes place exactly a week after a child is born. Whenever birth children who have been lost to a family are discovered, they are also outdoored at a naming ceremony and reintroduced to the family officially. Adopted children, or any who are brought permanently into a family, are taken through those rites of passage for the family to claim them as their own. We added the Ghanaian 'twin names' to my children's original names, as is customary, to complete the 'claiming-into-the-family' that is traditional to our Ghanaian culture. My Catholic priest also had a special ceremony to welcome the twins into our family and that of the parish. A lot of fuss was made of them, which they enjoyed very much because of the many gifts they received. They were baptised after the adoption order had gone through. We gave them four sets of godparents; each had two godparents from the Caribbean as a step towards integrating their Caribbean culture into our family. It opened the door to an enriched life of blending the Ghanaian and Caribbean cultures effortlessly into our lifestyle.

Fortunately for us, our relationship with social services continued very well because we were very open about the challenges that we faced, unlike many other families who feared being judged as ineffective parents. We asked for help when we needed it and soon got to know the issues we could rely on them for help with and the areas where they were woefully inadequate, such as racism. The biggest and most important issue with which every African and Caribbean adoptive family requires support is dealing with racism towards their adopted children at school. Throughout all of my experiences with my children, that has been the worst experience. No personal experience of racism could have prepared me for the intensity of racism that my children experienced at school. It takes almost super-human strength to support children to ensure they are not permanently damaged. This is why it is particularly important to ensure that all Black children end up in permanent homes with people who understand, who share their experience and who have enough empathy to be able to help them through these difficult periods at school. Once that chance is missed in any Black child's life, society ends up with damaged and angry young people with very little education.

Infertility and being a parent

As a very spiritual person – as most African and Caribbean people tend to be – my spiritual rationale for adoption is that God is so merciful that it does not make sense that he or she would bring a child into this world (who is so helpless that it cannot survive without the care of a mother or father) without also creating people who are perfectly good parent-material but who are unable to give birth to children. Surely it must be part of God's overarching plan for these two disparate elements to come together as a family?

The intimate knowledge that my children have of me sends chills up my spine. They read my non-verbal communication (which I am not even aware of) as clearly as if I was telling them. They unpick my thoughts, finish my sentences, fill in my lapses in memory and always just know what I went back in the house to get and suddenly couldn't remember! My 18 siblings are amazed at this because none of their children know them as well as my children know me. I was pleasantly surprised to find that this is a phenomenon that has been confirmed by a number of adoptive parents whose children are settled and feel a strong sense of belonging. A sense of belonging is crucial to the security of an adoptive child and parents who are infertile. It is what makes up for the feelings of loss that infertility invokes in parents and the loss of their original birth parents that adoptive children feel. The importance of little signs to confirm belonging to a family may seem irrelevant but they are important to an adoptive child. It almost feels like nature's way of endorsing their belonging to the family. The examples in our life are many:

- Being the same race and complexion as their parents is enormously important to my adopted children because comments about their resemblance to the family are more credible. It secretly amuses us but it makes my children feel so good.

- At the beach in Ghana one holiday, my daughter discovered she had a beauty spot on the same side of her face as all her five cousins. This was made more significant when they discovered that another cousin, twice removed, did not have it. For my child, it completely affirmed her position as one of the family.

- In the chronology of ages, my twins perfectly slotted into the one-year age gap that existed between all their cousins (my nieces and nephews) as well as having a wonderful and meaningful relationship with all of them.

- Travelling abroad to family activities, funerals and weddings, spending time with extended family in Ghana and America and engaging with family and other Black people within our network is enormously important to my children's self-esteem and sense of purpose and belonging.

- The children's perception of themselves, their nationality and their culture feeds into a shared history, shared experiences and shared living culture that aids their development of self, their confidence and, above all, their sense of belonging.

Their self-esteem did not remain consistently positive through the journey of their adoptive lives. There were lows and phenomenally precious highs that carried the family through the lows, until they reached their early twenties when all their upbringing and experiences came together to shape the direction in which their future will proceed.

Engaging with Black potential adopters

My experience and that of the many Black adoptive families that I have had contact with over the years leads me to conclude that a totally new approach is needed to engage African and Caribbean families in the UK. Apart from being put off, because of the discouraging responses from social services that they may have heard about, many who do gather the courage to put themselves forward for adoption do so with trepidation. There are some questions that Black families perceive as trick questions. Instead of giving straightforward answers, their guarded responses lead to them being further misunderstood, especially by white social workers. It is not a question of being racist; some social workers just do not know how things work within our community, how family members support each other and so on. Social services departments therefore need more African and Caribbean social workers (who understand the issues) in senior positions to be the first port of call to encourage new applicants from the BME communities.

We need to educate both sides: for instance, applicants from African and Caribbean communities are likely to have less angst about divulging information about a past criminal record to a Black social worker. They are more likely to share their full family history with a Black social worker than with a white one who, in their perception, may find their frame of reference or the nuances of their culture too difficult to understand. Most also need a mediator (ideally another adopter or foster carer from their community) who can offer support through their assessment process, like that I received from Jane. There is a great need for the Black community to be educated about the way things are done in social services departments and why social workers ask the questions they do. This can only be effectively done by a Black social worker or, ideally, a knowledgeable adoptive parent with whom they can identify and who shows that adoption approval can be achieved.

Media sensationalism about disaffected Black youth, without proper explanation of some of the causes of anti-social behaviours, further discourages potential adopters. Many are reluctant to take on children in care (those who may to fall into the category of 'hard to place' children) as they worry they may not have the tools to manage their behaviour effectively.

Training programmes run by experienced Black adopters of just such children are crucial in helping to allay their fears.

Conclusion

Can adoption therefore work effectively for infertile Africans in the UK? I would say, 'very much so'.

My marriage broke down four years after the children were placed and my ex-husband went on to have two birth children with his new wife. I now recognise the importance of couples making time for each other, when their focus is only on themselves, and of nurturing their relationship, which we never did. Adoption can be all-consuming and can take over one's life completely, if one lets it. Do something you really enjoy away from the children to recharge your batteries.

Adoption can work beautifully. Dealing with the internal and external forces that pull at you from inside and out when caring for adopted children can make for a very challenging journey. But as individuals and as a family you can come through it stronger and as better human beings. This has been the most important experience of my life and I would not give it up for anything. Every family in life deserves to go through the experience of fulfilment that I feel after 17 years of adoption and the profound sense of having achieved a worthwhile endeavour. The most heartening feeling for me is when my children tell me, 'Mummy, we are originally your children, only somebody else had to bring us into the world for you.'

CHAPTER 9

Infertility and Inter-Country Adoption

Gill Haworth, Peter Selman and Jan Way

Introduction

The UK is unusual within Europe in having many more domestic than inter-country adoptions (ICAs). In 2006, the ICA rate was 0.6 per 100,000 population compared to 5.4 in Italy, 6.5 in France, 9.7 in Sweden and 10.2 in Spain (Selman 2009b). ICA is a far less central response to infertility in the UK than in the Nordic countries or the Netherlands where there are now very few domestic adoptions.

Early international adoptions from Korea, the Philippines, Vietnam and Latin America reflected wider humanitarian concerns and often involved parents who already had birth children. Hoksbergen (2000) notes that 32 per cent of adopters in the Netherlands between 1971 and 1985 already had children, whereas previously over 90 per cent of domestic adopters had been childless. Feigelman and Silverman (1983) have termed this 'preferential adoption' – being motivated by reasons other than infertility.

In the 1990s the proportion of inter-country adopters who were infertile rose again, a pattern found also in Sweden (Andersson 2000) and West Germany (Textor 1991), and today a clear majority of ICAs involve 'traditional' adopters, couples adopting primarily because they are unable to have birth children. This was also the main motivation for domestic adoption by non-relatives in England and Wales, which reached a peak of more than 15,000 annually from 1965 to 1968 (Selman 1976). With the legalisation of abortion in 1967 and the growing acceptance of single parenthood, this number had fallen to 4000 a year by 1984 (Selman 2006b). Today, non-relative adoptions in the UK are mainly of children from the care system and many are older or have special needs, but a majority of adopters continue to be infertile.

ICA in Europe

The decline in domestic adoptions of infants began earlier in Sweden and the Netherlands and the response was to turn to adoption from abroad (Selman 2009a). By the late 1970s, in Sweden there were two children brought in from overseas for every hundred born in the country (Andersson 1986). In the Netherlands the number of ICAs rose from 142 in 1970 to nearly 1600 in 1980 (Hoksbergen and Bunjes 1986). Annual numbers fell in the 1980s and one reason suggested for the decline was the increased availability of assisted reproductive technology (ART), which was seen as more attractive (Andersson 2000) because of the long waiting lists for adoption, the 'gruelling and demeaning selection process', 'worries about adoption laws and the security of adoption' (Barth, Brooks and Iyer 1995), and concern over failure rates in overseas adoption, especially those involving older children (Hoksbergen 1991).

In Norway, where ICA numbers *increased* in the 1980s, it was suggested that this was because:

> New infertility treatments such as in vitro fertilisation are not widely practised and surrogacy is not allowed. Thus, the only option for most infertile couples in Norway is either to accept their infertility or apply for adoption of a child born abroad. ICA in Norway has been viewed as a private, acceptable, and respected way of creating a family if a couple cannot have their 'own' children. (Saetersdal and Dalen 1991, p.85)

The total number of ICAs worldwide had reached about 20,000 by the late 1980s (Kane 1993) and more than doubled in the next 15 years to over 45,000 in 2004 (Selman 2006a), despite the continued growth of ART and more couples travelling abroad for easier and cheaper access to egg donation or surrogacy. Demand seemed fuelled by increasing numbers of couples experiencing infertility associated with later marriage and delayed attempts at childbearing. There is little evidence that countries with high rates of ICA have above average rates of infertility or below average provision of ART. Italy, for example, has a very low fertility rate and does not permit egg and sperm donation whereas Spain (which also has very low fertility and an even higher rate of ICA) has easy access to ART.

ICA and infertility

ICA continues to be driven by the demand of childless Western couples wanting children 'for their own sense of fulfilment. They are not, in most cases, performing an act of charity' (Howell 2006). Most have already tried ART and a recent analysis of infertility in the USA indicated that 73 per cent of prospective adopters are subfertile or sterile and that seven out of ten women who had used infertility services had also considered adoption (US Department of Health and Human Services 2008). Feigelman and Silverman (1983) argue that the unique experience of infertile couples gives rise to different motivations and interests in adoption than among those with biological children.

The proportion of international adopters who are primarily motivated by infertility is usually put at about 75 per cent. For example, in a study of ICA in Ireland (Greene *et al.* 2007), only 22 per cent of adopters had birth children and a further 6 per cent had previously adopted domestically. However, significantly higher and lower figures have been reported in other studies. Saetersdal and Dalen (1991) studied 182 Norwegians adopting from Vietnam and India and found that half already had biological children, whereas Jaffe (1991) reported that 91 per cent of those in her study of ICA in Israel had infertility problems. In the United States, Rojewski and Rojewski (2001) found that infertility was cited as the primary reason for adopting from China by less than half of their sample and that there was a significant proportion of single female adopters, most of whom were childless but not infertile.

Infertility and the decrease in children available for ICA

The total number of children moving as a result of inter-country adoption fell from over 45,000 a year in 2004 to less than 38,000 in 2007, a decline of 17 per cent (Selman 2009c). This *decline* has taken place alongside a *rise* in demand, with waiting times growing longer each year in most countries and some approved applicants likely never to receive a child. In France, newspapers have reported as many as 25,000 families approved for international adoption (Moreau 2008), while the number of completed adoptions has fallen from 4136 in 2005 to 3162 in 2007. In Italy, there has been a constant increase in numbers wanting to adopt a foreign child and by 2009 the number approved was much greater than the number of adoptions each year, even though the number of adoptions increased in 2007 and 2008. Similar stories are found in Denmark, the Netherlands and Spain, where the ratio of approved adopters to parents receiving children had grown to over 2:1 by 2006 (Selman, Moretti and Brogi 2009). Worldwide prospective adopters are waiting longer for matches from China. By 2009 the number of UK couples approved for adoption from China had risen to 375 and the typical waiting time to 36 months.

In all of these countries the majority of applicants are older infertile couples, many childless, but others hoping to find a sibling for their first adopted child. In Italy, where 85 per cent of adopters have no birth children, many are applying to adopt an older child to minimise the waiting time and, as a consequence, some of the second children are older than the first (Selman *et al.* 2009). It is often assumed that ICA only involves young infants, but this is increasingly untrue. Although Korea and Guatemala send predominantly infants under the age of one, the majority of children from Brazil are aged five or older or have special needs (Selman 2006a). Throughout Eastern Europe it is mainly older children who are sent for ICA, as babies and young infants can be readily placed for domestic adoption (Selman *et al.* 2009).

The shortage of children available for ICA may also lead to more 're-productive tourism', fuelling the demand for surrogate mothers in India (Smerdon 2008–2009) and elsewhere, or to child-trafficking and other disturbing practices (Smolin 2004, 2006).

Infertility and ICA in the UK: Issues for practice

As indicated above, infertility is the predominant motivating factor in the majority of ICA worldwide. This picture is replicated within the UK.

The International Bar Association's (IBA 1991) study of inter country adopters in Britain found that only 20 per cent had birth children and a further 10 per cent had other adopted or fostered children. In a study of Romanian adoptions in the 1990s, virtually all the control group (who had adopted infants in the UK) were infertile and, while a third of those adopting from Romania had birth children, among the whole group some had birth children from a previous marriage only and/or had secondary infertility (Groothues, Beckett and O'Connor 1998).

Although most applicants are seeking to adopt a child not known to them, others have an existing relationship with the child they wish to adopt, sometimes genetic (so-called kinship adopters). In either group, the proposed adoption might be a same race or transracial placement.

The ICA process is arduous. Assessment can seem intrusive and the outcome uncertain – will approval be granted, will a placement be offered and, if so, will the child grow into a healthy and secure young adult?

For many, this experience resonates with and prolongs the emotional challenges already encountered during their quest for a birth child.

All inter-country adopters within England and Wales, whether adopting related children or not, follow a route that mirrors the domestic adoption process, but with additional components. In each stage of that journey, echoes of their infertility experience may be felt.

Enquiry, counselling and information gathering

At this stage prospective adopters may hold unrealistic hopes about the age of child or country from which they might adopt. The UK currently does not have accredited agencies with working arrangements with countries overseas and the central authorities'[1] role does not include proactively developing bilateral agreements or working relationships with states of origin. Consequently, the choice of country is very limited and this may provoke feelings of disappointment and anger, especially for those looking to specific countries for heritage reasons.

Accurate and objective information, verbal and written, is essential if individuals are to address the implications of overseas adoption. Group information sessions offer opportunities, perhaps for the first time, to share hopes and stories, to check out understanding and to find camaraderie amongst others with similar journeys. In the UK, ICA is still not universally accepted among adoption professionals. Charged with the responsibility to find families for UK children and frequently averse to transracial and trans-cultural placements, their response to ICA applicants can be experienced as a rebuff and rejection, perhaps confirming and compounding feelings held by applicants who are facing their own infertility.

A key element of early contact is to provide a setting where prospective adopters can engage in counselling both about their own readiness to adopt and about the implications of ICA, a task recognised internationally and enshrined in the provisions of the *Hague Convention on Protection of Children and Co-operation in Respect of Intercountry Adoption* (HCCH 1993). An open and informed professional approach is vital if the agency is to lay the foundation for an effective assessment process and an ongoing positive relationship.

---

1   Bodies designated by the concerned states to discharge the duties which are imposed by the Hague Convention upon such authorities.

Preparation

Practice in many countries recognises the importance of preparation for the task of adoptive parenting (Berry, Barth and Needell 1996; Duinkerken and Geerts 2000; Farber *et al.* 2003) and preparation serves a range of functions.

Developing an awareness that adoptive parenting is different from parenting birth children

Adoptive parenting brings constant reminders that a child is not born to the family, with the potential for unresolved pain and loss to surface. With the added dimension in transracial adoption of its visibility to others, prospective adopters need not only to acknowledge to themselves that they have relinquished the possibility of biological parenthood but also have to prepare to share this reality with the outside world. One attraction of ICA might be the belief that, unlike in domestic adoption, contact with the birth family is not required (Smolowe 1998). However, this is a fallacy; some overseas adopters meet the birth family and have ongoing contact. Intercountry Adoption Centre's (IAC's) experience is that preparation can play a major role in encouraging movement from a position where the birth family is not considered, and their role negated, to one where it can be held in mind and accepted as being part of the child and therefore part of the adopting family's life.

Most importantly, preparation aids the process of understanding as lack of information, particularly where a child has been abandoned, can pose a serious challenge to both the adoptee and adopters as the child matures. The use of film material or live speakers, for example, can enable the child's adoption plan to be seen through the eyes of the relinquishing birth parent(s) and the child themselves as an older adoptee, lowering feelings of fear and threat which may lie at the heart of views about birth families, contact and tracing.

Inter-country kinship adopters usually start from a different position about birth families, although it cannot be assumed that they will know either the child or family well, if at all. The diversity of motivation is vast: at one end of the continuum are those who are infertile and whose family members have conceived a child for them or who are 'gifting' children to them; at the other are those who would not have considered adoption but for the needs of related children in crisis (parental death, abandonment or rejection, or parental physical or mental ill health) (Haworth and Way 2007). The former group do not progress to an adoption application in significant numbers, probably because many will be advised at the pre-liminary stage that the arrangement does not meet UK immigration re-quirements and the child will be unable to obtain a visa to join them. Sometimes in these situations a transfer of parental responsibility has al-ready taken place in the state of origin and one consideration, therefore, is whether adopters should move (back) to the child's country in order to provide family life there for the child.

Kinship adopters are often among the most isolated of inter-country adopters and support services are rarely attuned to their needs.

Understanding the significance of past experiences

Many children placed from overseas have poor pre- and post-birth ex-periences, including neglect and abuse. The work of Rutter *et al.* (2009) records the potential difficulties that can result from institutional or poor early care. For those seeking to adopt a 'healthy' child with whom to enjoy 'normal' parenting experiences, this realisation can be hard to accept and, again, feelings of anger and disappointment can emerge.

Understanding the loss and pain at the heart of adoption

Applicants frequently attend preparation wishing to minimise their sense of loss and to invest only positive hopes and dreams in adoption. Preparation begins the process of helping applicants to own their pain, consider how it compares with that of birth families and adoptees and accept that shared vulnerability will remain for all parties.

Accepting uncertainty

Uncertainty in adoption is both short- and long-term. Prospective adopt-ers need to decide if they can manage this individually and within their partnership. Domestic placements can offer more medical and social in-formation, better professional support at placement and less complex legal processes and may appear more attractive for some. As a result, a small but steady core of prospective adopters moves from ICA to domestic adop-tion. A pilot study at IAC in 2006 showed that 18 per cent of prospec-tive adopters decided to switch post-preparation. In IAC's experience, the lengthy waiting period post-approval for placements from countries such as China also appears to contribute to later shifts.

Assessment

As infertility is at the heart of most adoption applications, the social worker's task is to assess applicants' accommodation between their inability to give birth and their suitability and readiness to nurture a child not born to them. Assessment offers the opportunity to understand the facts of the applicants' infertility and its meaning to them. Narrative coherence, emotional intelligence and availability, attitudes towards parenting, birth family, contact and disclosure all offer clues to their state of readiness (Millar and Paulson-Ellis 2009). In addition to core assessment work there will be further exploration in ICA assessments of the motivation to adopt from overseas, the links that exist or are being built with a country and culture, and individual understandings of attachment and institutional care. This is also the time to explore attitudes towards difference, identity and racism and to assist those pursuing a transracial placement to consider whether their lifestyle, supports and attitudes can sustain a child of difference within the family.

In essence, the assessment is trying to establish whether prospective adopters have sufficiently worked through their infertile status and have the capacity, flexibility and extended commitment to parent a child who may bring challenge into their lives in a way that birth parenting may not. Grotevant (2006) talks of 'adoption kinship networks' where individuals have to negotiate scenarios out of their comfort zone and which change and alter throughout the adoption journey, sometimes militating against them being 'the normal family' they wish to be. Potential adoptive grandparents, aunts, uncles and potential guardians may also be pushed out of their comfort zones as assessment enquiries extend to consider their support for the adoption. ICA is a new experience for many extended family members and work at IAC indicates that there is often a hidden reservoir of loss and pain associated with relatives' infertility. Worries and concerns about how a child who is 'different' will fit into their lives and homes need addressing with care. The openness of transracial adoption can feel particularly challenging to a generation for whom adoption would be considered a private family matter.

Adoption panel

Within England and Wales prospective adopters are invited to attend the adoption panel and our experience at IAC is that many choose to do so. This can feel like the final hurdle of the first leg of their journey and is anticipated with a mixture of fear and excitement. It raises feelings of helplessness as key decisions about their lives are entrusted to others and these can resonate with similar feelings associated with infertility. Knowledge and views about ICA vary across panels. This can dent prospective adopters' confidence in their impartiality and intensify any feelings of unfairness. Handling applications and prospective adopters with care is key.

Waiting for a placement

After approval, the professional emphasis changes to providing support as prospective adopters are left to await a match without any of the prescribed timescales that pregnancy affords. Many report this as a frustrating time, again with little control and often characterised by feelings of hopelessness and anxiety as to whether a match will be offered.

Unlike domestic adopters, inter-country adopters may have little ongoing contact with social workers and can feel isolated, using support (if at all) from parent support groups and internet chat rooms. UK agencies supporting those facing long waits can become the focus of anger, perhaps because this feels safer than showing or feeling anger towards the state of origin in which so much hope has to remain invested.

While this is neither the preserve of inter-country adopters nor of those motivated to adopt anyway as a result of infertility, a long wait can bring other challenges. Some may conceive, and this not only challenges their newly established identity as prospective adopters but also necessitates withdrawal from the adoption plan. For others, life events intervene – health concerns, getting older, change of job or country of residence, changes in priorities. Some take the hard decision that, after all the investment of time and emotion, a placement has come too late and life has moved on. Others may need professional support to arrive at the decision to let go. Adopters waiting for second or subsequent placements may feel that the age gap for an existing child would now be too great and choose to withdraw. Withdrawal almost always reawakens previous loss experiences.

Being matched with a child

The matching and introduction stages bring the adoption alive again, as the idea of having a child finally becomes a reality. However, for inter-country adopters, these stages are protracted. Unlike overseas adopters from other European countries, there are no UK specialist agencies accredited by the children's states of origin to act as a bridge to the overseas agency and 'their' child.

Different states of origin have different ways of matching prospective adopters with a child but, for virtually all those working regularly with the UK (with the exception of, for example, Pakistan and Kazakhstan), a match begins with the arrival of written information and a photograph of a child. This is a highly emotive time and, often, the time when 'claiming' the child begins as the photograph is shared and displayed among family and friends. Social and medical information may bring questions which need professional advice and guidance and, very commonly, the lack of information raises again issues of risk and uncertainty.

Current regulations in England and Wales require adopters (both, if a joint application) to have met the child overseas before they can confirm formally their acceptance of the placement, acceptance which they will have given provisionally at the matching stage. It can take months before the state of origin's invitation to travel, where required, is received or before otherwise being able to make the arrangements to meet the child. This can exacerbate uncertainty, with fears that events might intervene to prevent the adoption going ahead. Introductions, like matching, are variably managed by overseas countries; some provide graded introductory programmes comparable with UK domestic adoptions while others introduce and hand over the child at the same time.

During preparation, the expectation will have been espoused that inter-country adopters should seek support after the child joins their family. Indeed, once the child enters the UK, agencies in England and Wales have a duty to ensure that adopters know what services are available. However, unlike domestic adopters, they will rarely have had professional support at their introduction to their child (whatever the process). Many begin their long-awaited parenting experience overseas, away from their support networks and with a child who may be traumatised and distressed (Hoksbergen and van Dijkum 2001) and/or ill (Miller and Hendrie 2000). In addition, in order to progress the adoption, attendance at courts, offices, consulates and embassies is required, often with the child in tow. It is therefore not surprising that this period is often recalled as being stressful (Greene *et al.* 2007). Emotionally, it can become another roller-coaster ride. Fears about whether the child likes their 'new' parents, particularly children who are traumatised or ill or who show clear preference for one partner (in couple adoptions), can stir powerful emotions. Old infertility wounds can be reopened, including those that question self-worth and right to parenthood, and stimulate thoughts about whether bonding with a birth child might have been easier. Feelings of love and attachment to a child do not always come instantaneously and prospective adopters may question whether they have made the right decision. Although rare, some decide not to proceed and return home without the child, as the reality of parenting someone else's child proves too overwhelming. Feelings of grief and isolation invariably follow the loss of their dream of parenthood, as informal support networks built in readiness for adoptive parenting are no longer available.

Post-placement

Arriving home with a child is an exciting and long awaited moment but, for most, the new status brings challenges such as disturbed nights and worries about the child's health or feeding habits (Greene *et al.* 2007). Parents must also adjust to a new lifestyle; most UK agencies encourage at least one parent to be at home for a four to six month period after placement in order to encourage and foster a secure attachment. Sometimes the reality of parenting is very different from long-held expectations. As adoptive parents of toddlers or older children, they are not linked into the early support systems for birth parents and can feel isolated. Post-adoption blues are not uncommon, yet may provoke feelings of shame, such that adopters can find these feelings difficult to share with others (MacLeod and Macrae 2006). Ongoing attachment concerns, particularly in relation to children from institutions, can erode parental confidence unless they are supported to understand, persist and recognise any positive changes.

Post-adoption

Adoption is a lifelong journey for all concerned. Adopters' infertility and their accommodation to this will influence the development of the parent–child relationship and the outcome of the adoption for themselves and their child. As attachment and belonging grow, some parents' yearning for their child to have been born from them can turn into denial of adoption and 'forgetting' the associated tasks. Good preparation can help adopters to identify the ages and stages at which their infertility and the child's developmental stages may present enhanced challenges and provide strategies and tools with which to tackle some of the emerging issues.

Preparation should also have highlighted and normalised the potential need for adoption support. One of the earliest stages for this may be when the child asks questions about their birth, usually at around the age of three to four years: 'Was I born from your tummy, Mummy?' Research in both domestic and ICA indicates that openness about adoption and parental emotional availability are key components in aiding children's sense of integration and security (Rosenblum and Freeark 2006) and in promoting their longer-term mental health (Irhammer and Cederblad 2000), but may be affected adversely by cultural differences. Research in India (Bhargava 2005) illustrates how societal attitudes towards infertility and adoption can impact negatively upon parental openness and ability to communicate with their children. In IAC's experience, 'telling' is often viewed with significant trepidation by adopters. Where the adoption is a same race placement, there can be a temptation to avoid the subject until the child is older or, occasionally, to resist 'telling' at all. In transracial placements this route is not an option, so strategies need to be in place at an early age to both manage the questions from the outside world and assist the child themselves.

Children may yearn to be the biological child of their parents and this too can make it harder for parents to tackle the reality of the adoption and can reawaken their own pain at being unable to conceive. As the child's understanding grows and their thinking deepens, the pain of adoption with its multilayered losses can intrude into family life. Families are most likely to seek help when their children are aged seven to ten years, when behaviours triggered by a child's growing understanding that adoption brings losses as well as gains (so-called 'adoption bereavement') may occur, and during the teenage years when issues of sexuality and identity come to the fore (Brodzinsky 1990; Verhulst 2000). For infertile adoptive parents, the threat from birth parents can become very real as the adolescent compares their 'sexual' birth parents with their 'asexual and barren' adoptive parents. A particularly piercing question is whether or not their parents would have adopted them had they been able to have birth children.

Lack of information about the past – so prevalent in ICA placements – continues to challenge, whether in school where hidden disabilities might begin to emerge (Greene *et al.* 2007; Meese 2002; Ryvgold 1999) or during adolescence where understanding birth parents' motives and lifestyles may be hard to assimilate in the absence of concrete information. Adopters' hopes and dreams of academic achievement by their child, for example, may be thwarted by the impact of genes and past environment (Bhargava 2005; Dalen *et al.* 2006).

Where the placement is transracial and the adoption therefore 'visible', reminders of difference can feel constant if this prompts questions and responses from the outside world. Adoptees speak graphically of the impact of racism and stereotyping on their lives (Harris 2006; Lindblad and Signell 2008) and of the challenge to belonging that this brings. Adoptive parents will share the pain of these rejections and sometimes experience them alongside their child. At IAC, adoptive fathers and their teenage adopted daughters give powerful testament to the pain of their relationship being misconstrued by strangers as 'sexual' and 'bought', especially when the adoptee is presumed to be from a country associated with the sex industry and/or sex tourism.

Inter-country adopters also need to develop strategies for helping their child to understand something of the culture, language and heritage of the country of their birth. Although it cannot be assumed, same- race placements where the adoptive family are same-heritage adopters generally have ready access to the language and culture. Frequent homeland journeys may therefore be part of their lifestyle. For those adopting from a country where there are no such existing links, it is IAC's experience that most adopters are enthusiastic about this task and 'adopt' the country and its people. This might be achieved through creating and maintaining links with the institutions or people who assisted in the placement or through joining UK-based societies and support groups for adopters, many of whom offer heritage activities. Where the importance of cultural identity is denied, this may be driven by a family's wish to 'be a normal family' or because the parents' experience of the country at placement was not positive. Some studies have suggested that denial or avoidance can lead to adoptees having an increased interest in their origins (Irhammer and Cederblad 2000) whereas Lee and Quintana (2005) showed that positive interest on the part of adoptive parents was more likely to increase a child's interest in their heritage. Given that language forms part of cultural identity, some parents provide their child with access to their language through, for example, Mandarin Saturday classes. Other languages, such as Quichua (spoken in the Andes), provide a greater challenge to both child and parent.

The need to find a balance between encouraging and instilling a sense of cultural identity and highlighting differences to the point where a child's sense of belonging is undermined is a tension to which each adoptive family has to become attuned. Additionally, not all adopted children are interested in their country of origin in spite of a parent's best efforts and some find the pressure of learning an additional language beyond their capabilities. Faced with the knowledge that they should be offering these opportunities, parents can again feel anxious and guilty that they are not fulfilling their adoptive parenting duties.

Return visits to the birth country invariably carry meaning for the adoptive family. Seeing and experiencing a country for the first time is a powerful event for both the adoptee and adoptive parents, as visits re-awaken placement memories but also heighten anxieties about losing their child back to the country. Once mature, adoptees may choose to make these journeys alone or with other adoptees, which again can feel like a rejection for parents.

The search for identity can be especially complex for transracial inter-country adoptees (Hubinette 2004; Saetersdal and Dalen 2000; Silverman and Feigelman 1990). Potential searching and reunion may trigger anxiety in adoptive parents both about the security of their relationship with their child and about the adoptee undertaking a search without their on-hand support. 'Letting go' can be challenging, leaving adoptive parents feeling abandoned as their child searches for the alternative life they could have led. Where infertility was the driver to the adoption and ICA seen as an opportunity to avoid issues of birth family and contact, the child's interest in searching can reopen old wounds.

For many adoptees, having birth children of their own can be a turning point (Philips 2008). They see, usually for the first time, a person genetically related to them and in experiencing the birth of a child may feel empathy towards their birth mother. For adoptive parents, especially mothers who have had no experience of pregnancy and birth, this time can be a source of mixed emotions and prompt them to revisit their adoption journey and the range of feelings and memories associated with their quest for parenthood.

Conclusion

Adopting a child from overseas as a result of infertility is a complex parenting task and one which is never a solution to infertility, only to childlessness. The adoption journey that parents must go on with their child brings lifelong reminders that their child was not born to them. Acknowledging that some reminders will be painful is a key adoption task if parents are to have the emotional space and time to help their growing child process the meaning of adoption. While this applies to all adoptive placements, with ICA the challenges and hence the qualities required of inter-country adopters are greater.

References

Andersson, G. (1986) 'The Adopting and Adopted Swedes and their Contemporary Society.' In R. Hoksbergen (ed.) *Adoption in Worldwide Perspective.* Lisse: Swets and Zeitlinger.

Andersson, G. (2000) 'Intercountry Adoption in Sweden: The Perspective of the Adoption Centre in its 30th Year.' In P. Selman (ed.) *Intercountry Adoption: Developments, Trends and Perspectives.* London: British Association for Adoption and Fostering.

Barth, R.P., Brookes, D. and Iyer, S. (1995) *Adoption in California: Current Demographic Profiles and Projections through the End of the Century.* Executive Summary. Berkeley, CA: Child Welfare Research Centre.

Berry, M., Barth, R. and Needell, B. (1996) 'Preparation, support and satisfaction of adoptive families in agency and independent adoptions.' *Child and Adolescent Social Work Journal 13,* 2, 157–183.

Bhargava, V. (2005) *Adoption in India.* New Delhi: Sage Publications.

Brodzinsky, D. (1990) 'A Stress and Coping Model of Adoption Adjustment.' In D. Brodzinsky and M. Schechter (eds) *The Psychology of Adoption.* Oxford: Oxford University Press.

Dalen, M., Hubinette, A., Hjern, A., Lindblad, F., Rasmussen, F. and Vinnerljung, B. (2006) 'The Influence of Pre- and Post-adoption Factors on Intelligence Performance among Young International Adoptees.' Paper presented at the 2nd International Conference on Adoption Research, University of East Anglia, 17–21 July 2006.

Duinkerken, A. and Geerts, H. (2000) 'Awareness Required: The Information and Preparation Course on Intercountry Adoption in the Netherlands.' In P. Selman (ed.) *Intercountry Adoption: Developments, Trends and Perspectives.* London: British Association for Adoption and Fostering.

Farber, M.L.Z., Timberlake, E., Mudd, H.P. and Cullen, L. (2003) 'Preparing parents for adoption: An agency experience.' *Child and Adolescent Social Work Journal 20,* 3, 175–196.

Feigelman, W. and Silverman, A.R. (1983) *Chosen Children: New Patterns of Adoptive Relationships.* New York, NY: Praeger.

Greene, S., Kelly, R., Nixon, E., Kelly, G. *et al.* (2007) *A Study of Intercountry Adoption Outcomes in Ireland.* Dublin: Children's Research Centre, Trinity College.

Groothues, C., Beckett, C. and O'Connor, T. (1998) 'The outcomes of adoptions from Romania.' *Adoption and Fostering 22,* 4, 30–40.

Grotevant, H. (2006) 'Emotional Distance Regulation over the Life Course in Adoptive Kinship Networks.' Keynote speech, 2nd International Conference on Adoption Research, University of East Anglia, 17–21 July 2006.

Hague Conference on Private International Law (HCCH) (1993) *Hague Convention on Protection of Children and Co-operation in Respect of Intercountry Adoption.* The Hague: Hague Conference on Private International Law.

Harris, P. (2006) *In Search of Belonging.* London: British Association for Adoption and Fostering.

Haworth, G. and Way, J. (2007) *Adoption from Abroad of a Relative Child.* BAAF Practice Note 52. London: British Association for Adoption and Fostering.

Hoksbergen, R. (1991) 'Intercountry Adoption Coming of Age in the Netherlands: Basic Issues, Trends and Developments.' In H. Altstein and R. Simon (eds) *Intercountry Adoption: A Multinational Perspective.* New York, NY: Praeger.

Hoksbergen, R. (2000) 'Changes in Attitudes in Three Generations of Adoptive Parents: 1950–2000.' In P. Selman (ed.) *Intercountry Adoption: Developments, Trends and Perspectives.* London: British Association for Adoption and Fostering.

Hoksbergen, R. and Bunjes, L. (1986) 'Thirty Years of Adoption in The Netherlands.' In R. Hoksbergen (ed.) *Adoption in Worldwide Perspective: A Review of Programs, Policies and Legislation in 14 Countries.* Lisse: Swets and Zeitlinger.

Hoksbergen, R. and van Dijkum, C. (2001) 'Trauma experienced by children adopted from abroad.' *Adoption and Fostering 25,* 2, 18–25.

Howell, S. (2006) *The Kinning of Foreigners: Transnational Adoption in a Global Perspective.* New York, NY: Berghahn Books.

Hubinette, T. (2004) 'Adopted Koreans and the development of identity in the "third space".' *Adoption & Fostering 28,* 2, 24–26.

International Bar Association (IBA) (1991) *The Intercountry Adoption Process from the UK Adoptive Parents' Perspective.* London: International Bar Association.

Irhammer, M. and Cederblad, M. (2000) 'Outcome of Intercountry Adoption in Sweden.' In P. Selman (ed.) *Intercountry Adoption: Developments, Trends and Perspectives.* London: British Association for Adoption and Fostering.

Jaffe, E.D. (1991) 'Foreign Adoptions in Israel: Private Paths to Parenthood.' In H. Altstein and R. Simon (eds) *Intercountry Adoption: A Multinational Perspective.* New York, NY: Praeger.

Kane, S. (1993) 'The movement of children for international adoption: An epidemiological perspective.' *The Social Science Journal 30*, 4, 323–339.

Lee, D.C. and Quintana, S.M. (2005) 'Benefits of cultural exposure and development of Korean perspective-taking ability for transracially adopted Korean children.' *Cultural Diversity and Ethnic Minority Psychology 11*, 2, 130–143.

Lindblad, F. and Signell, S. (2008) 'Degrading attitudes related to foreign appearance: Interviews with Swedish female adoptees from Asia.' *Adoption & Fostering 32*, 3, 46–59.

MacLeod, J. and Macrae, S. (eds) (2006) *Adoption Parenting: Creating a Toolbox, Building Connections.* Warren, NJ: EMK Publications.

Meese, R.L. (2002) *Intercountry Adoptions in School.* Westport, CT: Bergin and Garvey.

Millar, I. and Paulson-Ellis, C. (2009) *Exploring Infertility Issues in Adoption.* London: British Association for Adoption and Fostering.

Miller, L. and Hendrie, N. (2000) 'Health of children adopted from China.' *Paediatrics 105*, 6, 40–44.

Moreau, F. (2008) 'Attendent enfants désespérément.' 'Desperately waiting for children.' *Sud Ouest*, 17 January 2008.

Philips, Z. (2008) *Mother Me.* London: British Association for Adoption and Fostering.

Rojewski, J. and Rojewski, J. (2001) *Intercountry Adoption from China: Examining Cultural Heritage and Other Post Adoption Issues.* Westport, CT: Bergin and Garvey.

Rosenblum, K. and Freeark, K. (2006) 'Family Processes that Promote Emotional Competence and a Sense of Belonging in Young Internationally Adopted Children.' Paper presented at the 2nd International Conference on Adoption Research, University of East Anglia, 17–21 July 2006.

Rutter, M., Beckett, C., Castle, J., Colvert, E. *et al.* (2009) 'Effects of Profound Early Institutional Deprivation: An Overview of Findings from a UK Longitudinal Study of Romanian Adoptees.' In G. Wrobel and E. Neill (eds) *International Advances in Adoption Research.* London: John Wiley.

Ryvgold, A. (1999) 'Intercountry Adopted Children's Language and Academic Skills.' In A. Ryvgold, M. Dalen and B. Saetersdal (eds) *Mine – Yours – Ours and Theirs.* Oslo: University of Oslo.

Saetersdal, B. and Dalen, M. (1991) 'Norway: Intercountry Adoption in a Homogeneous Country.' In H. Altstein and R. Simon (eds) *Intercountry Adoption: A Multidisciplinary Perspective.* New York, NY: Praeger.

Saetersdal, B. and Dalen, M. (2000) 'Identity Formation in a Homogeneous Country: Norway.' In P. Selman (ed.) *Intercountry Adoption: Developments, Trends and Perspectives.* London: British Association for Adoption and Fostering.

Selman, P. (1976) 'Patterns of adoption in England and Wales since 1959.' *Social Work Today 7*, 7, 194–197.

Selman, P. (2006a) 'Trends in intercountry adoption 1998–2004: Analysis of data from 20 receiving countries.' *Journal of Population Research 23*, 2, 183–204.

Selman, P. (2006b) 'Towards a demography of adoption: making sense of official statistics on child adoption and the search for origins.' Paper presented at the *Second International Conference on Adoption Research.* University of East Anglia, 17–21 July 2006.

Selman, P. (2009a) 'Intercountry Adoption: Research, Policy and Practice.' In G. Schofield and J. Simmonds (eds) *The Child Placement Handbook: Research, Policy and Practice.* London: British Association for Adoption and Fostering.

Selman, P. (2009b) 'Intercountry Adoption in Europe 1998–2007: Patterns, Trends and Issues.' In K. Rummery, I. Greener and C. Holden (eds) *Social Policy Review 21: Analysis and Debate in Social Policy.* Bristol: Policy Press.

Selman, P. (2009c) 'The rise and fall of intercountry adoption in the 21st century.' *International Social Work 52*, 5, 1–20.

Selman, P., Moretti, E. and Brogi, F. (2009) 'Statistical Profile of Intercountry Adoption in the European Union.' In *International Adoption in the European Union*. Final report to the European Parliament's Committee on Civil Liberties, Justice and Home Affairs. Florence: Istituto degli Innocenti.

Silverman, A.R. and Feigelman, W. (1990) 'Adjustment in interracial adoptees – An overview.' In D.M. Brodzinsky and M.D. Schechter (eds) *The Psychology of Adoption*. New York, NY: Oxford University Press.

Smerdon, U.R. (2008–2009) 'Crossing bodies, crossing borders: International surrogacy between the United States and India.' *Cumberland Law Review 39*, 1, 15–85. Available at www.ethicanet.org/ Smerdon.pdf, accessed on 19 February 2010.

Smolin, D. (2004) 'Intercountry adoption as child trafficking.' *Valparaiso Law Review 39*, 2, 281–325. Available at http://works.bepress.com/david_smolin/3, accessed on 29 January 2010.

Smolin, D. (2006) 'Child laundering: how the intercountry adoption system legitimizes and incentivizes the practices of buying, trafficking, kidnapping, and stealing children.' *Wayne Law Review 52*, 113–200. Available at http://law.bepress.com/expresso/eps/749, accessed on 26 April 2010.

Smolowe, J. (1998) *An Empty Lap: One Couple's Journey to Parenthood*. New York, NY: Simon and Schuster.

Textor, M.R. (1991) 'International Adoptions in West Germany: A Private Affair.' In H. Altstein and R. Simon (eds) *Intercountry Adoption: A Multinational Perspective*. New York, NY: Praeger.

US Department of Health and Human Services (2008) *Adoption Experiences of Women and Men and Demand for Children to Adopt by Women 18–44 Years of Age in the United States, 2002*. Washington, DC: US Department of Health and Human Services.

Verhulst, F.C. (2000) 'The Development of Internationally Adopted Children.' In P. Selman (ed.) *Intercountry Adoption: Developments, Trends and Perspectives*. London: British Association for Adoption and Fostering.

CHAPTER 10

A Child at Last:
Adoption after Infertility

Anthea Hendry and Penny Netherwood

Introduction

The changing pattern of adoption over the last two decades has brought close attention to the consequences of pre-placement histories of children when assessing and working with post-placement difficulties (for example Golding *et al.* 2006). In contrast, the pre-placement experiences of the adoptive parents are comparatively neglected both in the literature and in practice. The main exception to this is in relation to the role that the adoptive parents' attachment style plays in developing a secure attachment in the adopted placement (Steele *et al.* 2003). Far less emphasis has been given to other factors influencing the adoptive parents' capacity to parent effectively. Since, for the majority of adoptive parents, infertility is a key experience in the decision to adopt, the impact of this needs to be considered. Most work in this area has focused on the immediate transition to adoption following infertility (for example Daniluk and Hurtig-Mitchell 2003; Salzer 1999). However, like adoption, infertility is lifelong and its emotional impact can re-emerge across the lifespan, creating additional challenges for adoptive families to negotiate.

In this chapter, the developmental life stages model (Erikson 1963) and the family life cycle model (Carter and McGoldrick 1989) are used as a framework for examining infertility and adoption after the placement of children, to emphasise the lifelong nature of both and the way they interweave with life stages and life events. This builds on the work of Brodzinsky, who adapted Erikson's model to include the additional tasks and challenges facing adoptive families (1987) and used it to consider the impact of infertility (1997). His model has been well endorsed in the literature (for example Bingley Miller and Bentovim 2007; Scott and Lindsey 2003) and has proved clinically useful in our own work, as has the integration of systemic and psychoanalytic approaches in general.

The settings we draw experience from include: a social services adoption unit, a voluntary sector post-adoption service and a child and adolescent mental health service (CAMHS). In this chapter, four vignettes – composites from the many families and individuals we have worked with – provide the basis for commentary and discussion around key developmental stages. We conclude by drawing out some implications for practice from the research and practice-based evidence we have highlighted.

Becoming a family

Barbara and Neil lived on a council estate in a large city. A white British couple, they had both lived and worked in the area all their lives. They were keen to start a family as soon as they married in their mid-twenties but, after extensive medical investigations over several years, their infertility remained unexplained. They tried IVF once but found the whole process too stressful and financially prohibitive. After three years of disappointment they decided to make a family through adoption.

The process from making this decision to Dylan being placed with them took two years: this too was an anxious time of scrutiny, waiting and uncertainty. When Dylan finally arrived at the age of 15 months, they felt as if they had completed a very long and painful journey to parenthood. Then, to their astonishment and delight, six months later Barbara found she was pregnant.

When she gave birth to a daughter they called Tiffany, they were overjoyed and felt that their family was now complete. They did not foresee the complications of parenthood that awaited them. Dylan was now a strong-willed, active boy of two and a half. He had always been a handful, particularly for Barbara, who was placid and quiet by nature. Dylan reacted very negatively to Tiffany's arrival. He became aggressive towards Barbara and extremely defiant. Barbara was soon exhausted and overwhelmed. When Tiffany was just six months old Dylan bit her hand so hard she bled. In despair, Barbara talked to their GP about Dylan who referred him to CAMHS.

Anecdotes of spontaneous conception after long-term infertility are familiar to adoption agencies. In the 1950s and 60s, it was hypothesised that adoption could act as a 'cure' for infertility, but evidence for this was lacking (Humphrey and MacKenzie 1967). While recent advances in reproductive technologies are likely to have reduced the incidence of spontaneous conception after adoption, we know it does still occur. The best evidence of this is from a relatively recent study of spontaneous conception following unsuccessful infertility treatment. Kupka *et al.* (2003) reported that spontaneous conception occurred in 32 out of 226 couples, a rate of 14 per cent. Of these spontaneous conceptions, 84 per cent occurred within two years of treatment ending, which roughly corresponds with the time period in which an adoptive placement could have begun. The psychological and biological mechanisms that enable spontaneous conception after long-term infertility are complex and yet to be understood fully. However, there are clear consequences when this happens after an adoption placement has been made.

The experience for Barbara and Neil was that, just as they are adjusting to adoptive parenting – the stage at which the reality of grief regarding infertility can be triggered (Tollemache 1998) – suddenly they are facing the new reality of becoming birth parents. Tiffany's birth opens them up more clearly to the part of Dylan's life they have missed and to the differences in parenting an adopted child. However much they try, they can never make Dylan's position in their family the same as Tiffany's: he is not of their genealogy, they did not share his first birthday and early milestones. Acknowledging the differences and losses for them at this stage will be important (Kirk 1964).

Dylan has a story that he will need to be told as he gets older. Brodzinsky (1987) identified that, during the infancy and toddler stage of an adopted child's life, adoptive parents need to develop realistic expectations of adoptive parenthood and cope with the anxiety and uncertainty surrounding the initial telling process. In order to do this, Cudmore (2005) describes how adoptive parents must be able to tell their own story of infertility to themselves but, in this case, it will be hard to develop a coherent story about Dylan's arrival that makes any sense to him as he gets older. Barbara and Neil's awareness of the difference adoption brings may be heightened at this stage but, with Tiffany's arrival, their capacity to work on this to the benefit of Dylan may be inhibited. There is now a risk factor for the placement.

The challenges of middle childhood

Two brothers, Liam aged one year and Jason aged two and a half years, were placed for adoption with Linda and Richard, a white British couple in their early thirties. This followed four years of unsuccessful treatment for dual factor infertility. They had both desperately wanted their own birth children but they resigned themselves to the fact that this was not to be. Linda gave up her nursing career to stay at home with the boys while Richard worked long hours in computer programming in order to maintain their relatively comfortable lifestyle. They were given a life story book for the boys, including photos and basic information about their birth families. They found it difficult to think about the boys' experiences of abuse and neglect before coming to live with them. They put the life story book in the attic to think about later.

Six years later, Jason, now nine, is a quiet, compliant and rather anxious boy who has never caused Linda and Richard any major concern until a parents' evening at his school some months ago. His teacher commented that he seemed more distracted in class than usual, he had fallen out with his one friend and his work was not progressing as expected. The teacher asked if anything had happened at home. At first, Linda and Richard could not think of anything but, later, they reflected that there had been a deterioration in Jason's relation with his brother. In need of advice, Linda contacted the local authority post-adoption support service who suggested she and Richard join their support group for adoptive parents. In one of the sessions, they learnt about a stage of grieving that many adopted children go through around eight to nine years of age, as they become able to understand that they have lost something very significant, their birth family. However settled the child may have been in the adoptive family, they can go through a stage of psychological disturbance as they adjust to this reality. Linda and Richard agreed it was time to get some help in talking to the boys about why they had been adopted. They decided to begin by asking the placing agency for some up-to-date information about the boys' birth mother. When Linda learnt that their birth mother was now settled in a more stable new relationship and had given birth to two daughters, whom she was parenting herself, she was thrown into an unexpected state of turmoil. A confusing mix of outrage, bitterness, jealousy and grief overwhelmed her for weeks. In the process of doing what she knew was right for her adopted sons, old wounds relating to her own infertility had been re-opened. She needed to address these feelings before she could think about telling the boys that they had two half-sisters living with their birth mother. She needed to be emotionally available to help them through the impact of this news.

Theories of cognitive development and family life cycle development indicate that telling children about adoption is best done as an ongoing process, adapting the information given in step with the child's unfolding intellectual and emotional development (Burnell 1990). Ideally, this process should begin early, encouraging openness and a positive view of being adopted. Having a coherent narrative to explain the reasons for adoption is associated with better adjustment in adopted children and young people (see Hudson 2006 for a review). To be coherent, this narrative needs to include the parents' motivation to adopt, which for possibly 80 per cent of adopters will be infertility (Cudmore 2005).

While this guidance may seem straightforward, many adoptive parents struggle with the process of telling because, like for Linda and Richard, it is a poignant reminder of their infertility. Thinking and talking about the child's birth parents can revive feelings of envy of others' fertility and a sense of defectiveness in themselves or their partner (Schechter 1970). When trying to make sense of unsuccessful attempts to conceive a child, both men and women can start to wonder whether this indicates they are just not 'cut out' to be parents. After adoption, these doubts about entitlement to parenthood can re-emerge, along with doubts about their ability to parent (Brodzinsky 1997). Parental self-doubt and vulnerability make talking about adoption feel even more threatening. Kirk (1964) proposed that adoptive family relationships are built on a foundation of loss: loss of fertility and biological children for the parents, loss of the birth family for the child and loss of the child for the birth parent. Brinich (1990) describes the 'collusive denial' that families can engage in about the losses that preceded adoption, particularly the loss of the imagined biological baby. He suggests that the fantasy of this loss often remains hidden until the arrival of the adopted child, but hidden does not mean inactive. Cudmore (2005) eloquently describes the importance of coming to terms with infertility-related losses sufficiently to be psychologically available to the adopted child: 'There clearly needs to have been sufficient mourning for there to be enough room for a child who needs a home in the new parents' minds' (Cudmore 2005, p.307).

In this example, Linda and Richard have avoided processing their own feelings of loss, which prevented them from noticing the changes in Jason until his teacher shared her observations. Linda's experience of a sudden re-emergence of infertility-related feelings following new and unexpected information about the boys' birth mother illustrates how emotionally charged any form of contact with birth parents can be, particularly for adoptive parents who have experienced infertility.

Negotiating adolescence

We know that adolescence is a time of great change for all young people and for their families. Family life cycle models (for example Erikson 1963; Preto 1989) identify particular tasks which need to be negotiated at this stage and psychological conflicts for the young person to resolve. Rapid bodily transformation tends to precipitate feelings of confusion for most young people, who begin to question who they are and who they are going to become. In modern Western society, developing a separate self identity typically draws attention to the wider social world and venturing away from the family unit. The challenge for parents is to adapt to changing dynamics around interdependence while remaining a continuous source of emotional support and connection. Preto (1989) describes how parents can feel a void as they are no longer needed in the same way, with adolescence marking the loss of their child. For adoptive families, additional tasks have to be negotiated at this stage and negotiating the common tasks can be more complicated (Brodzinsky 1987). When parents have experienced infertility, the normative and adoption-specific tasks of this stage of development can be unexpectedly difficult to negotiate, as the following vignette indicates.

> Joy remarked to her husband Keith that their adopted son, Jack, was taller than him. It was true. Jack at 15 was not just tall for his age but confident, sociable and attractive. He seemed like a magnet for girls at his high school. It was not long before Keith had to face the reality of his son being sexually active. This was so unlike any experience Keith had had at this age. He had been a late developer, withdrawn and shy. Joy was his one and only girlfriend. They had met when they were 19. Even at that age Joy knew she could not have children because of a medical condition. This did not seem important to Keith at the time. He loved Joy, they married and later she suggested adopting and he thought that would be fine. He had not bargained for what Jack's adolescence stirred in him. It was something Keith found deeply disturbing and it unsettled not just him but his marriage. Keith fantasised about the possibility of his son getting a girl pregnant and this led to fantasies of getting someone pregnant himself. His sense of loss and grief at not having his own birth child hit him with full force for the first time. His relationships with both his son and his wife suffered a severe set-back which he could neither talk about nor fully understand. He suffered from difficulty sleeping. His GP gave him medication but he was not offered any psychological help.

Both systemic and psychodynamic theorists suggest that when a young person passes through this significant phase of psychosexual development it can reactivate emotional issues for parents from their own development (Preto 1989; Schechter 1970). For infertile adoptive parents the realisation that their adoptive child is sexually mature and could potentially conceive a child can often expose or reawaken feelings of envy towards fertile men and women. For Keith, his son's virility and assumed fertility triggered something new and troublesome for him.

For adopted young people the identity confusion in puberty can be particularly pronounced. The sense of discontinuity from their younger self is increased because of the earliest months or years living outside their current adoptive family. When similarities in physical and character traits between the young person and their adoptive parents are few and information about their birth family is limited, feelings of uncertainty and incompleteness are often experienced. Sants (1964) named this 'genealogical bewilderment'. At the same time, adoptive parents can also become acutely aware of emergent physical and character differences between themselves and their adopted teenager, reactivating feelings of loss of their own genetically related child and reminding the adoptive parents of their child's genetic heritage and its partial influence on the child's unfolding development.

Similarly, previous experiences of attachment, separation and loss are also likely to be reactivated as an adopted young person gains more independence. For adoptive parents this will include the losses associated with infertility as well as possible earlier unresolved losses. Some adoptive parents struggle to allow the process of separation and individuation to unfold. Schechter (1970) observed that any disengagement of a child from the parents places them back in the state of being childless again. If this coincides with the adopted young person openly beginning to search for their birth parents, the fear of rejection and loss of their child will be heightened.

Preto (1989) describes how, for all families, unresolved conflicts can resurface at this stage of the family life cycle. In this case, conflict has emerged in Keith and Joy's relationship that seems likely to have remained unresolved from the time of the decision to adopt. Blum (1983) describes how each partner will bring to the task of adoptive parenting conflicts from their earlier history and, when infertility is part of that history, these conflicts might well include feelings of anger towards the infertile partner, a sense of defectiveness experienced by the infertile partner and adoption as an agreement for the marriage to continue.

Grandparenting

Here we will explore the grandparenting role at two key stages in the adoptive family life cycle: first, in the early stages of the adoptive placement and second, when the adopted person has a child of their own. Both types of grandparenting are neglected areas in the adoption literature. In our experience, this life stage holds particular relevance for families formed by adoption after infertility, which has implications for post-adoption support.

Blum (1983) suggests that the acceptance or not of the adopted child by the adoptive grandparents can be a critical factor in helping or hindering integration of the child into the family. From his psychoanalytic view it is not just the grandparents' actual attitudes towards the adopted grandchild that are important but also their fantasised reactions in the minds of the adoptive parents, for example that their parents will fear that 'bad' blood is coming into the family. An example of this phenomenon is explored in the vignette later in this section. Blum concludes that adoptive parents need their parents to give full support as, without it, both their identity as a parent and as a son/daughter will be damaged. Similarly, the adopted child needs to feel accepted by the adoptive grandparent in order to develop a sense of being 'good enough' to be part of the family's generational continuity.

Pitcher (2009) reports findings from a qualitative study which seem to confirm this view. He found that adoptive parents carefully compared how grandparents treated their adopted child and any biological grandchildren. Adoptive parents were also alert for positive signs of acceptance of the adopted child as a true grandchild. Pitcher concluded that adoptive grandparents have a symbolic function as witnesses to the family's legitimacy, viewing them as 'figures whose approval enables the parents' anxieties about the acceptability of their family structure, and the acceptability of the actual child, to be assuaged' (p.63). These studies suggest that rejection of the adopted child by adoptive grandparents is not only problematic for the child but deeply wounding for the adoptive parents, as it can feed a sense of inadequacy and disappointment connected to infertility.

At a very different family life stage, adoptive parents might hope to become grandparents themselves. This too can have added complications for people who have never borne children of their own as the following case vignette describes:

> Diane was a widow of African Caribbean origin in her late fifties. She lived in an outer London suburb and worked part-time as a school dinner lady. Her only adopted daughter, Melanie, whose birth mother had parted with her at birth, was of dual heritage (African Caribbean/ white British). Melanie's husband was white British.
>
> When Melanie rang to tell her the news of her pregnancy, Diane found it difficult to respond positively, which Melanie found bewildering

and hurtful. In the weeks that followed Diane felt increasingly overwhelmed by waves of private grief connected with her own inability to have children. She avoided asking Melanie anything about the progress of her pregnancy and this began to cause a gulf between her and her daughter. For Diane, any anticipation of becoming a grandparent was subsumed by feelings she had had as a much younger woman, desperately trying to become pregnant. Feelings of envy and bitterness were dominant. Coping with this was a lonely experience not helped by her own mother's attitude. Her mother, Winnie, had never completely accepted Melanie as her granddaughter, which Diane had struggled to comprehend until Melanie went through a rebellious stage during her adolescence. Winnie's barbed remark that 'it's the bad blood in her that's the trouble' left Diane in no doubt that Melanie was never going to have her grandmother's full approval. This had proved to be true and had soured family relationships. 'She'll be no good as a mother' was Winnie's immediate comment to Diane when she learnt of the pregnancy.

The final straw for Diane came when she learnt that Melanie had made indirect contact with her birth mother, a white British woman, and now wanted to meet her. She had fantasies of Melanie's birth mother reclaiming her and becoming the legitimate grandmother. Her identity as both a mother and a future grandmother felt very threatened. She rang the local post-adoption service and was able to access some helpful support over the next few months.

For adopted people, becoming a parent can have particular resonance. This life stage is inevitably a reminder of their own beginnings and often invites new questions. Research confirms that becoming a parent is a frequent trigger of the search for birth parents by adopted people (Howe and Feast 2000). Nervous reactions by adoptive parents to adopted people searching are not uncommon (Howe and Feast 2000), as this is an inevitable reminder of the difference adoptive parenting brings and of infertility. Triseliotis, Feast and Kyle (2005) interviewed 77 adoptive parents whose adult children had had reunions with their birth mothers. Twenty-one per cent openly acknowledged that feelings of sadness relating to their infertility persisted after they adopted children, and some of these emphasised that the loss of the experience of pregnancy and birth was still felt keenly. Diane's experience will not be uncommon among this group of adopters and was exacerbated by the birth mother having a different ethnicity, more similar to the expected baby's. The attribution of the adoptive grandmother, Winnie, that Melanie's birth parents were responsible for her poor behaviour in adolescence and her likely inability to parent a child adequately highlights the fact that adoption has long been a fascinating area of research for the study of hereditary and environmental influences. The 'bad blood' theory, a real concern for some adoptive parents, may prove easy to turn to when an adopted child shows unwelcome behaviour or unwanted characteristics.

Again, not very evident in the literature but familiar in our practice are scenarios of adoptive parents becoming very active grandparents to their adopted children's children in sometimes difficult circumstances. We have worked with adoptive parents whose older-placed children had experienced early neglect and abuse prior to adoption. For some of these children, being placed in a safe and nurturing environment will not make up for these early disadvantages (see Scott and Lindsey 2003 for a review). Unplanned pregnancy can occur in teenage years when they are not psychologically ready for parenting. This can be an opportunity for adoptive parents to participate in their closest experience to pregnancy and birth. While painful in some areas, this can also be rewarding. Some grandparents may need to formally take over the parenting of grandchildren. This can be a powerful healing experience for infertile adoptive parents who finally have a baby to care for, though this can lead to role confusion for all three generations in later years. Others stay in the grandparenting role, supporting their child all they can emotionally, financially and practically. This can also be a reparative time after a stormy adolescence.

Implications for practice

We have highlighted the key developmental stages that can present additional challenges for some adoptive families after infertility. These sit alongside the complex needs that children placed for adoption bring with them. For some adoptive parents, the experience of infertility investigation and treatment prior to adoption seems to strengthen their psychosocial resources, which may help them to manage these additional challenges (Daniluk and Hurtig-Mitchell 2003). However, many adoptive parents will still seek outside help after the adoption, and recognition of their needs is growing (for example Bingley Miller and Bentovim 2007). Some, initially or exclusively, will go to generic services such as the GP, practice counsellor or private therapy for such help. Others will seek help from the range of specialist adoption support agencies in the voluntary sector, such as the national self-help organisation Adoption UK and local post-adoption services. Some families will need multi-agency support through social care, education, CAMHS or other health services (Hendry and Vincent 2002; Kenrick, Lindsey and Tollemache 2006). A few families will require highly specialised and intensive input such as that provided by Family Futures Consortium (Archer and Burnell 2003).

When seeking support, it is unlikely that infertility will be at the forefront of what parents think is troubling them. If they are still parenting an adopted child at home, this is much more likely to be concerns about the child's behaviour or development. However, if infertility was a motivation for adoption, the practitioner needs to hold this in mind as a possible factor when seeking to understand the presenting concerns. When considering support services for adoptive parents who experienced infertility, the following key factors should be held in mind:

- The reality of a placed child is likely to trigger further feelings of loss associated with infertility, so it can be early on in a placement that infertility-related counselling is most beneficial. However, individual counselling/psychotherapy may be indicated at any stage of the adoptive parents' life cycle.

- During the process of treatment for infertility, some couples withdraw from parts of their social network to protect themselves from painful encounters, unbearable emotions or stigma. Being treated differently or feeling different to others can continue after adoption, exacerbating feelings of social isolation. Support groups for adopted parents are particularly helpful to normalise experiences and may be a safe place for infertility issues to be revisited.

- A psychological division of labour often emerges to help cope with infertility. For example the woman experiences more emotional pain while the man provides support and energy to continue with infertility treatment (Cudmore 2005). This can become a dysfunctional split, particularly after adoption, under the strain of emotional and behavioural manifestations of the child's earlier experiences. If left unaddressed, this can lead to difficulties in the couple's relationship, highlighting the importance of couple counselling at any stage when adoptive parents present themselves as needing help.

- An attachment therapies model of family work (Golding *et al.* 2006; Hughes 1997, 2007) may be indicated to facilitate the attachment relationship between adopted child and adoptive parents and to develop a coherent story of how the adoptive family came to be formed. This will include not only the child's pre-placement history but also the parents' infertility. Such work needs sensitive preparation with adoptive parents before launching into dyadic work with the adopted child.

- Adoptive parents' infertility can have an impact at all stages of the life cycle and for all parties to an adoption. The impact of adoption does not stop when the adopted child leaves the family home, as our final vignette clearly demonstrates. For practitioners, this is just as likely to be evident in counselling/therapy with adopted people. They may struggle to understand that difficulties in relating to their adoptive parents, which emerge when they themselves become pregnant, start parenting or have a reunion with birth family members, may stem from their parents' infertility.

Conclusion

Loss is a fundamental part of all adoptions for everyone involved and will impact on earlier significant losses, such as those encountered through infertility. Both adoption and infertility are experiences that are lifelong and will influence how different life stages and life events are experienced. Rather than resolving all the issues surrounding them, the emphasis needs to be on acknowledging and making sense of experiences in the past to understand how they are influencing the present. Adoptive parents need to have resolved issues around their infertility sufficiently to have room in their minds for the emotional needs of their adopted child when she or he first arrives and of that child as it grows and becomes adult. As we have highlighted in this chapter, there are key developmental and life cycle stages when managing to do this will often require expert help.

References

Archer, C. and Burnell, A. (eds) (2003) *Trauma, Attachment and Family Permanence.* London: Jessica Kingsley Publishers.

Bingley Miller, L. and Bentovim, A. (2007) *Assessing the Support Needs of Adopted Children and their Families.* London: Routledge.

Blum, H.P. (1983) 'Adoptive parents: Generative conflict and generational continuity.' *Psychoanalytic Study of the Child 38*, 141–163.

Brinich, P.M. (1990) 'Adoption from the Inside Out.' In D.M. Brodzinsky and M.D. Schechter (eds) *The Psychology of Adoption.* Oxford: Oxford University Press.

Brodzinsky, D.M. (1987) 'Adjustment to adoption: A psychosocial perspective.' *Clinical Psychology Review 7*, 25–47.

Brodzinsky, D.M. (1997) 'Infertility and Adoption Adjustment: Considerations and Clinical Issues.' In S.R. Leiblum (ed.) *Infertility: Psychological Issues and Counselling Strategies.* New York, NY: Wiley.

Burnell, A. (1990) *Explaining Adoption to Children who have been Adopted.* Post-Adoption Centre Discussion Paper 3. London: Post-Adoption Centre.

Carter, B. and McGoldrick, M. (1989) *The Changing Family Life Cycle: A Framework for Family Therapy.* Boston, MA: Allyn and Bacon.

Cudmore, L. (2005) 'Becoming parents in the context of loss.' *Sexual and Relationship Therapy 20,* 3, 299–308.

Daniluk, J.C. and Hurtig-Mitchell, J. (2003) 'Themes of hope and healing: Infertile couples' experiences of adoption.' *Journal of Counseling and Development 81,* Fall, 389–399.

Erikson, E. (1963) *Childhood and Society.* (2nd edn). New York, NY: W.W. Norton.

Golding, K.S., Dent, H.R., Nissim, R. and Stott, L. (eds) (2006) *Thinking Psychologically about Children who are Looked After and Adopted.* Chichester: Wiley and Sons.

Hendry, A. and Vincent, J. (2002) 'Supporting adoptive families: An interagency response.' *Representing Children 15,* 2, 104–117.

Howe, D. and Feast, J. (2000) *Adoption, Search and Reunion.* London: The Children's Society.

Hudson, J. (2006) 'Being Adopted: Psychological Services for Adopting Families.' In K.S. Golding, H.R. Dent, R. Nissim and L. Stott (eds) *Thinking Psychologically about Children who are Looked After and Adopted.* Chichester: Wiley and Sons.

Hughes, D. (1997) *Facilitating Developmental Attachment: The Road to Emotional Recovery and Behavioural Change in Foster and Adopted Children.* Northvale, NJ: Aronson.

Hughes, D.A. (2007) *Attachment-Focused Family Therapy.* New York, NY: W.W. Norton

Humphrey, M. and MacKenzie, K.M. (1967) 'Infertility and adoption: Follow-up of 216 couples attending a hospital clinic.' *British Journal of Preventative and Social Medicine 21,* 90–96.

Kenrick, J., Lindsey, C. and Tollemache, L. (eds) (2006) *Creating New Families: Therapeutic Approaches to Fostering, Adoption and Kinship Care.* London: Karnac.

Kirk, H.D. (1964) *Shared Fate.* New York, NY: Free Press.

Kupka, M.S., Dorn, C., Richter, O., Schmutzler, A., van der Ven, H. and Kulczycki, A. (2003) 'Stress relief after infertility: Spontaneous conception, adoption and psychological counselling.' *European Journal of Obstetrics & Gynaecology and Reproductive Biology 110,* 2, 190–195.

Pitcher, D. (2009) 'Adopted children and their grandparents: Views from three generations.' *Adoption & Fostering 33,* 1, 56–67

Preto, N.G. (1989) 'Transformation of the Family System in Adolescence.' In B. Carter and M. McGoldrick (eds) *The Changing Family Life Cycle: A Framework for Family Therapy.* Boston: Allyn and Bacon.

Salzer, L.P. (1999) 'Adoption after Infertility.' In L. Hammer-Burns and S.N. Covington (eds) *Infertility Counselling: A Comprehensive Handbook for Clinicians.* New York, NY: Parthenon Publishing Group.

Sants, H.J. (1964) 'Genealogical bewilderment in children with substitute parents.' *British Journal of Medical Psychology 37,* 2, 133–141.

Schechter, M.D. (1970) 'About Adoptive Parents.' In E.J. Anthony and T. Benedek (eds) *Parenthood: Its Psychology and Psychopathology.* Boston, MA: Little, Brown.

Scott, S. and Lindsey, C. (2003) 'Therapeutic Approaches in Adoption.' In H. Argent (ed.) *Models of Adoption Support: What Works and What Doesn't.* London: British Association for Adoption and Fostering.

Steele, M., Hodges, J., Kaniuk, J., Hillman, S. and Henderson, K. (2003) 'Attachment representations and adoption: Associations between maternal states of mind and emotional narratives in previously mal-treated children.' *Journal of Child Psychotherapy 29,* 2, 187–205.

Tollemache, L. (1998) 'The perspective of adoptive parents.' *Journal of Social Work Practice 12,* 1, 27–30.

Triseliotis, J., Feast, J. and Kyle, F. (2005) *The Adoption Triangle Revisited: A Study of Adoption, Search and Reunion Experiences.* London: British Association for Adoption and Fostering.

CHAPTER 11

Nature and Nurture: What Do Theory and Research Tell Us?

Olga van den Akker

Introduction

This chapter addresses the psychological and socio-cultural context of research and theory into successfully becoming a parent with or without a full or partial genetic link to one's child. Across the world, family models are hugely diverse, ranging from the normative ones of naturally conceived offspring within 'traditional' family units to adoptive, one parent, same sex or heterosexual families as recognised in the early 1970s, to the genetically fragmented make-up of families formed through assisted reproduction from the 1980s onwards. The diversity and complexity of family formations in the twenty-first century require analyses from a broad range of perspectives. Three major topics will be discussed:

- the social and cultural context within which comparisons of families based on genetic differences are made

- the significance of a genetic link in a nature/nurture context

- the importance of family and parent–child dynamics in relation to genetically related or unrelated offspring.

The social and cultural context within which comparisons of families based on genetic differences are made

Family compositions have changed substantially over the last few decades and the consequences are under-studied. Furthermore, little theory has been applied to compositely different family units. In social terms, the traditional biological/genetic family consists of a mother, a father and one or more naturally conceived (and therefore usually) genetically related children. This normative pattern is culturally the most familiar and most accepted family unit, even among young, white Western couples (Langridge,

Connolly and Sheeran 2000). Consequently, as I will discuss later, when people whose fertility is challenged are asked their preferences for a future family, they respond much as shown in Figure 11.1. They strongly favour one which mimics the traditional, 'natural' and normative family by affording both full genetic and gestational links or the closest possible to that (van den Akker 2007).

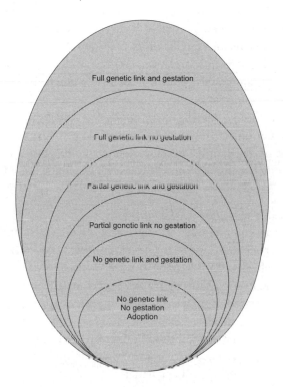

Figure 11.1: Spiralling of preferences of genetic, gestational and social links between parent(s) and child(ren). Adapted from van der Akker, O.B.A. (2007).

The historical, social and cultural theoretical context of families

The social organisation and regulation of families has been rooted historically in biological and genetic (or blood) relatedness (Kirkman 2004). Biologically legalised, identifiable family units were effectively aided by the social regulations of the state, as described by Engels (1884), leading to the formulation of the structural-functionalist theory of the family (van den Akker 2001a). The structure of a biological family had a function to contain diversity and encourage unity in provision. Traditional family theories therefore describe it within an institutionalised and legitimised structure. More recent postmodern interpretations, on the other hand, reflect the changing fabric of socially reconstructed family units (Bernardes 1997), including all their present-day diversity, such as genetically unrelated or partially related family units (van den Akker 2001b). However, although postmodern interpretations of the family oppose long-standing beliefs surrounding nuclear families, they continue to be cognitively outside people's traditional comfort zone. This leaves today's political discourses of the family, social policy, family law and fertility legislation to continue to fuel, and be fuelled by, traditional normative formulations and assumptions of 'the family', despite their disparity with the lived experiences of family life in over half the Western population (Land 1999).

Families created through social changes
With the loosening of family ties, increasing divorce rates and the creation of families outside marriage or stable relationships and/or headed by same sex couples, alternatives to the norm are increasingly common. Indeed, diversity exists even within normative heterosexual two-parent families. A previously married or unmarried person with offspring may start a new family with someone who already has children from a previous relationship and they may create additional offspring from their union. Children can be singletons yet have half- and/or step-siblings living in the households of their parents' previous partners.

Families created through adoption and assisted reproduction
The options for overcoming involuntary childlessness are much the same as outlined for the socially reconstituted families described above in terms of the disparity from the norm, nature and tradition. Those affected may use assisted reproductive technology (ART) to have offspring who are fully genetically related, maternally or paternally related (i.e. where egg or sperm donation or genetic surrogacy[1] has been used), linked through pregnancy only (i.e. where embryo donation has been used) or not linked

---

1   Genetic surrogacy involves the use of the commissioning father's sperm and the surrogate's egg with the pregnancy being carried by the surrogate.

either genetically or through gestation (i.e. through gestational surrogacy[2] or adoption).

The way infertile families manage to achieve parenthood through adoption and ART undermines naturalist and normative conceptions of traditional families. Here, even more than before, the family unit is achieved outside the biological and sexual domain of reproduction (Segal 1999). Despite their high population incidence, many are described as not 'normal' and not 'natural' (Purewal and van den Akker 2007). The striving for 'normality' and as natural a family semblance as possible also influences many infertile couples' choices to overcome their infertility (Bartholet 1993). Van Balen, Verdurmen and Ketting's (1997) and van den Akker's (2000) research has shown that, once women and men are faced with infertility, they favour treatments which allow them a full genetic link and only opt for treatments using donated gametes, surrogacy or adoption if all else fails. The drive for biological relatedness is also demonstrated in research on adoption. Berry (1993) reported that adoptive couples who went on to conceive naturally at a later date reported that they strongly preferred being biological parents. Miall (1989) found that although adoptive mothers were positive about adoption, a biological child would have been preferred.

Adoptive parents and couples commissioning a baby through surrogacy do not undergo the stages associated with biological parenthood, such as gestation and childbirth, and rarely undertake breastfeeding – experiences that have been associated with being necessary for the development of loving, caring parenting relationships. However, Badinter (1981) critiqued the myth of the maternal instinct in bearing and raising children and argued against the validity of the use of the positivistic attitudes of pronatalists at the expense of the plight of those unable to bear their own children naturally. Nevertheless, the gold standard of biological (genetic and gestational) motherhood and the assumed ability to parent among biological birth parents is ingrained in most societies, despite the abundance of knowledge demonstrating that sex and reproduction are now firmly separated and the growing evidence that reproduction today appears to emanate as much from social pressures and demands as from biological drives. State and health care systems continue to reflect the enduring concerns about families (and parenting) where there is genetic difference by distinguishing clearly between 'natural' and assisted or

---

2   Gestational surrogacy is where the egg and sperm from the commissioning parents are used and the surrogate carries the pregnancy, though the baby has no genetic link to her.

adoptive parenthood, in so far as it is only the latter two groups that have to satisfy the appropriate authorities about their fitness or suitability to parent (Bernardes 1997).

In a recent review of the critical components of research into family functioning following surrogacy, the perspectives of the commissioning parents, as well as those of the relinquishing parents and the offspring, were considered (van den Akker 2007). Significant uncertainty of family belonging was apparent between the genetic, gestational and/or social parent(s) as well as the offspring. In surrogacy, as in any assisted conception procedure, preferred cognitions (a fully genetically related baby) may not have been consonant with actions (a partially or non-genetic or not gestated baby).

The review also showed that the popularity of assisted conception is affected by a number of factors including stigma, as well as the importance of a genetic link and perceptions of normative beliefs and attitudes. It appears that some of those who use ART thus employ cognitive dissonance to enable them to go against their prior perceptions of their preferred or ideal family and enter treatment. This is not always sustainable once their family is formed.

The significance of a genetic link in a nature/nurture context

The relative importance of independent and shared contributions to the nature versus nurture debate has shaped psychological thoughts for decades and continues to be of importance today and into the future. Advances in the Human Genome Project[3] will help our understanding of the function of every gene, allowing us to predict who will be prone to major diseases or who will display (un)desirable behaviours.

Genetic and environmental influences

Developments in human genetics have the potential to inform the extent to which people's genetic make-up and lifestyles contribute to the onset of disease or to characteristics and behaviours – issues of particular concern to non-biological parents. For example, we already know that some

---

3   The Human Genome Project was a joint international project set up to identify, describe and store all the genes in human DNA (www.ornl.gov/sci/techresources/Human_Genome/home.shtml).

diseases are entirely genetically determined (such as some of the sickle cell anaemias) or are linked to specific genes (such as schizophrenia) (Harrison and Owen 2003), whereas other diseases, conditions or traits are likely to be at least 50 per cent due to nurture. Nurture, or environmental factors, includes our social environment (for example, poor diet, lack of stimulation, inadequate parenting, availability of health care, poor housing) but also our biological environment (for example, effects transmitted during pregnancy). Stable aspects of personality or intelligence are likely to be determined to a very large extent by environmental factors. However, the importance of the interactions between our specific genetic constitution and our specific environment in shaping a large part of our being means that genes also play a part in shaping our personality, intelligence and identity (Plomin *et al.* 2001). Of course, these genetic and intrauterine influences are not always determined by prospective parents, as they may have little or no control over these dimensions. Their effects on subsequent family functioning are not yet fully investigated.

Human rights to genetic information

There are a number of fundamental concerns about the importance of nature versus nurture, including whether knowledge of one's genetic origin, for social, personal and biological reasons, is a human right. It has been argued that it is the right of every adopted and ART-conceived child to know the likelihood of developing certain traits or characteristics and conditions (Blyth 1998). Disclosure of genetic origin in adoption and gamete and embryo donation, in order to allow access to potentially crucial medical information (for example, to enable the recipient to opt for early screening or initiate appropriate lifestyle changes to minimise genetic risk), is now well recognised (Blyth 1998). Disclosure that is intended to minimise any potentially negative impact on family functioning where there are non-genetically related offspring is more disputed, reflecting the more controversial debates about the genetic transmission of personality characteristics.

Parents' views on the significance of genetic links

Research on infertile women choosing surrogacy to overcome involuntary childlessness has found that most 'intended' or 'commissioning'[4] mothers believe a genetic link is important, even when they commissioned a genetic

---

4 Both these terms are used in surrogacy circles.

surrogacy (see earlier explanation) (van den Akker 2005). Other research suggests men are more favourable than women towards maintaining a genetic link (Ravin, Mahowald and Stocking 1997). This may relate to the culturally ingrained paternalistic importance of maintaining 'blood lines', so that inheritances, land and the family name are passed on from generation to generation of individuals connected by 'blood' or genes. Indeed, it has been suggested that patriarchal societies where offspring take on the father's family name are especially threatened by the use of sperm donation (Becker 2000).

Coping behaviours towards, adaptation to and interactions with a partially or non-genetically related child are, therefore, an area worthy of further study (Kirkman 2004). Since the use of ART is on the increase – not only by infertile couples but also for 'social' needs, for example by single women and lesbian and gay couples – it is important to consider the research on parent–child dynamics, because most medical intervention ends at the delivery suite, leaving the new families alone to operate in an untested vacuum. This point is returned to below. The reported stigma still associated with technological intervention in conception does not help those opting for assisted conception in knowing how, when and why to tell their children and others of the nature of their conception and of their genetic difference.

Genetic identity and origins
The magnetic pull of genetics in relation to identity has been reported in numerous studies of families where there is genetic difference. Adolescent donor offspring tracing their donor believed they could learn more about themselves if they knew more about their genetic parent (Scheib, Riordan and Rubin 2003). Scheib and Ruby (2008) also reported a study of parents who used donor conception treatment and later traced their children's donors in the belief that involving the donor and/or using information about them would enhance their child's well-being and contribute to them feeling more that they were part of a family. This was confirmed by Freeman *et al.* (2009) who reported that some ART parents, especially single mothers, search for their child's donors to aid the child's development of a sense of 'identity'.

Similarly, searches for genetic origins, identity and genealogical history have been reported in research on adoption (Haimes and Timms 1985). Howe has written and researched extensively on adoptive families from the perspectives of the children and their adoptive parents and describes how the birth mother's 'presence' was there throughout the adoption (Howe 1996). Howe has also revealed that, contrary to previous beliefs, most parents involved in open adoptions admitted that they considered that the influence of genes on the expression of their children's stable personality traits was undeniable. These beliefs were strengthened when adoptive parents and children met the birth parents.

Haimes and Timms (1985) reported that many adopted adults found it difficult to explain the reasons for wanting to search for birth parents. Whatever the expressed reasons are, according to Howe and Feast (2000) this is likely to include a desire to 'discover something about one's identity and origins' (p.15).

There is a need for more research to help us to understand better how far these various parties considered genetics to be a formative influence (for example, in determining 'who' the offspring was) and how far their 'need to know' was fuelled by other influences such as notions of kinship and what might predispose some people to give more weight to one than the other.

The importance of family and parent–child dynamics in relation to genetically related or unrelated offspring

With the socially and medically created alternative families that now comprise large proportions of the population, we need to ask what the enduring attraction is of a genetically gestated child within a traditional fully genetically related family unit and what impact genetic difference has on parent–child dynamics and family functioning.

Interpreting research into family functioning if there is genetic difference
There is little research or theory explicitly extrapolating genetic relatedness in families (see van den Akker 2006) but it is possible to draw on related theory and research. However, before comparisons are made, the inherent differences in so-called 'relinquishing parents' need to be described. Differences between those relinquishing gametes, babies or children are profound and will affect attitudes towards openness of information or contact. Additionally, a number of problems with the research are apparent:

- The adoption literature does not always clarify if the adoptive parents being studied were infertile, although their (in)fertility status is likely to have a differential effect on disclosure, openness and a preference for a genetic link.

- Little health information on birth and adoptive parents is available.

- Infertile couples undergoing treatment may be affected by long-term effects of stigma, anxiety and depression; it is methodologically difficult to separate the effects of these on parent–child dynamics and family functioning from any to do with genetic difference per se.

- It is methodologically complex to separate the effects of other features of family life (such as income, employment, education levels, ethnicity and so on) from those associated with responses to infertility and genetic links.

- Research evaluating family functioning may be particularly prone to respondents giving answers that reflect what they consider to be socially desirable.

Parent–child dynamics in early infancy

The dynamics between parents and children will be affected by the experiences of those 'new' to parenthood, regardless of mode of conception. For example, there is ample research demonstrating that the transition to any kind of parenthood is a psychologically sensitive period (Moller, Hwang and Wickberg 2008). Thus, those who have largely exhausted their psychological, social, supportive, economic, employment, time and other resources in their quest to become a family are likely to face additional difficulties than those whose transition was smoother. Typically, those becoming parents following fertility treatment or through adoption have a longer and more arduous transition to make than do those who conceive naturally.

The treatment process following a diagnosis of infertility is cumbersome, expensive and time-consuming, has an uncertain outcome and may result in anxiety and depression (van den Akker 2002). It is possible that those individuals or couples most at risk of developing problems are those who use maladaptive (or unhelpful) coping strategies to cope with the stress. There is some concern that, where adjustment is maladaptive, any negative affective states developed during treatment may linger on into parenthood (Klock and Greenfeld 2000). Concerns have therefore been expressed that parents who fail to come to terms with their infertility may have trouble forming optimal bonds with their future child. For example, the child may be a reminder of the negative experiences and emotions the parent experienced during fertility treatment. Conversely, there have also been concerns that parents may feel that having a child will *remove* any psychological conflicts and feelings about their infertility (Colpin 2001). This may lead parents to develop unrealistic expectations of their (future) children (McMahon *et al.* 2003) and bring about possible additional problems including enhanced risk of separation anxiety and parents being overprotective. Furthermore, the alienation of the male partner from much of the fertility treatment process may put a strain on the marital relationship and on his relationship with a future child.

Theoretically, research on women has shown that, following natural conception, attachment to the foetus begins in pregnancy (Rubin 1984) and carries on following delivery when the bonding process begins, strengthened by nurturing and caring behaviours including breastfeeding. Few studies have assessed attachment patterns following successful fertility treatment despite concerns, for example, that bonding in recipient mothers of surrogate babies may be compromised by the lack of biological connectedness and gestational involvement (Fisher and Gilman 1991). Furthermore, the pain of childbirth not experienced by women using surrogacy or adoption means they may be forfeiting that part of the bonding process too.

Parent–child dynamics in relation to disclosure of origins

Parent–child dynamics must be assessed contextually. Any parent, whether female, male, lesbian, gay, unmarried, married, older or younger, needs to address the opportunities for disclosure to a child of their origins where these are in relation to adoption or donor conception. Disclosure issues can affect parent–child dynamics: research has shown reluctance on the part of gamete recipients, for example, to disclose for fear of their child not loving them as a parent (Brewaeys *et al.* 1997). In surrogacy, recipient parents have stated their intention to disclose the child's origins (van den Akker 2000, 2005) and this translated into actual disclosure in Golombok and Murray's (2004) study. However, use of donor gametes and disclosure may not always sit comfortably in a social context.

Parent–child dynamics and stigma

Reports of stigma associated with ART families have been found to affect family functioning, particularly where the child was conceived using donated gametes (van den Akker 2002). Kirkman's (2004) large and seminal qualitative investigation of parents, donors and offspring revealed a complex interaction in the meaning of genes and relationships as negotiated within their social contexts, with no single narrative fitting all interpretations. Different issues took on importance at different stages among these individuals, hence complicating interpretations.

Parent–child dynamics in reconstituted and lesbian families
Looking to the research into a different group of families with genetic difference presents a different picture. Empirical research into maternal functioning in divorced heterosexual and lesbian families who conceived in previous heterosexual relationships has shown no differences in parent–child dynamics between these mothers. McCandlish (1987) studied a small number of planned lesbian families and reported that the biological and the social mothers developed strong attachments to their children, with little difference between social and biological mothers. In fact, higher quality of parent–child interactions involving social mothers has been reported (Brewaeys *et al.* 1997) and better parenting awareness skills in planned lesbian mothers when compared to fathers in heterosexual relationships (Flaks *et al.* 1995). However, differences have been reported in some studies: for example, Golombok *et al.* (2003) reported lower levels of emotional involvement with the children in social lesbian planned mothers (who do not have the genetic link) than in fathers of heterosexual couples (who do have a genetic link). However, these results may have emerged because many of the women were in fact stepmothers to the children, adding another dimension to the interpretation of these data.

Parent–child dynamics in adoptive families
Parent–child dynamics in adoptive families have also been studied, suggesting that in adoption the measurement of dynamics between adopted child(ren) and parents differs according to the type and timing of the adoption. For example, Rosenthal and Groze (1990) have described the changes in traditional adoption practices over the last 30 years away from the adoption of white infants by white, middle class, infertile couples towards the adoption of children of wider age groups and ethnicities by less well-educated and more socio-economically, ethnically diverse couples, as well as by single, lesbian and gay people. These factors inevitably will affect parent–child dynamics because the older child, particularly if he or she has experienced a traumatic childhood, will react to their new parents

differently to an infant placed in a traditional, relatively well-to-do home (Barth and Miller 2000).

Family functioning over time following ART treatment

Segev and van den Akker's (2006) review of psychosocial and family functioning research following ART found that, in general, the short- and long-term implications are positive, regardless of the method of ART used. ART families are no more likely than 'traditional' families to need extra clinical or social care in the years following the birth. In a study of Australian families with genetically related ART infants, parents were found to be comparable on parenthood-specific adjustment, social support and marital adjustment to those who conceived without medical assistance (Gibson *et al.* 2000). Golombok *et al.* (2005), in the UK, found that IVF mothers (but not fathers) had better psychological adjustment to parenthood than did naturally conceiving mothers, although, in their Australian sample, Gibson *et al.* (2000) found that IVF fathers did not report any differences in their adjustment to parenthood. Unfortunately, the participation rate for fathers was considerably lower than that of mothers and these results must therefore be interpreted with caution. ART in itself, therefore, did not appear to have a significant negative effect on the relationship between the parent and child, family functioning and the psychosocial development of the child. The differences found were negligible, suggesting that the effects of ART treatment change little over time and show no lasting negative consequences.

Although a number of those studies were limited to families where both parents were genetically related to the child, ART children with genetic difference have also been found to have secure, positive attachments and responsiveness to their parents (Barnes *et al.* 2004; Brewaeys 2001; Söderström-Anttila 2001). However, it is important to stress that the functioning of families where there is genetic difference is under-studied; this is particularly true for families where there has been no disclosure. If this group of families were studied there may well be a different and potentially more problematic picture.

Family functioning and adoption

The experience of loss and separation or, in many cases, of early deprivation can undoubtedly affect the emotional development and psychological functioning of adopted children and, in turn, parent–child relationships. Early adoption services (like early sperm donation services) were practised under the umbrella of 'natural' parenting whereby couples were advised to 'mimic' biological parenting. More recently there has been a shift towards encouraging positive acknowledgement of differences in relation to loss, separation, identity and belonging, in the belief that this is more likely to promote effective family functioning, similar to that found in positive biological family functioning. If children are placed for adoption following unstable, negative previous experiences they may not have the skills to adapt positively to their adoptive family and there could be risks to its stability and functioning (Brodzinsky 1987). It is possible that the well-being of adoptive families may be influenced by:

- the psychological state and age of the child

- the conditions that led to adoption (such as mental illness, imprisonment or youth of birth parent(s)); how straightforward the pathway to adoption was and the extent of openness within the adoption

- the ability of the adoptive parents to meet the extra needs of the child

- their own perceptions of the quality of parenting that is needed where there is no biological link to the child

- the potential disappointment of their own inability to reproduce and associated feelings of stigma.

The adoptive parents' feelings can also affect the parent–child relationship and pose additional factors, affecting interpretations of the research reports of these families. For example, people adopt for a variety of reasons including to overcome unresolved issues or disappointments within their own lives and reproductive histories. However, issues of 'belonging and difference are unavoidable and inherent in the experience of being adopted' and, while 'feeling different is not necessarily perceived or experienced as a negative state' (Howe and Feast 2000, p.98), it does limit what we can say about family functioning where there is genetic difference.

From the point of view of genetic relationships and family functioning, it has been reported previously that adopted children who were brought up in families which did not function well were more likely to search for their birth parents (Raynor 1980). However, other studies have not confirmed this link (Campbell, Silverman and Patti 1991). Reuter *et al.* (2009) studied family interactions in 284 adoptive families with adolescent children and compared these to 208 non-adoptive families. Their research found that, although adoptive families reported more problems, no differences in parental behaviours were found, suggesting that the children who were adopted were more likely to show conflict behaviours, rather than their parents, especially if placed when older. It was further suggested that the age of adoption influenced these children's ability to display warmth.

Conclusion

The differential contribution of nature and nurture in adoption, ART and surrogacy remains under-studied. Issues of the contributions of nature and nurture are complex and should not be overlooked in practice. In general, although there are exceptions, family functioning in families with adoptive and ART-conceived offspring appears to be similar to that reported in those with 'naturally' conceived and reared offspring (Hammarberg, Fisher and Wynter 2008). In a society where ART treatment is becoming increasingly used and there are associated increasing numbers of less traditional families, it is encouraging to find that the research carried out so far suggests that successful treatment does not appear to have significant, long-term, detrimental effects on families. Research on families where there is no genetic link, as in adoptive families or families with donor-conceived children, has shown there are issues of belonging and difference which are not reported in ART families where donated gametes have not been used or in naturally conceived families. These results are likely to be influenced by numerous other unexpected and unaccounted-for factors which may also influence under-studied socially reconstituted families, such as age at adoption or when entering a new family with step-parents and/or half-siblings. There is no doubt that some characteristics are inherited and expressed to a greater or lesser extent in children where or however they are reared. What, in my view, is more interesting, and what appears to be more important for optimum nurturing, support and warmth, is the meaning people attach to the opportunity to be part of a full- or part-genetic/gestational or adoptive family.

References

van den Akker, O.B.A. (2000) 'The importance of a genetic link in mothers commissioning a surrogate baby in the UK.' *Human Reproduction 15*, 8, 110–117.

van den Akker, O.B.A. (2001a) 'The acceptable face of parenthood: Psychosocial factors of infertility treatment.' *Psychology Evolution and Gender 3*, 2, 137–153.

van den Akker, O.B.A. (2001b) 'Adoption in the age of reproductive technology.' *Journal of Reproductive and Infant Psychology 19*, 2, 147–159.

van den Akker, O.B.A. (2002) *The Complete Guide to Infertility: Diagnosis, Treatment, Options.* London: Free Association Books.

van den Akker, O.B.A. (2005) 'A longitudinal pre-pregnancy to post-delivery comparison of genetic and gestational surrogate and intended mothers: Confidence and gynecology.' *Journal of Psychosomatic Obstetrics and Gynecology 26*, 4, 277–284.

van den Akker, O.B.A. (2006) 'A review of gamete donor family constructs: Current research and future directions.' *Human Reproduction Update 12*, 2, 91–101.

van den Akker, O.B.A. (2007) 'Psychosocial aspects of surrogate motherhood.' *Human Reproduction Update 13*, 1, 53–62.

Badinter, E. (1981) *The Myth of Motherhood: An Historical View of the Maternal Instinct.* London: Souvenir.

van Balen, F., Verdurmen, J. and Ketting, E. (1997) 'Choices and motivations of infertile couples.' *Patient Education & Counselling 31*, 1, 19–27.

Barnes, J., Sutcliffe, A.G., Kristoffersen, I., Loft, A. *et al.* (2004) 'The influence of assisted reproduction on family functioning and children's socio-emotional development: Results from a European study.' *Human Reproduction 19*, 6, 1480–1487.

Barth, R. and Miller, J. (2000) 'Building effective post-adoption services: What is the empirical foundation?' *Family Relations 24*, 4, 447–455.

Bartholet, E. (1993) *Family Bonds: Adoption and the Politics of Parenting.* New York, NY: Houghton Mifflin.

Becker, G. (2000) *The Elusive Embryo: How Women and Men Approach New Reproductive Technologies.* Berkeley, CA: University of California Press.

Bernardes, J. (1997) *Family Studies: An Introduction.* London: Routledge.

Berry, M. (1993) 'Adoptive parents' perceptions of, and comfort with, open adoption.' *Child Welfare 77*, 3, 231–253.

Blyth, E. (1998) 'Donor assisted conception and donor offspring rights to genetic origins information.' *International Journal of Child Rights 6*, 237–253.

Brewaeys, A. (2001) 'Review: Parent–child relationships and child development in donor insemination families.' *Human Reproduction Update 7*, 1, 38–46.

Brewaeys, A., Ponjaert, I., van Hall, E. and Golombok, S. (1997) 'Donor insemination: Child development and family functioning in lesbian mother families with 4–8 year old children.' *Human Reproduction 12*, 6, 1349–1359.

Brodzinsky, D. (1987) 'Adjustment to adoption: A psychosocial perspective.' *Clinical Psychological Review 7*, 25–47.

Campbell, L., Silverman, P. and Patti, P. (1991) 'Reunions between adoptees and birth parents: The adoptees' experience.' *Social Work 36*, 4, 329–335.

Colpin, H. (2001) 'Parenting and psychosocial development of IVF children: Review of the research literature.' *Developmental Review 22*, 644–673.

Engels, F. (1884) [1972] *On the Origins of the Family, Marriage, Private Property and the State.* New York, NY: International Publishers.

Fisher, S. and Gilman, I. (1991) 'Surrogate motherhood: Attachment, attitudes and social support.' *Psychiatry 54*, 1, 13–20.

Flaks, D., Ficher, I., Masterpasqua, F. and Joseph, G. (1995) 'Lesbians choosing motherhood: A comparative study of lesbian and heterosexual parents and their children.' *Developmental Psychology 31*, 105–114.

Freeman, T., Jadva, V., Kramer, W. and Golombok, S. (2009) 'Gamete donation: Parents' experiences of searching for their child's donor siblings and donor.' *Human Reproduction 24*, 3, 505–516.

Gibson, F., Ungerer, J., Tennant, C. and Saunders, D. (2000) 'Parental adjustment and attitudes to parenting after in vitro fertilization.' *Fertility and Sterility 73*, 3, 565–574.

Golombok, S. and Murray, C. (2004) 'Families created through surrogacy: Parent–child relationships in the first year of life.' *Fertility and Sterility 80*, 3, S50, 133.

Golombok. S., Jadva, V., Lycett, E., Murray, C. and MacCallum, F. (2005) 'Families created by gamete donation: Follow-up at age 2.' *Human Reproduction 20*, 1, 286–293.

Golombok, S., Perry, B., Burston, A., Murray, C. *et al.* (2003) 'Children with lesbian parents: A community study.' *Developmental Psychology 39*, 1, 20–33.

Haimes, E. and Timms, N. (1985) *Adoption, Identity and Social Policy: The Search for Distant Relatives.* Aldershot: Gower.

Hammarberg, K., Fisher, J. and Wynter, K. (2008) 'Psychological and social aspects of pregnancy, childbirth and early parenting after assisted conception: A systematic review.' *Human Reproduction Update 14*, 5, 395–414.

Harrison, P. and Owen, M. (2003) 'Genes for schizophrenia? Recent findings and their pathophysiological implications.' *Lancet 361*, 9355, 417–419.

Howe, D. (1996) *Adopters on Adoption: Reflections on Parenthood and Children.* London: British Association for Adoption and Fostering.

Howe, D. and Feast, J. (2000) *Adoption, Search and Reunion: The Long-term Experience of Adopted Adults.* London: The Children's Society.

Kirkman, M. (2004) 'Genetic connection and relationships in narratives of donor-assisted conception.' *Australian Journal of Emerging Technologies and Society 2*, 1, 1–20.

Klock, S. and Greenfeld, D. (2000) 'Psychological status of in vitro fertilization patients during pregnancy: A longitudinal study.' *Fertility and Sterility 73*, 6, 1159–1164.

Land, H. (1999) 'Families and the Law.' In J. Munchie, M. Wetherell, M. Langan, R. Dallos and A. Cochrage (eds) *Understanding the Family.* London: The Open University.

Langridge, D., Connolly, K. and Sheeran, P. (2000) 'Reasons for wanting a child: A network analytic study.' *Journal of Reproductive and Infant Psychology 18*, 4, 321–338.

McCandlish, B. (1987) 'Against All Odds: Lesbian Mothers' Family Dynamics. Gay and Lesbian Parents.' In F.W. Bozett (ed.) *Homosexuality and Family Relations.* New York, NY: Harrington Park.

McMahon, C. Gibson, F., Leslie, G., Cohen, J. and Tennant, C. (2003) 'Parents of in vitro fertilisation children: Psychological adjustment, parenting, stress and the influence of subsequent in vitro fertilisation treatment.' *Journal of Family Psychology 17*, 361–369.

Miall, C. (1989) 'Reproductive technology versus the stigma of involuntary childlessness.' *Social Work Care 70*, 1, 43–50.

Moller, K., Hwang, P. and Wickberg, B. (2008) 'Couple relationship and transition to parenthood: Does workload at home matter?' *Journal of Reproductive Infant Psychology 26*, 1, 58–68.

Plomin, R., DeFries, J., McClearn, G. and McGuffin, P. (2001) *Behavioural Genetics* (4th edn). New York, NY: Worth Publishers.

Purewal, S. and van den Akker, O. (2007) 'The socio-cultural and biological meaning of parenthood.' *Journal of Psychosomatic Obstetrics and Gynecology 28*, 2, 79–86.

Ravin, A., Mahowald, M. and Stocking, C. (1997) 'Genes or gestation? Attitudes of women and men about biologic ties to children.' *Journal of Women's Health 6*, 639–647.

Raynor, L. (1980) *The Adopted Child Comes of Age.* London: Allen and Unwin.

Reuter, M., Keyes, M., Iacono, W. and McGue, M. (2009) 'Family interactions in adoptive compared to nonadoptive families.' *Journal of Family Psychology 23*, 1, 58–66.

Rosenthal, J. and Groze, V. (1990) 'Special needs adoption: A study of intact families.' *The Social Service Review 64*, 3, 475–505.

Rubin, R. (1984) *Maternal Identity and the Maternal Experience.* New York, NY: Springer.

Scheib, J. and Ruby, A. (2008) 'Contact among families who share the same sperm donor.' *Fertility and Sterility 90*, 1, 33–43.

Scheib, J., Riordan, M. and Rubin, S. (2003) 'Choosing identity-release sperm donors: The parents' perspective 13–18 years later.' *Human Reproduction 18*, 5, 1115–1127.

Segal, L. (1999) 'A Feminist Looks at the Family.' In J. Munchie, M. Wetherell, M. Langan, R. Dallos and A. Cockrage (eds) *Understanding the Family.* London: The Open University.

Segev, J. and van den Akker, O.B.A (2006) 'A review of psychoscoial and family functioning following assisted reproductive treatment.' *Clinical Effectiveness in Nursing 9*, Suppl.2, e162–170.

Söderström-Anttila, V. (2001) 'Pregnancy and child outcome after oocyte donation.' *Human Reproduction Update 7*, 1, 28–32.

CHAPTER 12

Infertility and Adoption: The Search for Birth Parents and the Impact on Adult Family Relationships

Julia Feast

Introduction

When people make the decision to adopt because of infertility, it is natural for them to have thoughts and questions about whether they will be able to love a child to whom they have no genetic relationship. Will the child satisfy their desire to create a family? Will feelings of loss and sadness be lessened through adopting? Will their relationship with the child be strong and enduring? Making a decision to adopt is a life-changing decision which involves the deepest and most intense of feelings. These questions and issues will be considered during the preparation and assessment process of applying to adopt, a process designed to enable prospective adopters to make an informed decision and for the adoption agency to satisfy itself that they have the necessary qualities to meet a child's needs throughout his or her childhood and beyond.

Adoption is a lifelong process that does not end with the making of an adoption order. Feelings such as loss and sadness may resurface across the lifespan for the adopted person, the birth family and the adoptive parents. It is important that they are acknowledged and addressed. Other key areas to be explored during the assessment process are how to manage talking with a child about their origins including the reasons they were adopted. Prospective adopters will also need to explore how they may feel and react if their son or daughter decides that they want to find out more information about their origins and to make contact with birth family members. Will they be able to understand the reasons why? Will they be anxious that their role as parents might be usurped by the birth parent? Will they fear losing the love and affection of their son or daughter?

In 2005, findings from the first British study to explore the individual experiences and perspectives of adopted persons, birth mothers and adoptive parents about the adoption search and reunion experience were published (Triseliotis, Feast and Kyle 2005). The postal questionnaire study provided an insight into how relationships fared across the adoption lifespan and in particular the impact of the search and reunion process on adoptive parents and their relationship with their child. Using the findings from this study (hereafter referred to as the 2005 study) together with examples from practice, this chapter also explores how issues and feelings relating to the adoptive parents' infertility were helped or hindered by the family's communication and openness about the adoption, the closeness of the relationship during childhood and adolescence, and whether any residual infertility-related feelings of loss and sadness were heightened during search and reunion experiences.

The study
The findings from the 2005 study are based on the experiences of 93 adoptive parents, 93 birth mothers and 126 adopted people, together with a small sample of birth fathers. These adoptions took place mainly before 1975. The study extended and built on the findings of a previous study (Howe and Feast 2000), which reported on the experiences of 472 adopted people who had either searched for or been contacted by birth relatives. It was unique in that it highlighted the shared and different experiences, reactions and feelings of (i) pairs of adopted people and their birth mothers, (ii) pairs of adopted people and their adoptive parents and (iii) triads of adopted people and their birth mothers and adoptive parents.

All the adopters were white European, just over half (55%) describing themselves as infertile and just under half (45%) having birth children as well as adopted children. The latter group included some who had adopted as a result of their infertility but then gone on to have birth children. The overwhelming majority (80%) had had children placed with them when they were babies under the age of one. In 16 per cent of the families the adopted person was the only child. The average age of the adoptive parent when their son or daughter sought contact with a birth relative was approximately 59 years and the average age of the adopted person was 30 years.

Why people adopted

The desire to have a family was the most common motivating factor with more than half (55%) unable to create a family of their own because of infertility problems.[1] The adoptive parents described a range of feelings on learning that they were not able to have biological children, including 'sad', 'devastated', 'deeply upset', 'very disappointed', 'grief and sadness', 'unhappy' or 'absolutely heartbroken' as well as 'disorientation', 'frustration', 'anger' and 'sense of loss'.

> I was increasingly sad and became emotionally upset each month when my periods continued regularly. My husband was more patient and philosophical about it.

Twenty-five per cent of adopters in the study wanted to adopt because of their wish to enlarge their existing family. Of these, most had been told either not to risk another pregnancy or that another conception would not be possible. Adoption seemed to them the obvious way to fulfil their wishes:

> We had planned on having more children, but a miscarriage and subsequent hysterectomy prevented this – we knew that many children were in need of homes.

Managing sadness and loss of infertility

Almost 8 in 10 (79%) of the adoptive parents in the 2005 study reported that the feelings of loss and sadness they experienced when learning about their infertility did not persist over the years. They described the adoption as a healing factor:

> Adopting our daughter helped me overcome the sadness of not being able to have any further children myself.

> Adopting a family satisfies all my longing to have children. It was a wonderful gift to us. It would have been very precious to have our own children and see the likeness to me and my husband; however, being able to love our adopted children totally took this away.

> The feelings did not persist. Why? Because we decided it was the right way for us and had no regrets. Our two children (adopted) were our pride and joy and much loved.

---

1   At the time of these adoptions, fertility treatments were not so readily available or advanced as today, so adoption was often the only option available for those unable to conceive naturally.

However, for some parents (21%) they did persist. One adoptive parent explained that, because of feeling that marriage was about having your 'own' children, the sense of loss remained. Others described how they missed 'the birth process', 'the actual giving birth' or having a 'blood' relationship. One adoptive mother found that such feelings became more intense when her children were giving birth to their own children.

Openness and communication

The adoptive parents in this study believed that it was important to be open with their child about his or her adoptive status, with the majority (86%) telling their son or daughter before the age of four. They recalled following the advice of the adoption agency to disclose as early as possible and to introduce the word 'adoption'. Some said that they read stories to their child about how she or he came to them, even before the child was able to understand:

> Having told her from the time she was in her cot there was never any dramatic 'telling' time.

> Sometimes, when D was not too well he would sit on my knee for a cuddle and say tell me my story.

Many felt that keeping the adoption a secret could damage the relationship and break the trust between parent and child. Many did not want the child to find out from another source instead of them. As several adopters said, with the truth 'you can't go wrong', 'not to tell would have lost his trust in us' and they 'always believed in being honest'.

In the previous study about adopted people (Howe and Feast 2000) it was reported that 75 per cent of adopted people felt uncomfortable talking to their adoptive parents about their adoption and asking questions about their birth family background. They were afraid that their adoptive parent(s) might feel hurt, or that they would be seen to be disloyal to them. Interestingly, when asked in the 2005 study, adoptive parents did not share this view or experience. Ninety-seven per cent reported feeling comfortable talking about the adoption and 89 per cent said they did not find it difficult to share background information. Most (76%) had shared what background information they had about the birth family, viewing it as their duty, as the child's right to know or as the best policy to follow. Many said that they tried to pass information on in stages, depending on the child's age and the type of information to be shared. The teenage years were a popular time for sharing more information. However, 10 per cent of adoptive parents said that they found it difficult to share background information; this sometimes related to its distressing nature. For example, one parent avoided sharing the information that a birth mother became disabled following a failed suicide attempt until her daughter was 18 years old and 'able to cope':

> Gradually gave S all the information we had except one, that her mother was paralysed after she tried to kill herself by jumping from a bridge... I felt this was too big a grief to put upon a child until she began to search about her past.

Although the great majority of parents said that they remembered bringing up the subject of adoption frequently or periodically, a minority had not raised it and waited instead for the child to take the initiative before talking about adoption and answering questions:

> Shared it with her when she wanted to know.

However, the study showed that the more the child spoke about their birth relatives during adolescence, the better the emotional health of the adopters as measured via the General Health Questionnaire, which was one of the tools used in the study. Some adoptive parents would have liked more information about their son or daughter's origins as they did not always feel able to answer the questions that were raised.

The adoptive parent's relationship with their child

Nearly all the adoptive parents in the 2005 study reported having had no difficulty getting close to their child during childhood with 99 per cent reporting 'very close' or 'close' relationships. Not surprisingly, this dropped to 65 per cent during adolescence (when the turmoil of that stage of development including separation from parental figures and independence come to the fore). Adolescence is typically a time when young people explore their identity; for adopted young people, this can be more complex. One adoptive parent commented, 'Have you tried adolescence?'; others said 'she was a nightmare' and 'adolescence is not easy either for daughters or parents'. However, closeness had recovered by the time the adopted child reached adulthood, though not back to the levels of closeness experienced during childhood.

The study asked adoptive parents how easily they felt their child made a relationship with them. Eighty-nine per cent said that their child was responsive or very responsive during their childhood, with the rest saying that the responses were mixed, including some where the child was not very responsive. Much has been written in recent years about how attachment can be affected by experiences in the early years (Cairns 2002; Howe 2008; Iwaniec 2006; Prior and Glaser 2006; Simmonds 2008). Whether the less responsive relationships were due to the child's early life experiences or relationships within the adoptive family, they can be a cause of concern and worry. What the study did show was that there were strong positive associations between the parents' overall satisfaction with the adoption experience and their reported closeness to their adopted child. Those parents who reported the persistence of infertility-related feelings rated their closeness to their adolescent child to be lower than those where such feelings had dispersed.

Of those adopters who had biological as well as adopted children, over 87 per cent found the relationship similar with each:

They are all my children. I love them but they are all different.

The remainder (13%) described the relationship with each as 'different' but were keen to add that the difference was in nature not depth.

Where parents reported differences between *parenting* their birth and their adopted child, they explained that, although all their children were treated the same, the relationships were not exactly the same because their adopted child(ren) had no genetic relationship with them and also had different needs, traits and personality. Some said that, while they loved all their children 'just as much', they found it easier to understand their birth children and what 'made them tick' because they were more like themselves and it was easier to predict their behaviour. As one reported:

you know your children in a way you don't know your adopted child.

The adopters in these situations said that they could recognise some family traits with which their child was born. For parents who had had birth children after adopting a child, there was a wish to try to minimise any feelings of difference and explain or make up for this to the adopted child. They wanted to ensure that the child did not feel any less loved as a result of a genetic child being born into the family. It almost seemed as though they were afraid the adopted child might feel less valued or wanted now that they had a birth child, and so they worked hard to try to prevent this feeling from arising.

The outcome of searching and impact on the adopted adult's relationship with their adoptive parent(s)

It was not until the Children Act 1975 that adopted people in England and Wales were given the legal right to request identifying information that would enable them to apply for a copy of their original birth certificate.[2] The information on the birth certificate then enabled them to begin a search for birth relatives if they so wished. The legislation was retrospective, giving all people adopted from 1926 the right to information about their origins. For the majority of the adoptive parents in the 2005 study, this had been a major change, as the assumption at the time of the adoption was that all legal ties with the birth family had been severed and that, providing the adoption proved to be 'happy', there would be no 'need' for later searching. However, the majority (90%) were aware of it; almost two-thirds (61%) said that they were pleased about it, with the remainder divided between being indifferent (14%) or angry or worried (13%).

The 1975 legislative change came about in recognition that adoption is in reality a lifelong process. It acknowledged that some adopted people felt the need to seek information about their origins in order to help build a fuller sense of identity. The earlier study referred to above (Howe and Feast 2000) found that the main reason for adopted people searching and contacting birth relatives was a basic and 'natural' curiosity rather than because they had an unhappy adoption experience. They wanted answers to questions such as 'Who am I?', 'Where do I come from?' and 'Who do I look like?'

Even prior to an adopted person's decision to begin searching actively for background information and/or birth relatives, many adoptive parents had been aware that their son or daughter had been considering doing so and had been aware that their child had unanswered questions and therefore might begin to search in the future. The majority could understand this need, as reflected in comments such as 'to satisfy natural curiosity', 'learn more about her background' and 'a deep desire to know who she looked like'.

While some adoptive parents had indicated that they would be willing to help in the search, others, while not opposed to the idea, felt that they should only get involved at the instigation of their son or daughter:

---

2   In Scotland adopted people always had the right to obtain a copy of their original birth certificate at the age of 18 – subsequently 17 – and in Northern Ireland this right was given to adopted people in 1987 and was also a retrospective right.

She discussed it with us before she started making contact. Went ahead with my blessing – I always said I would help her if she ever wanted to trace her family.

A quarter (26%) said that they had always been aware that their son or daughter was considering searching as it had been an open discussion within the family over time, so there was no 'formal sitting down' and being informed about the decision. Just over half (51%) had been told either as the search began or just before contact was made, and the remainder (23%) had only learned after contact had been made. Where parents were only informed later, this was usually because the adopted person wanted to avoid causing them upset. Some chose to delay sharing until they had met the birth family member, on the basis that if the contact was going to be short-lived then there would be little point in causing unnecessary distress to their adoptive parent(s).

Practice example 1

Henry was 35 years old when he approached the adoption agency for information about his origins and subsequently made a decision to trace his birth mother. The search took less than three months and his birth mother was delighted to hear from him. Henry felt unable to tell his adoptive parents about his search and contact with his birth mother as he was always aware of their distressed looks whenever he brought up the subject of his adoption.

Henry developed a close bond with his birth mother and they saw each other regularly. After two years the burden of the secret he was keeping from his adoptive parents became too much. He decided that they needed to know but felt unable to be completely upfront. He therefore introduced them gently to the idea by telling them that he had contacted the adoption agency with the hope of searching for his birth mother. He decided that he wanted to give them time to adjust to this first before telling them that he was in touch with her. He decided not to tell them that all this had happened two years ago.

The 2005 study showed that those adoptive parents who had always known about their son or daughter's desire to search, or had known it before the process began, were more positive about the experience than those who were informed afterwards. Indeed, many in the former group felt compassion towards the birth mother and could understand that the contact might be particularly beneficial if she had been longing for contact over the years. Such understanding did not necessarily mean that they were not concerned and worried about how this might impact on their own relationship with their son or daughter. While most were confident about the strength of their relationships, some feared that the love and bond between them would be lessened. Some adopters were also anxious that their son or daughter would be hurt in the process of the search and reunion, and may even be rejected by the birth parent:

> The fear that he might be 'rejected' again and let down, but also the worry that he might go off and join his original family.

> I was worried she might feel rejected, as she had felt rejected as a baby, so it would be a double rejection.

> I have always felt loved by our daughter so it caused no concern that she should trace her birth parents. The only concern was that what she might discover would cause her distress.

A small number (8%) felt negative or unsure about the outcome. The vast majority, however, described the experience as positive for their son or daughter and, despite the initial fears and concerns, they were pleased that it had happened. They reported that their son or daughter had benefited greatly, mainly because it had helped strengthen their sense of identity and improved their understanding about why they had been adopted. Almost 80 per cent said that the search and reunion had been a positive experience for themselves as parents.

Contrary to their fears, almost all adopters said that the contact with the birth family made no difference to their own family life. They were reassured that their sons and daughters could have more than one relationship without the one being at the expense of the other. Ninety per cent continued to have frequent indirect forms of daily or weekly contact with their now adult sons and daughters, unaltered as a result of the relationship that had been formed with the birth family. Most (94%) reported that, after the contact with the birth parent, they felt close or very close to their son or daughter; for almost two-thirds (65%) this represented no change to the relationship and, for almost a quarter (22%), the relationship was reportedly enhanced. Only 13 per cent felt it had deteriorated. The following quotations sum up what the experience was for the vast majority of adoptive parents:

> Concerns that he would leave us were groundless…he is even more sure he is 'ours' after the experience. We are happy that he has at last met his mother and made a friend of her.

> We were both apprehensive about our daughter's contact with her birth mother but generally feel it was worthwhile for her sake. Our close relationship with our daughter continues.

I feel very satisfied that our son's birth parents know of his continued existence and well-being and that he is aware of his origins. It seems right that this should be so. I am glad that he was happily settled in his life. I can imagine that contact at say 18 years of age might have been more difficult and perhaps unsettling.

Discussion

When discussing these findings, it is important to acknowledge that the majority of this group of adoptions took place before 1975 and are therefore very different to present-day adoptions. The profile of children adopted in the UK today has altered considerably, away from mostly healthy white babies and towards those who have complex needs and backgrounds resulting from maltreatment (or significant risk of such), who are older and may be part of a sibling group (Department for Children, Schools and Families 2008; Simmonds 2008; Triseliotis et al. 2005).

In contemporary adoptions, some link with the birth family is often maintained either through exchanging letters (usually through an adoption agency to maintain confidentiality) or face-to-face meetings. This means that adoptive parents are reminded constantly that the child has another set of parents with whom they have a genetic relationship. Also, those placed when older may have some memory of their family of origin and/or the foster family with whom they lived prior to adoption. This means that the subject of adoption or origins cannot be ignored, forgotten or put to the back of their mind, as was the case with some parents in the 2005 study.

Contemporary adopters are also more likely to have tried a range of fertility treatments before turning to adoption. They may well have had more assessment and preparation about how issues relating to their infertility may resurface if and when their son or daughter decides to seek out and establish relationships with birth family members. The majority of the adoptive parents in the 2005 study said that there were no enduring feelings of sadness about their infertility and that the child they had adopted brought immense joy and made them feel they were a family. It could be argued that one reason for this is that in the past fertility treatments were not as available and advanced as today, so these adoptive parents were better able to 'come to terms with' their infertility and set aside their quest and desire to have their own genetic child.

While the majority in the study said that their adoption experience helped them to overcome their infertility-related feelings of loss and sadness, for nearly a quarter this was not the case. However, this did not appear to stop them having full and successful relationships with their adopted children. Nevertheless, adopters prior to the 1970s were unlikely to have the same opportunities to address issues relating to their infertility and the impact this might have on the adoption and on their relationship with their adopted son or daughter. For example, how would they feel if their adopted son or daughter did not live up to their hopes and expectations in terms of academic ability or compatibility in terms of interests? Would the fact of their infertility and sadness about not producing a child that was more like them overshadow their relationship with their adopted child?

Practice example 2

Anna and Mike were really delighted when they were approved as adopters and overjoyed when their daughter Gemma was placed with them at the age of three months. Anna and Mike were both professional people; Anna was a teacher and Mike a lawyer who enjoyed swimming, playing tennis and rowing. They wanted Gemma to have the privileged upbringing they had had. They ensured that she had the 'best' education and was involved in a range of sporting activities. They had high expectations and were sure that, with the environment and opportunities that they would provide, Gemma would do well and be just like them. However, as the years progressed it became clear that Gemma struggled at school. She failed to get any 'A' levels and therefore was not able to go to university as her parents had hoped and expected. She also had no interest in sport but preferred to watch TV soaps and read magazines.

Both Anna and Mike tried not to show their disappointment that Gemma had not turned out as they had expected their own child would have done. The fact that Gemma was so different to them was a constant reminder of their infertility, of the fact that she was not theirs. The sadness they felt about not having their own child permeated their relationship with her.

Practice example 3

Mary had been widowed for many years and had a very close relationship with Georgina, her adopted daughter. They had often talked about Georgina's origins and the reason for the adoption. Mary had explained that Georgina's birth mother had loved her but was too young to look after her. Mary felt nothing but compassion for Georgina's birth mother and was very accepting and understanding when Georgina decided to locate and make contact with her. She was therefore totally taken aback by the feelings of jealousy and insecurity that she encountered when Georgina actually made contact with her birth mother and began a relationship with her. The relationship with Georgina became very strained and Mary was left feeling that her maternal status had been usurped by Georgina's birth mother.

Practice example 4
June was delighted when her adopted daughter told her that she was expecting a baby and therefore that she would become a grandparent. However, June was really surprised that she could not feel engaged as the pregnancy progressed. She avoided talking about clinic appointments, scans and birth as it made her feel very sad and resentful that she had never experienced a pregnancy or birth of her own child.

At the time that the adoptions in the 2005 study took place, adopters were told that adoption meant that all legal and emotional ties with the birth parent had been severed and that adopted people therefore had no legal right to search for their birth family. It could be expected that this would mean that any infertility-related feelings of sadness and loss would/might be reactivated when they learnt that their son or daughter had now decided to search for, or indeed had had contact with, their birth family. It could be expected that this would rekindle feelings of sadness and loss and remind them that they were not the genetic parents. What the study revealed was that, although some adoptive parents felt concerned or slightly uneasy that the relationship with their son or daughter would be undermined by the search and reunion process, the long-term outcome was that they still remained 'mum and dad', even when close relationships were developed with the birth family. However, some adoptive parents did describe feeling hurt and rejected when their child first announced that they wanted to find or had already found a birth parent.

Anxieties about the parental role being undermined or usurped are not only confined to that of parent–child, but can also be an issue for grandparents:

Practice example 5
Ruby's daughter Helen had traced her birth mother Anita eight years ago and the reunion had gone very well. There was regular contact not just with Helen but also Ruby and her husband. To some extent they felt that they had just extended their family as everyone got on well and they had a lot in common.

However, Ruby was taken aback by a comment made by her eight-year-old granddaughter when she came with Helen for tea one afternoon. They had spent a very happy time together and, as Helen kissed her adoptive mother goodbye and said 'Thanks, Mum. Bye,

Mum', Ruby's granddaughter piped up: 'She's not your mum, Mummy. Anita is.'

Although Ruby's granddaughter meant no harm or malice by saying this, Ruby was overwhelmed with the feelings that this statement generated in her. She said that it made her feel sad and worthless and reminded her of her infertility and that Helen was not her genetic child, although until this point she had always felt she was. Ruby had thought that after all this time she had come to terms with her own infertility but this event brought into sharp focus that she had not. She decided to seek some counselling.

The findings from the 2005 study show that it appears possible for people to come to terms with their infertility sufficiently for it not to compromise their ability to love their adopted children. The study revealed that adoptive parents were able to form close and loving relationships with their adopted son or daughter to such an extent that they felt the child was as if born to them. This does not mean that they did not acknowledge the fact that their son or daughter was adopted or deny them information about their origins.

Summary

This chapter has presented findings from a study that increases understanding about adoptive parents' feelings about their infertility following adoption. It explores how adoptive parents react when their son or daughter decides to search for background information about their origins and make contact with birth relatives, including how this impacts on their relationship with their child. A clear message from the study is that 'parenting' is a complex matter. Adoptive parenting involves all the normal tasks of parenting but has additional elements, for example acknowledging and embracing the child's origins and their different genetic background. The study showed that parenting was not just about biological ties; close and enduring relationships can be forged between the adopted child and his or her adoptive parents where there is no genetic relationship. For the majority, the initial sadness felt by the adoptive parents about their infertility and inability to have their own genetic child was alleviated enormously by the fact that they were able to adopt children and become a family. For some adoptive parents, issues about their infertility did surface throughout the adoption but for the majority they did not. This did not mean that they were not concerned about how their relationship would fare or be affected as a result of their son or daughter's search for information about origins or contact with birth relatives. However, for the overwhelming majority these concerns were not realised: adoptive parents remained 'mum and dad'. The study reported that open communication enhanced the strength of relationships, aiding feelings of closeness to their adopted son or daughter and helping them to feel less threatened by the adopted child's search and reunion with their birth parent and other family members.

References

Cairns, K. (2002) *Attachment, Trauma and Resilience: Therapeutic Caring for Children*. London: British Association for Adoption and Fostering.

Department for Children, Schools and Families (2008) *Adoption: Access to Information and Intermediary Services. Practice Guidance*. London: Department for Children, Schools and Families.

Howe, D. (2008) 'The Impact of Histories of Abuse and Neglect on Children.' In G. Schofield and J. Simmonds (eds) *The Child Placement Handbook: Research, Policy and Practice*. London: British Association for Adoption and Fostering.

Howe, D. and Feast, J. (2000) *Adoption, Search and Reunion: The Long-term Experience of Adopted Adults*. London: The Children's Society.

Iwaniec, D. (2006) *The Emotionally Abused and Neglected Child: Identification, Assessment and Intervention. A Practice Handbook*. London: John Wiley.

Prior, V. and Glaser, D. (2006) *Understanding Attachment and Attachment Disorders: Theory, Evidence and Practice*. London: Jessica Kingsley Publishers.

Simmonds, J. (2008) 'Adoption: Development Perspectives within an Ethical, Legal and Policy Framework.' In G. Schofield and J. Simmonds (eds) *The Child Placement Handbook: Research, Policy and Practice*. London: British Association for Adoption and Fostering.

Triseliotis, J., Feast, J. and Kyle, F. (2005) *The Adoption Triangle Revisited: A Study of Adoption, Search and Reunion Experiences*. London: British Association for Adoption and Fostering.

Final Thoughts

'We don't get afternoon naps any more!'

We wanted to end where we started – with the words of those who have 'adopted after infertility'. We asked Joanne, John, Mary, Louise and Oliver to share their thoughts with us as they look back on their experiences. Louise (and Oliver) pick up the story:

One day life was normal – we got up and went to work. The next day all was different, too different – life had changed. The route I was following had gone wrong, very wrong, and my happy-go-lucky life had changed. I was no longer the invincible, carefree girl looking at life through rose-tinted glasses but had suddenly become an adult with real problems. I wanted to let Oliver go, I wanted him to pursue a different life and have a chance of a family with a proper woman – a woman who could give him children; I didn't want to stand in his way.

We went for fertility treatment, lots of it. We made textbook embryos, kept writing the cheques and kept trying, again and again and again! The medical services kept us going down different routes, different drugs, different this, different that, telling us we'd get there next time. The long and short of it was that in 11 years we'd had five fresh cycles and six frozen cycles – the result: no baby, no holidays.

It suddenly hit us that while ever we kept writing cheques we would never get refused. We kept being given false hope and promises. IVF is a great thing; it works for so many and it is an amazing procedure. We have no regrets attempting IVF but it wasn't working for us.

After 11 attempts, a mixture of fresh and frozen embryos, our consultant suggested we get donor eggs from a younger woman to give us a better chance of conception. So, the textbook, grade 1 embryos we'd been making since I was 27 were no longer worth using. We came home, cried, talked, drank a bottle of wine or two, cried some more, then decided that IVF ends here. It was scary, it had been such a big part of our lives that it was difficult to imagine life without it. The transition from IVF to adoption didn't happen overnight. We'd discussed it many times but while ever we were being egged on by the infertility experts we kept putting adoption to the back of our minds.

Now, everything felt different, like I'd woken up with somebody else's body, or life. I couldn't put my finger on it until 'bang', all of a sudden it hit me – a great weight had been lifted from my shoulders. I could see clearly, everything looked bright. I know this sounds dramatic and made up but it's true – I realised that I'd left IVF behind. I was looking forward to the adoption process, I had a spring in my step and realised that I was doing what I was meant to do all along. I was meant to adopt a child.

I wish we hadn't carried on with the IVF treatment for as long as we did – but we did, driven by a combination of the medical services pushing us, and our hope and desperation not to be failures. But really we have no regrets, I don't believe in regrets, life is about choices. Whatever choice or decision you make at any point in your life is because it feels right at the time and so you must live with it and realise that it was the right thing to do at that point in your life.

Somehow our relationship strengthened through it all. Sometimes in life, people who go through the mill together seem to connect on a more profound level than those who just calmly sail along. This really summed us up.

When we finally decided to go further with adoption we had to attend an open meeting which was long, quite boring and slightly condescending. However, we met a lovely trainee social worker there who asked if anyone would be happy to be interviewed at home by herself and an assessor as part of her course. We agreed and told her that after years of IVF it would be great to speak to professionals without me having to take my clothes off! She thought this was really funny and that we had the right sense of humour to adopt – we held on to this.

When we started the process we seemed to grow closer still. We're certainly not perfect and we still have our ups and downs but the adoption process gave us a really special bond and has put us in a really good place. Everything that happened could have destroyed us but if we hadn't endured what we did we certainly wouldn't be the people we are today. Apparently at the adoption panel, everybody was moved when they quizzed us about the transition from IVF to adoption. They just knew from our honesty and openness that we were ready to take the next step.

People look from the outside and say all the usual stuff about adoption, how they can't understand how women keep knocking out kids and they should be sterilised. To be honest, when we went into adoption we had the same stereotypical views. Our views soon changed when we met a birth mother on the preparation course who'd had numerous children taken into care. When we first saw her we both thought, 'Hmmm – just what we expected.' When we listened to her story we both sat there crying. It was heartbreaking. I won't tell you her story because it's hers to tell, not mine, but she never really stood a chance. She was so brave to come and speak to us all. I really admired her. Nobody broke the cycle of life for her but this is what we hope we have done for our little girl; to give her a chance and a good old crack at a happy life.

In some adoptions, you are able to meet your child's birth mother. I dearly wanted to do this to reassure her that I would look after and love her daughter and do the best I possibly could for her... I wanted to do it for my daughter also. My real father died when I was seven years old. My mum remarried and my stepfather has been a great dad. I always remember him telling me about meeting my dad via mutual friends and them having a couple of pints together. He thought my dad was a really great bloke – this gave me so much comfort and sort of made me realise it was OK to love my stepdad.

When it comes to the nature or nurture debate all I can say is we've had our daughter since she was 11 months old and, believe me, she is like me in so many ways. She displays my character, my habits, my facial expressions. We know that one day we will have to explain to her about her background and that we are not her biological parents but we'll cross that bridge or rather climb that massive mountain when we come to it.

For anybody considering adoption and worrying about when their adoptive children come of age, have access to their records and want to meet their real parents, just bear in mind that children are only ever on loan: be they biological children or adopted children, they all grow up and leave home – you don't own them. Just love them and guide them, help them onto the right path, never make demons out of their biological parents; after all, you might one day all be together at your child's wedding!

Mary, who adopted as a single parent rather than pursuing fertility treatment, picks up the thread:

Twelve years after holding my child for the first time and weeping to know that my joy came as a result of the pain of another woman, I revisit that time often as he seems to struggle with so much of himself and the world around him. When he has an aggressive, violent, frightening 'wobble' and it's easier to think 'it must come from his birth family...' and when he struggles to read and write and workers say 'perhaps he has inherited some of his parents' learning difficulties' and when he gently cradles a newborn child and people say 'look at the love he has got from you', the question of nurture/nature, of what he has taken from his birth parents and what he has taken from his time with us is oh so real. It's like a form of 'racism' or 'classism', a 'mothering' that never gets talked about – why is it that all the 'bad' and challenging parts of him are so easy to associate with his birth parents, the 'others' – and that the beautiful and wonderful parts of him are claimed by 'us', his adoptive family? How does this help my child to gain a positive sense of who he is; how does that begin in any way to repay my debt to his birth mother?

The final words go to Joanne and John:

All in all, we were trying for a family for ten years before we turned to adoption. It was unexplained really, there was no firm diagnosis. We'd been trying for six years to get pregnant naturally and then had a miscarriage. After that, the doctors weren't interested in helping us because they said we could manage it. We ended up going private for IVF but it was a lot to go through. There was travel every day, getting up at 5 a.m. to get to the hospital as it's that far away. Financially, we still haven't really recovered from it years later. After the second cycle of treatment, I miscarried again. I couldn't face another so that's when they agreed to do the tests. They discovered I had a chromosome abnormality which meant it would be virtually impossible to carry full-term and if I did there would be a serious chance of birth defects so we decided to go for adoption. We always say we should have gone straight for adoption, but I suppose we had to go through it to get to where we are now. Adoption was always on the cards though; we always had it in mind.

It wasn't the loss of having a biological family that was the biggest overwhelming thing for me, it was what we went through when I lost the baby, the miscarriage, and that still haunts me sometimes. When we talk about it, it brings back the overwhelming sadness, the way we were treated. That overwhelms the fact that we haven't got biological children. But I'll always be sad that I never went through a pregnancy and gave birth and all that; that will always be there. At one time I couldn't walk down the baby aisle in the supermarket, we couldn't watch anything on the television to do with babies or pregnancy. When my best friend was pregnant I avoided her and the baby was a week old before I could bear to see her. But she had another baby after we had our boys placed and I couldn't wait to get there, the contrast was unbelievable. We've learnt to deal with it; it's not as important as it used to be.

The adoption process was brilliant; it was just positive all the way through, we had a brilliant social worker. It was dead easy to shift to adoption because we were ready for it. We had got to the stage where not being able to have our own children was not an issue. It was never an option not to have children in our lives; we would have carried on until we got children one way or another.

Infertility ruled our lives for a long, long time but the time was right for us to come to terms with it. All right, we may have suffered infertility but to us we just wanted to be parents, and when it came down to it, it really didn't matter how it came about; it wasn't a major shift.

The message that we would like to put across is not to focus too much on the infertility and focus instead on the couple; we were ready and didn't need to wait any longer. We totally understand that you have to weep for the children you are not going to have but we grieved less for that than for the babies we lost.

We found out about our boys in June and the social workers came to see us in July. They gave us photographs which weren't very flattering, in fact they were awful really, they picked the worst photographs. We met the foster carers in August and they gave us a DVD – and then we were constantly on the phone to them. We used to phone up for the silliest of reasons like 'What size shoes?', 'What washing powder do you buy?' and things like that, so there was that connection there.

We just think that our social worker made the perfect match. She always used to go on about how the longest wait would come after approval panel because she had to be sure that she matched us properly and the children's social worker has to be sure that they get the right parents. So when it happened so quickly we just thought she'd given us a worst case scenario, but we just think that the match she made was spot on. She said she could imagine our oldest standing outside in his overalls helping Daddy tinker with the car and that's exactly what he does!

We were told our oldest had issues, but we didn't know the first thing about attachment, or about therapeutical parenting. Half the time we don't know if we're doing the right thing, we just have to go with it and do the best we can. I think that's the same whether you are natural parents or not. The first few months were not the nicest, in fact they were overwhelming at times. He used to cry, throw massive tantrums, do head-banging. You'd put his dish on the table and he would just swipe it on the floor. It took quite a while for him to settle down and even now we have to admit that we struggle a bit sometimes. He has issues with socialisation which go back to his early experiences. You can't blame that on the adoption because it's not actually the adoption that's caused it, it's what happened before and we're just having the backlash. But he's our son just like he is and we'll always be here for them and hopefully he'll turn out OK.

Everyone says that they are ours the way they act and go on. It's really funny when we go for walks across the fields and John's walking ahead with his hands behind his back and the kids behind him with their hands behind their backs in just the same way. Their characteristics are ours and the things that are coming out in them are coming from us. Sometimes you can look at them and just get a fleeting glimpse of their mum, they've got her eyes – but we don't know enough about her or how she is to compare. This nature versus nurture thing, there's got to be something in it, but we haven't picked up on it yet.

We have the letterbox contact with their birth mother which we hate doing but we understand the reasons for doing it. We've got photographs of her and storybooks, so we are building on that part of the story as they get older. The life we lead is normal for us; it may be extraordinary for some people but it's all we know. Yes, there are the additional issues there with the adoption, but I think they will rear their heads more as the kids get older and start asking more questions and we'll just deal with them as they come.

We've really just 100 per cent got on with life. We start at half past six in the morning and there is no break until they go to bed. We don't get afternoon naps any more but they are just ours and we can't imagine life being any different now.

Biographies

Olga van den Akker is Professor of Health Psychology and Head of the Department of Psychology at Middlesex University, London. She is a chartered health psychologist with specialist research interests in health psychology and reproductive health, having published over 200 journal articles, scientific conference presentations and media outputs and authored two books: *The Complete Guide to Infertility: Diagnosis, Treatments, Options* (Free Association Books 2002) and *Reproductive Health Psychology* (Wiley-Blackwell (in preparation) 2010).

Sally Baffour is an adoptive parent of 19-year-old boy and girl twins. In 2002 she founded the Thank U Charity whose aim is to promote adoption and fostering to the hitherto difficult to reach Black and mixed heritage community using innovative engagement methods. She is also the TV presenter of the charity's *Adoption Matters* show, a unique outreach and training recruitment programme. She sits on the London Borough of Haringey's Permanency (Adoption) Panel, is a trustee of the Race Equality Foundation and a member of the General Social Care Council's (GSCC) Conduct Committee.

Rachel Balen is Principal Lecturer in Social Work in the Centre for Applied Childhood Studies at the University of Huddersfield. She leads a masters course in child welfare and safeguarding and has research interests in research with children and the psychosocial needs of children with cancer and their families. She is co-editor, with Marilyn Crawshaw, of *Sexuality and Fertility Issues in Ill Health and Disability: From Early Adolescence to Adulthood* (Jessica Kingsley Publishers 2006).

Marilyn Crawshaw is Senior Lecturer in Social Work at the University of York. She has practice and research experience concerning different aspects of the impact of fertility difficulties on couple and family relationships. She chairs the UK multi-agency Project Group on Assisted Reproduction (PROGAR), is a national adviser to UK DonorLink, the Voluntary Information Exchange and Contact register for adults genetically related through donor conception, and is a past external adviser and inspector for the Human Fertilisation and Embryology Authority.

Lorraine Culley is Professor of Social Science and Health at De Montfort University, Leicester. Her research interests are in diversity, health and health care and social aspects of infertility. Current research projects include an ESRC study of 'fertility tourism' and an NHS-funded study of endometriosis and cultural diversity. She has published widely in the field including a recent co-edited book with Nicky Hudson and Floor van Rooij *Marginalized Reproduction: Ethnicity, Infertility and Reproductive Technologies*, (Earthscan 2009), and a co-authored book with Simon Dyson, *Ethnicity and Healthcare Practice* (Quay Books 2009).

Julia Feast is a policy, research and development consultant at the British Association for Adoption and Fostering (BAAF). She is an experienced social worker and researcher. She has particular interests in the identity and information rights and needs of adopted people, postcare adults and donor-conceived people. She is co-author of *Adoption, Search and Reunion: The Long-term Experience of Adopted Adults*, 2nd edn (BAAF 2003), *The Adoption Triangle Revisited: A Study of Adoption, Search and Reunion Experiences* (BAAF 2005) and *A Childhood on Paper: Accessing the Child Care Files of Former Looked After Children in the UK* (University of Bradford 2005).

Jenny Gwilt is an independent consultant in the field of looked after children and adoption services. She worked in children's services in both the statutory and voluntary sectors for nearly 30 years, followed by a secondment to the Department for Education and Skills as a professional adviser on adoption, where she worked on the development of the regulations and guidance for the Adoption and Children Act 2002. She has also worked on inspection of safeguarding and services for looked after children. She has chaired adoption panels for many years.

Gill Haworth is a registered social worker and Director of Intercountry Adoption Centre, a registered voluntary adoption agency in London. She has worked in adoption since 1973 in both the statutory and voluntary sectors. She is Chair of the Adoption Agencies Consultant's Group on Intercountry Adoption (AACGICA) and Vice-Chair of the Network for Intercountry Adoption (NICA).

Anthea Hendry is an art psychotherapist working in private practice. She has previously worked as a social worker in fostering and adoption, as the manager of After Adoption Yorkshire (a voluntary organisation providing services to all parties to adoption) and as a principal art psychotherapist in the Leeds Child and Adolescent Mental Health Service.

Nicky Hudson is Senior Research Fellow in the School of Applied Social Sciences at De Montfort University, Leicester. She is a sociologist with an interest in infertility, assisted reproductive technologies, health, gender and ethnicity and co-editor with Lorraine Culley and Floor van Rooij of *Marginalised Reproduction: Ethnicity, Infertility and Reproductive Technologies* (Earthscan 2009).

Gayle Letherby is Professor of Sociology in the School of Applied Psychosocial Sciences at the University of Plymouth. Her research and writing interests include reproductive and parental identity (including infertility, involuntary childlessness, pregnancy loss, teenage pregnancy and young parenthood and the experience of pregnancy complicated by pre-existing diabetes) and method, methodology and epistemology.

Penny Netherwood is a consultant clinical psychologist, working in the Leeds Child and Adolescent Mental Health Service, part of NHS Leeds. She has carried out doctoral research looking at the psychological impact of infertility

Lone Schmidt is an associate professor at the Institute of Public Health, University of Copenhagen. Her research field is in reproductive health with a focus on the psychosocial consequences of infertility and treatment and on outcomes of fertility treatment. She leads courses in reproductive health and medical sociology.

Peter Selman is Visiting Fellow in the School of Geography, Politics and Sociology at Newcastle University. He is Chair of NICA (Network for Intercountry Adoption) and a trustee of BAAF (British Association for Adoption and Fostering). He has many publications in the area of inter-country adoption, including *Intercountry Adoption: Developments, Trends and Perspectives* (BAAF 2000).

Petra Thorn is a social worker and infertility counsellor who has been working in private practice for over 15 years. She is Chair of the German Society for Fertility Counselling and Coordinator of the ESHRE (European Society for Human Reproduction and Embryology) Special Interest Group Psychology and Counselling. She has published widely on psychosocial aspects of infertility and has a special interest in third-party conception.

Jan Way is a registered social worker who has specialised in inter-country adoption since 1986. She is a training and development manager at Intercountry Adoption Centre, London, and also undertakes both pre- and after-adoption work for local authorities and voluntary adoption agencies in the inter-country adoption field. She is an adoptive mother and an adopted person.

Subject Index

Author Index